READ OUR LIPS (from *The Bitch in the House*)

"Here are a few things people have said about me at the office: *You're unflappable. Are you ever in a bad mood? You command respect as soon as you walk into a room.* Here are things people—OK, the members of my family—have said to me at home: *Mommy is always grumpy. Why are you so tense? You're too mean to live in this house and I want you to go back to work for the rest of your life!*"

—KRISTIN VAN OGTROP

"I believed myself to be a feminist, and I vowed never to fall into the same trap of domestic boredom and servitude that I saw my mother as being fully entrenched in; never to settle for a life that was, as I saw it, lacking independence, authority, and respect."

—E. S. MADURO

"Of course nobody thinks to ask me and Michael—my partner of eleven years and the father of our two-year-old son—why we're not married until we're all at a *wedding*, which is kind of awkward, at best. 'Um, maybe because marriage is a tool of the *patriarchy*?' I could say, and smile and take another bite of poached salmon and wink across the table at the bride and groom."

—CATHERINE NEWMAN

"Why, come to think of it, hadn't I been warned of this—the loss of identity, the potential claustrophobia, the feeling of being utterly trapped—by those who had gone before me, afloat in yards of tulle and demurely holding their bouquets?"

—DAPHNE MERKIN

"If and when we did have this child, I didn't want to be a bad mother. I wanted to be *my* mother—safe, protective, rational, calm—but (and here's the catch) without giving up *all* my anger, for if it sometimes scared and shamed me, it also fueled me: my drive, my ambition, my work....I didn't want to bury it completely—only to tame it....I was terrified of what my anger might make me capable of."

—ELISSA SCHAPPELL

Praise for *The Bitch in the House*

"[This] new collection of essays by angry women is an event worth marking. . . . Drawing parallels between *The Bitch in the House* and [Betty] Friedan's work is unavoidable."
—*Boston Globe*

"This often-hilarious collection of new pieces by women is starkly revealing of their thoughts on the conflicts and stresses of womanhood today, the constant attempts to be all things to all people: professional, nurturing, accomplished, erotic. Here is unvarnished truth and more than a smidgen of anger about marriage, motherhood, solitude, and sex from such writers as Pam Houston, Ellen Gilchrist, Hope Edelman, Natalie Angier, and northwesterners Karen Karbo and Natalie Kusz."
—*Seattle Post-Intelligencer*

"Asked to explore a significant element of her life, each of the twenty-six remarkable women in this impassioned anthology does so in thoughtfully introspective, honorably truthful, and candidly self-revelatory essays that feel less like contemporary feminist rhetoric and more like late-night, soul-searching conversations between best friends. . . . The writing is superb: smart, sassy, and honest—oh, are they honest . . . in this must-read for every woman."
—*Booklist*

"The great thing about *The Bitch in the House* . . . is knowing how many of us are out there: perfectly delightful women who turn into shrews when faced with yet another sinkful of dishes/demand to hear *Hop on Pop*/dating suggestion from Mom. This book will have a place on the bedside table—if you don't throw it at somebody first."
—*O, The Oprah Magazine*

"The chief truth that emerges from these essays . . . is that even when women's choices seem somewhat similar, the lives of no two women are alike. . . . There are gems among these essays, and some of the best ones are light and funny and telling."
—*New York Newsday*

"Any woman who has ever felt confused about personal choices she has had to make, or might have to make, should pick up this articulate and insightful collection of essays."
—*Daily News* (New York)

"Combining motherhood and marriage and a career is an intricate affair. . . . This book of deeply personal essays contains . . . exceptional writing."

—*San Francisco Chronicle*

"Here are thoughtful, graceful writers . . . ruminating on choices they've made and lessons they've learned. . . . Giving voice to their 'private lives' is not so easy for the writers collected in *The Bitch in the House*. For them, speaking out is a labor of love, and all of us—men and women—would do well to listen."

—*Boston* magazine

"Powerfully thought-provoking. . . . This 'House' may be full of angry women, but it is also full of smart ones, and their words and life stories are instructive."

—*Austin American-Statesman*

"A hot new collection of essays, all of them interesting."

—*The Atlantic Monthly*

"A rollicking, free-flowing, double-barreled think piece."

—*Hartford Courant*

"A classy list of contributors. Will ring true for many readers. . . . Others may find it comforting to know that even smart, articulate, successful women can have deeply unsettled inner lives."

—*Publishers Weekly*

"Amusing, ferocious, whiny, and wise."

—*Elle*

"Deserves a place on your nightstand."

—*USA Weekend*

"These remarkable essays by remarkable women are written with a breathtaking candor that makes the reader feel that the words are being whispered into her ear; as if one's best friend is confessing feelings—of anger, frustration, love, confusion, commitment—not meant for publication."

—*The Women's Times* (MA)

"The twenty-six very good writers gathered here offer thoughtful personal accounts that address important questions. . . . These are honest voices . . . and if the picture they paint is accurate and sometimes a little bitter, it is also often wickedly funny. . . . [It] will offer comfort to real women living real lives."

—*Library Journal*

"What a book, for men and women both. There is no bitterness here, only the eloquence of honesty. Different voices present themselves forthrightly; ultimately, there is something so open, and openhearted, in the way these women offer up their versions of marriage, work, children, divorce, affairs, and dress sizes, that the reader is tempted, in the face of such truthfulness, to set the book down and say 'Thank you.'"

—Elizabeth Strout, author of *Amy and Isabelle*

"Every once in a while a book comes along to remind you that you are not alone, that everything you think is true is, and that you are not crazy. *The Bitch in the House* is that book. It is smart, funny, wise, honest, and very probably—and I speak from experience here—the story of your life."

—Cynthia Kaplan, author of *Why I'm Like This*

"I devoured these essays, and took great guilty pleasure in trespassing into these private lives. May the high IQs and elegant writing represented on these pages take no offense when I say 'Move over, *True Confessions*.'"

—Elinor Lipman, author of
The Dearly Departed and *The Inn at Lake Devine*

"This fascinating volume presents a range of voices and visions regarding what women want in work and play, in love and out of love. It is a fine contribution to the literature of the unspoken and meaningful extension of Virginia Woolf's thinking on women and their predicaments."

—Lauren Slater, author of
Love Works Like This and *Welcome to My Country*

"Not a variation on *The Surrendered Wife* or a man-trapping manual like *The Rules*. . . . Explore[s] the reality of modern women, some of whom are trying to juggle kids, careers, housework, and husbands. Others are trying to find love amid society's conflicting messages about money, sex, and matrimony."

—*USA Today*

"With a title like *The Bitch in the House*, you know that what lies ahead is no Stepford Wives' manual, no perpetually perky June Cleaver/Donna Reed guide to the married life. . . . Snarls without apology."

—*Pages*

"Stark, moving essays. . . . Like a conversation over coffee."

—*Pittsburgh Pulp*

"Reading this book is like having a long lunch with a good friend. Like painting your toenails cherry red. . . . The essays are uniformly well written, almost always interesting, often funny, and occasionally wise."

—*Women's Review of Books*

"Angry and engaging. . . . Twenty-six mothers, lovers, and single women write candidly about what fuels their rage. The authors wrestle with the fundamental issues of modern female life (sex, stress, work, motherhood) and look honestly (and with a sense of humor) at why they feel so dissatisfied."

—IndieBride.com

"So intimate are some of these essays that they are too much to own up to, even in this confessional era. One anonymous writer describes her 'open marriage.' Another broods over giving up first-rate sex."

—*Massachusetts Union-News*

"A lively collection of capable writers. . . . An engaging collage of contemporary voices."

—*Daily Hampshire Gazette*

Ellen M. Augarten

About the Author

CATHI HANAUER, the author of the novel *My Sister's Bones,* has written articles, essays, reviews, and fiction for *Elle, Mirabella, Self, Glamour, Mademoiselle, Parenting,* and many other magazines. She has been the monthly books columnist for both *Glamour* and *Mademoiselle,* and was the relationship-advice columnist for *Seventeen* for seven years. She lives in western Massachusetts with her husband, writer Daniel Jones, and their daughter and son.

Featuring all-original essays by

Ellen Gilchrist

Hope Edelman

Pam Houston

Daphne Merkin

Natalie Angier

Vivian Gornick

Jill Bialosky

Helen Schulman

Chitra Divakaruni

Karen Karbo

Kate Christensen

Elissa Schappell

Veronica Chambers

Susan Squire

. . . and many more

Bitch in the House

26 Women Tell the TRUTH About Sex, Solitude, Work, Motherhood, and Marriage

Edited by

Cathi Hanauer

Perennial
An Imprint of HarperCollins*Publishers*

Grateful acknowledgment is made for permission to reprint the following copyrighted materials:

"Comment," copyright 1926, © renewed 1954 by Dorothy Parker, from *The Portable Dorothy Parker* by Dorothy Parker, edited by Brendan Gill. Used by permission of Viking Penguin, a division of Penguin Putnam Inc.

"Greed" by Nina Cassian, translated by Stanley Kunitz, from *Life Sentence: Selected Poems* by Nina Cassian, edited by William Jay Smith. Copyright © 1990 by Nina Cassian. Used by permission of W.W. Norton & Company, Inc.

Excerpt from "Professions for Women" in *The Death of the Moth and Other Essays* by Virginia Woolf, copyright 1942 by Harcourt, Inc., and renewed 1970 by Marjorie T. Parsons, Executrix, reprinted by permission of the publisher.

Lyrics from "The Story," by Shawn Colvin, John Leventhal © 1989 WB Music Corp. (ASCAP), Scred Songs (ASCAP) & Lev-A-Tunes. All Rights o/b/o Scred Songs administered by WB Music Corp. All Rights Reserved. Used by Permission. Warner Bros. Publications U.S. Inc., Miami, FL. 33014

Pages 291 and 292 constitute a continuation of this copyright page.

A hardcover edition of this book was published in 2002 by William Morrow, an imprint of HarperCollins Publishers.

First Perennial edition published 2003.

The Library of Congress has catalogued the hardcover edition as follows:
The bitch in the house : 26 women tell the truth about sex, solitude, work, motherhood, and marriage / edited by Cathi Hanauer ; featuring all original essays by Ellen Gilchrist . . . [et al.].—1. ed.

p. cm.

ISBN 0-06-621166-2

1. Women—United States—Social conditions—Case studies. 2. Interpersonal relations—United States—Case studies. I. Hanauer, Cathi. II. Gilchrist, Ellen.

HQ1421.B523

305.42'0973—dc21 2002023026

ISBN 0-06-093646-0 (pbk.)

05 06 07 ❖/RRD 20 19 18 17 16 15 14 13 12

For Dan, of course

You who come of a younger and happier generation may not have heard of her—you may not know what I mean by The Angel in the House. I will describe her as shortly as I can. She was intensely sympathetic. She was immensely charming. She was utterly unselfish. She excelled in the difficult arts of family life. She sacrificed herself daily. If there was chicken, she took the leg; if there was a draft she sat in it—in short she was so constituted that she never had a mind or a wish of her own, but preferred to sympathize always with the minds and wishes of others.

— Virginia Woolf, "Professions for Women,"
a paper presented to the Women's Service League

I am greedy. Puritans scold me
for running breathlessly
over life's table of contents
and for wishing and longing for everything.

— Nina Cassian

Contents

IV. Look at Me Now

Introduction

THIS BOOK WAS born out of anger—specifically, my own domestic anger, which stemmed from a combination of guilt, resentment, exhaustion, naïveté, and the chaos of my life at the time. But ultimately, it is not an angry book. It's a book that shows us that the trials and tribulations of our work and relationships, children and homes and sex lives—complete with their passions, dysfunctions, and frustrations—are not ours alone but the same or similar struggles of so many others. It's a book that reveals that if the grass sometimes seems greener, sometimes it is. And sometimes, it's decidedly not.

The book began two years ago, after my family—my husband, Dan, and our two children, then aged four and one—had just left New York City to move to a small town in Massachusetts where the kids could each have a room and Dan could work part-time from home instead of full-time from an office, enabling him to write his second novel and do his part of the co-parenting arrangement we'd both always (if vaguely) envisioned. The move came, for me, after an autonomous decade in my twenties indulging in all the things I had come to value—a rewarding, lucrative career combined with exercise, romance, solitude, good friends—followed by six whirlwind years that included marrying, moving three times, and birthing and nursing two children, all while contributing my necessary share of the family income by writing a monthly magazine column, publishing a novel, and completing a second novel under contract. By the end, I'd worked my way up to roughly two-thirds time hired child care, much of it taking place in our apartment (in which I also worked). Our final year in New York had been a veritable marathon: nursing a baby at the computer while typing to make a deadline; sprinting home from my daughter's nursery school, both kids in tow, to return phone calls; handing the children off to Dan the instant he walked in at night so I could rush out to a coffee shop to get *my* work done. When we moved, I expected things to finally be different. I'd be able to work purely and efficiently—to focus as I had years ago—knowing Dan was on during those times. We'd be calm, we'd take family bike rides . . . our New Lives would begin.

Instead, my life, my marriage, my schedule, felt more overwhelming than ever. The phones rang nonstop. (We had three different "distinctive rings"—Dan's work line, my work line, and the family line. Total nightmare.) FedEx packages and cartons of books I was supposed to be reading—I was writing *Mademoiselle*'s monthly books page at the time—arrived by the week, to be added to the still-unpacked boxes that rimmed every room, dust bunnies breeding around them. I rarely managed to cook a good dinner, as my own mother had virtually every night, and I rushed my children through the hours so I could get to all the things *I* had to do, furious when they wouldn't go to bed, when they were up calling me in the night. Dan was doing more parenting than he ever had (and feeling, I imagined, like a better father than those of previous generations simply by virtue of being around), yet I still felt *I* was the one who managed and was responsible for the kids—from their meals to their clothing, activities, schoolwork, baby-sitters, birthday parties—as well as handling all the "domestic" things I'd always done (grocery shopping, cooking, laundry, school and social responsibilities, and so on). I still had the same work—my income was now even more important—and, it seemed, less time than ever to do it. My days were nonstop at high speed, my brain flooded with lists and obligations.

All day long, I stomped around barking orders, irritable and stressed out. I was angry at the cat for waking me, at the car for having no gas when I got in it (late for something—always late), at the toy I'd just tripped on . . . and at Dan. Because he'd used up the coffee filters or

Cascade without putting them on the list; because he'd finished his work and had time to check out the *New York Times* and *Salon* while I struggled to find time for mine; because I was always more anxious and frantic than he was. Of course, I'd fallen in love with him partly because of this very calm, but now his ability to relax when I never seemed to felt unfair, oblivious, even rude. I resented him and this chaos I found myself in—even as I never stopped being grateful for the elements that created it. Two healthy children, a nice home, an interesting job . . . what could I possibly be mad about? And yet, mad I was.

So, night after night, once the kids were asleep (sort of), I left laundry unfolded, phone calls unreturned, school forms unfilled out, and my own work undone to go online and fire furious e-mails to my friends to try to figure it out. And I began to realize something. A lot of these women—particularly those who, like me, were ambitious women (often writers) juggling jobs and marriages and, sometimes, small children—also were resentful, guilty, stressed out. "I want a partner in my husband, not another child," one fired back at me. "I told him if something doesn't change, I'm leaving, even though we just got married," said another, adding, "Yesterday I actually had a fantasy that we got a divorce, moved back into our separate apartments, and just dated each other again." "I'm fine all day at work, but as soon as I get home, I'm a horror," said a third. "I'm the bitch in the house."

The bitch in the house. That's exactly how I felt. The opposite of what Virginia Woolf called The Angel in the House—but with anger to boot. Sometimes my friends and I would get on the topic of our sex lives, or—in the case of the married ones, it seemed—lack thereof. "Put me anywhere near a bed and I just want to *sleep,*" said one mother. The recently wed woman mourned the loss of the "hot sex" she'd had with her husband before they'd tied the proverbial knot. One young single friend who'd just moved in with her boyfriend already felt the waning of her desire. (In the same breath, she spoke of how it scared and amazed her how angry she got at him sometimes—how she'd walk in from work and see a sinkful of dishes and explode with rage, while her poor boyfriend watched, baffled, from the couch, beer in hand, newspaper spread before him, stereo blaring the Dave Matthews Band.)

Newspaper and magazine stories appeared regularly to echo our feelings. "Why Women Hate Their Husbands," screamed a cover line on *Talk* magazine. (The article's subtitle: "Love, sex, family, career—it was all supposed to be so easy for the modern woman. Then why are this therapist's patients so furious?") In a piece in the *New York Times Magazine,* a modern working couple visited the Love Lab (a Family Research Lab in Seattle that, after watching a couple interact, predicts whether they will divorce), and, the male half of the couple reported, "In ten minutes, my wife chalked up one hundred and thirty moments of criticism. I displayed one hundred and thirty-two moments of defensiveness." (His wife, he went on to say, "was a keen critic of an institution into which she had twice been recruited. Marriage, she said, was advertised falsely—the myth of enduring romantic love—and its responsibilities sharply limited a woman's growth.")

Women's number one issue in sex therapy had shifted from not being orgasmic to lacking desire; a doctor friend in California confided to me that the top two complaints of her female patients were lack of libido and "inexplicable rage." One friend (full-time working mother, two small kids) told me: "Every woman I know is mad at her husband, just mad mad mad at everything. Every time I bring it up to a woman like me, she just goes bananas. . . . R and I had a fight the other night that involved him saying he feels like I resent him all the time and I feel like he's always failing me. . . . We have that fight about once a month."

Naturally, this outpouring of anger interested me. I began to ask these women about their thoughts and experiences—to dig deeper—and to consider and compare potential reasons for this seeming epidemic of female rage.[1] At the same time, I started reading a new book called *Flux,*

[1] A few that came to mind: Too much to do in too few hours. Not enough help from society and, sometimes, spouses. Invasion of technology into our lives, further accelerating our already fragmented time. Financial responsibility combined with the responsibility and inherent desires of motherhood. The wish, regardless of financial responsibility, to have a fulfilling career, for which we've prepared all our lives. Pressure, thanks to a society obsessed with appearance combined with growth in the plastic surgery, cosmetic, and weight-loss industries, to look not only flawless

in which journalist Peggy Orenstein, after interviewing 200 women in their twenties, thirties, and forties, concludes that "Women's lives have become a complex web of economic, psychological, and social contradictions, with opportunities so intimately linked to constraints that a choice in one realm can have unexpected consequences (or benefits) ten years later in another." Orenstein calls the modern world a "half-changed" one, in which "old patterns and expectations have broken down, but new ideas seem fragmentary, unrealistic, and often contradictory." And I began to wonder if, far from being irrational (or me just being a spoiled brat), my anger—and that of my friends—had clear-cut wellsprings, sources that didn't go away because we had more choices than other generations of women or because we had loving, sensitive partners or even because we led full, privileged lives.

At the end of *Flux,* Orenstein offers suggestions for women, one of which is to share their experience with one another, to "talk across lines of age and circumstance." As I read those words, I realized that this was what I was already doing: gleaning comfort and advice, sympathy and wisdom, from friends of all ages in all situations. The more women I spoke to—whether they were angry or not—the better I felt, and the more insight I gained into my own life and the lives of other women also struggling, whatever their issues happened to be. And I saw that I could expand this correspondence I'd been having and ask many more women to join in the sharing and revelations: women who'd grown up in homes like mine and in less traditional or middle-class ones; women who'd chosen to marry but not to have children, or to have children but not to marry; women who'd

but younger than we actually are. Lack of role models in our lives for what we're trying to do. (At my age, my mother was in the midst of a fifteen-year interruption of her career in order to cheerfully raise four children, head the PTA and the Brownie troop, and serve our family three home-cooked meals a day, plus meet my father's every demand; my mother-in-law had mostly given up her career to aid my father-in-law's career and raise their two boys.) Lack of help from our extended families. (My mother had resumed that interrupted career and, at sixty-three, was at its pinnacle, working full-time while overseeing the care of my ninety-two-year-old grandmother and nursing-home-confined younger brother—not to mention still waiting on my father, who, conveniently for him, was stuck back in the 1950s.) The ideas and belief—courtesy of a culture ever more mired in materialism, consumerism, and false advertising—that we should have it all, do it all, and be it all, and be Happy. And if we're not, by God, something is wrong.

divorced, sometimes twice or more. Women who'd remained single and without children. Women with "unusual" arrangements—open marriage, for example, or becoming someone's mistress. To name a few.

Ask I did: the most interesting, eloquent women I knew and knew of. I approached mostly novelists and professional writers, but also a handful of other smart, thinking women who I knew had a story to tell. I requested of these potential contributors that they explore a choice they'd made, or their life situation—or their anger, if they felt it—in an essay; that they offer an interesting glimpse into their private lives, as if they were talking to a friend at a café. One after another, they signed on. And this book was launched.

By the time I sat down to put it together, I had much more than I had ever hoped for. The authors range in age from twenty-four to sixty-six; their topics and experience incorporate a great breadth and range. Anger, domestic and otherwise, is covered in many incarnations, particularly in the book's third section, "Mommy Maddest": one writer, Hope Edelman, furious because her husband wasn't present enough when their baby was young; another, Laurie Abraham, because hers was so present it made her feel threatened and competitive as a mother. Novelist Helen Schulman describes being overwhelmed by simultaneously caring for her ailing, aging parents and her two young kids, not to mention her marriage and her career. And two women, Pulitzer Prize–winning science writer Natalie Angier and novelist Elissa Schappell, both write candidly about their own longtime anger and what it means—and what they hope for—when it comes to their children.

But as the book evolved, anger turned out to be only one small part of a much greater picture. Many of these women weren't enraged, in some cases because earlier discontent had led them to pursue a less traditional road, challenges notwithstanding. In the first section, "Me, Myself, and I," Kerry Herlihy tells of finding herself pregnant by a married man—after once being betrayed by another married man—and deciding to have the baby on her own, asking for and expecting nothing from the father (though also welcoming whatever he wanted to give); later in the book, Pam Houston details *her* chosen path—one of autonomy and adventure—and her own debate, at age thirty-nine, about whether or not to have a baby. Jen Marshall shares her story of moving into a Massachusetts apartment with her longtime boyfriend, quickly finding herself stifled and depressed, and ultimately moving back out—and then to New York—opting instead for long-distance romance with the man she continues to love faithfully.

In the book's second section, "For Better and Worse," Catherine Newman—bisexual in her twenties—ruminates about how and why, finding the institution of marriage politically and socially offensive, if not downright absurd, she now lives with her lover (and the father of her son) *without* becoming his lawfully wedded wife. Novelist Hannah Pine unveils her choice of open marriage: how it came to be, how it works, what she gets out of it, and how she deals with the inevitable jealousy of being alone and awake at five o'clock in the morning knowing her husband is out with another woman.

Many other authors—in this section and in the book's final one, "Look at Me Now"—also raise the shade on their own marriages or sex lives (or both) to show us their passions and processes of enlightenment. Cynthia Kling reveals how she learned to use her imagination—and to maintain her creative and "forbidden" side—in her current marriage in order to keep it sexy and sexual; novelist Kate Christensen offers some similar sentiments in presenting her struggle, at age thirty-five and as the daughter of a mother who ended three marriages, to learn how to be a wife—something she initially found almost unbearable. Novelist and poet Jill Bialosky confesses to a loss of intimacy and sexual desire in her marriage after her son was born, while Hazel McClay contemplates why she ultimately chose a man she loves over men with whom she's had passionate sex, even though her current and true love "has never wrapped me in his arms, never covered my mouth with his and kissed me until I gasped for breath."

Daphne Merkin's piece about her ill-conceived wedding—the uncomfortable if perhaps appropriate prelude to her equally ill-conceived marriage—reiterates that divorce, idealized fantasy though it might be for most married women at one time or another (and valid and necessary solution that it is for many a bad marriage), is hardly nirvana, particularly as one gets into middle age, when, as she puts it, "everyone else suddenly seems to be married—safely tucked in for the night in their tidy Noah's Ark of coupledom—while you're out in the lonely forest scavenging for a warm body to huddle up against." Memoirist Natalie Kusz depicts a different kind of loneliness—and victory—in her essay about being an overweight woman in an unsympathetic and insensitive society.

That's just a sampling of the words and topics that make up this book, subjects covered with grace, wit, humor, depth, irony, sadness, and striking candor. Many of the twenty-six contributors contemplate decisions and aspects of their life that they've never explored publicly before; they get down and dirty in ways that may shock and titillate. Their pieces reflect, in a chorus of different voices, the elations and disappointments of our lives as fervent and ambitious women today.

As for me, my life, and the anger that spawned this book, I conclude it, thankfully, from a somewhat less pissed-off place, partly because my family and I have settled into this town (found baby-sitters, a house-cleaning service, out-of-home office space for Dan) and our children have aged from four and one to six and three (more sleep, less physically exhausting/all-consuming care), and partly because, with practice, we've gotten better at co-parenting: I've learned to *ask* for the things I need (rather than doing them myself while seething in silent resentment), Dan to carry out his share regularly and efficiently. Though as the mother I'll probably always feel that I bear the main responsibility for my children's care and upkeep (as Daphne Merkin once put it, feminism can come and go, and egalitarian fashions can prevail or not prevail, but it's the rare household where the brunt of the solicitude and concern for the children—and, I would add, for the community—falls on the father)—

and though this will continue to infuriate me at times when my life feels overcrammed—I also relish the sense of importance being a mother brings to my life, as much as I thrive on the satisfaction that comes with my career. I am not willing to give up any of it, even if the price is exhaustion. And reminding myself of that, as often as I have to, is calming and liberating.

In fact, in many ways—at least during the good months (enough income, absence of overwhelming deadlines, no one down with the flu)—my life now is probably as close to what I envisioned, moving here, as it'll ever be. Which is not to say I don't find plenty to be furious about. The claustrophobia of marriage—even with its security and coziness. The chaos of raising children—despite their funny sayings and sweet little breath. The stress of combining a career with both of the above—a career that keeps me vital and self-possessed. And so on. In considering it all, I can't help thinking of a T-shirt I once saw, touting a whitewater river known for its currents, that read "This place sucks. Let's stay." I've chosen this life, and I'd choose it again in a heartbeat, but like many of the women in this book, I'm a perfectionist and a malcontent with a too-full schedule, eager to reap every morsel I can from my brief time on this earth. And if that means I'll never be The Angel in the House—and it does, as I've learned—may my family forgive me.

But enough about that. I turn you over to twenty-six other women: provocative, intriguing, deeply contemplative women, gloriously exposed. May they move, amuse, and enlighten you as they did me.

—Cathi Hanauer

Me, Myself, and I

Oh, life is a glorious cycle of song,
A medley of extemporanea;
And love is a thing that can never go wrong;
And I am Marie of Roumania.

—Dorothy Parker, "*Comment*"

Excuse Me While I Explode

My Mother, Myself, My Anger

E. S. Maduro

Y PARENTS MET and started dating on the same day, at the age of thirteen. Forty-five years later, my father still glows when he tells the story of seeing my mother on her first day at his school, and how he offered to walk her home that very afternoon. They dated throughout high school, went to the same college, and got married the day before their graduation, at age twenty-one—three years younger than I am today. After college my father went to graduate school and eventually became a history professor; my mother worked as a schoolteacher for a while; they bought a cheap house in the countryside and started a family. Presto, the American Dream.

When my older sister was born, my mother stopped working out of the house and became the mom I know her as. The mom who maintained a spotless house and a balanced checkbook and found the time to praise and nurture two growing children, all while having dinner ready and waiting, on the table, every night by 6:30. The mom who put off a career until her mid-forties so she would be available to her family—which she still is—though that is not to say she didn't work. My mother's job included, but was never limited to, pickling cucumbers, making jam, doing laundry for four people, changing diapers, teaching two children to read, doing all the grocery shopping for a family, cooking three meals a day (making sure a vegetable was included at dinner), cleaning the house, doing art projects, building snowmen, feeding a dog, driving to the doctor's office, picking kids up from piano lessons, going to parent-teacher conferences, sewing hems in school uniforms, ironing men's button-down shirts . . . and so on. I think there are few résumés out there that could top my mother's were she ever to think it worthy of writing—which she never would.

As a young child—naturally, I suppose—I don't really remember being aware that my mother existed between the time I left for school in the morning and the time she arrived at the bus stop to meet me coming home. Laundry and dusting and shopping were far outside my elementary-school-age mind, and if chores were done when I got home, it certainly didn't catch my attention. As I grew older, however, my awareness of our household began to change. My mother went back to school and, at age forty-five, became a special ed teacher. After that, she often came home exhausted at 5:30 and began making dinner. Saturdays and Sundays she woke up early to rush all over, cleaning, cooking, shopping, organizing the calendar. Monday mornings she'd be up at 4:30 to write a report that had been neglected over the weekend, then she'd make me breakfast before school and zip off to work. Gradually, I began to notice that she never seemed to have a moment to herself. Simultaneously, I realized that my father, who took care of all the "manly" household chores—chopping wood, killing mice—still had time for a well-respected career and a whole slew of regular hobbies. The setup began to seem drastically unfair to me. Free time, to my high school mind, was an absolute necessity, and I was witness to the fact that my mother seemed to be getting none of it.

This is not to say that I suddenly dropped to my knees before my mother, realized the saint that she was, and thanked her. Instead, I became disappointed in her and—to my current shame and regret—ridiculed her for being so undemanding about her own needs and so willing to dedicate herself to maintaining the house and serving us. I became angry at both of my parents: at my father that his chores (take apart and reassemble the kitchen sink, work in the garden, snow-blow the driveway) seemed interesting and challenging and were always impressive to friends and relatives, while my mother's endless chores seemed layered in routine and monotony. Both my parents had careers now, but it still fell to my mother to do every trivial and mindless thing that needed to be done, and I was frustrated with her for never seeming to mind this or to demand more help from my father.

I spent hours as a teenager talking to her (rarely listening) about why she was so accepting of her role in our family. I would recount the way my father would stride into the house after work and she would politely have dinner waiting for him; the way there was an unspoken sentiment in our house that his career was more important than hers. "Why don't you divorce him and find a husband who will offer to clean up the kitchen after dinner and let you sit down for once?" I would yell; or, "How come his job takes precedence over everything else while yours has to fit around all the other things you do and have always done?" Somehow, my mother was always able to shrug me off—to reply that she was fine, that someday I would understand. But I wasn't at all sure that I would, or that she was. What's more, I believed myself to be a feminist, and I vowed never to fall into the same trap of domestic boredom and servitude that I saw my mother as being fully entrenched in; never to settle for a life that was, as I saw it, lacking independence, authority, and respect.

. . .

I met my own boyfriend, Paul, during my senior year of college. He was absolutely the furthest thing possible from my father, which was exactly what I was looking for at the time. Though I love my father passionately, I was certain that the man of my life would know how to cook dinner and clean the house, would offer to do the dishes, would fold the laundry without being asked. My goal was to avoid the domestic life that my mother had found for herself; the first step was to have a liberal, open-minded boyfriend. I found one with dreadlocks, a nose ring, and a passion for that most nonacademic of subjects, music—just the opposite of my traditional and overly intellectual father.

On our first date, Paul offered to cook me dinner, and when it was over he did all the dishes. When I'd stop by his house (which he shared with three other male friends), I would marvel at the way he seemed to take care of cleaning up the kitchen, the way he would look disapprovingly at his housemates' dirty underwear on the bathroom floor. His books were neatly arranged on a shelf in his bedroom, his clothes were well folded in drawers, and he even had a laundry bag with his name on it. I was hooked. This man seemed to know how to do all the things my own father couldn't or wouldn't ever do. After a few months of dating, I called a friend from home one night and talked at length about how this guy seemed so perfect; how he was so responsible, so thoughtful; how I just couldn't imagine him ever expecting me to take care of all the housework, the child care, the dinners, were we ever to get married.

My mother and I had long conversations about how she had gone from her father to her husband without ever spending a segment of her life independently. She commented often about how lucky I was, and how glad she was for me, that I was part of a generation that got to make educated decisions about how their lives would go. "You have choices," she'd say. "Be thankful that you're so aware of the qualities that are important to you in a husband, before you run off to get married. When I was your age, girls didn't even realize what they were getting into when they got married. It was just the thing to do." Once, during one of these conversations, I asked her if she'd do it over again differently if she could. In one of her most open and honest moments with me, she said, "Yes. Definitely." Though I realize now that her answer had to do with more than just household responsibilities, at the time I felt so lucky knowing that I would never repeat her domestic lot, that I would not go from my father's home to my husband's. I felt proud that I would create a home with my husband based on shared responsibility and input; proud that I was, in fact, already on the road to doing it.

. . .

Then I visited Paul's family.

Paul and I were upstairs watching a movie when his mother called us down to dinner. The table was set, the food was ready, and we sat down. In a few moments Paul's father arrived and instantly complained that his favorite hot sauce was not on the table. His mother leapt up to get it. Dinner was over in about eight minutes, and almost as if by a feat of magic, everyone was gone from the kitchen before I had even put down my fork. Paul was on the piano, improvising a song to play for me; his father was upstairs reading the paper. Paul's mother and I spent the next twenty minutes cleaning up, loading the dishwasher, and putting the food away. A mother of two sons, she immediately loved me and has been fond of me ever since. She was delighted with Paul's choice.

I, on the other hand, suddenly felt my first twinge of anger and resentment toward Paul. *Surely he can't realize I'm still in the kitchen, washing his plate,* I thought. But I knew he did. And it was as if, in a matter of minutes, his personality had a whole new side I hadn't noticed before. This man, who had been so different from my father, was immediately just like him, all because of what he didn't do or even notice. And I believe, looking back on that evening, that had I not already been so filled with a kind of rage at the ease with which so many men seemed able to overlook the daily tasks that women did for them, I would not even have really minded doing dishes with Paul's mother. Certainly, I would not have suddenly decided to be on the lookout for this trend in him—would not have begun the awful, silent process of tallying up and storing away and keeping tabs on what he helped out with and what he did not.

. . .

Now it is almost three years later, and the same boyfriend is lying in our bed, in our apartment, trying to recover from a winter flu. I glance at him while writing these words, and seeing his peaceful breaths rise and fall under our soft down comforter, I feel total affection for him. He is delightful—considerate, attentive, and kind—and I feel lucky to share my life with him. I look the other way, however, into our kitchen, and upon seeing a pile of dirty dishes in the sink, I fall back into a silent conversation that has been going on in my head since we happily, if blindly, moved in together last fall.

It begins something like this: "Does it just not occur to him that I worked all day and might like to come home to a place where I don't immediately have to start cleaning in order to feel some sense of peace with where I am? Am I the only one who cares that our house is a mess?" And then the list of things he hasn't done, or has done wrong, comes flooding, pouring, rushing into my mind. I count the number of times I stopped at the grocery store on my way home this week and compare it with the number of times he has voluntarily done the same. I replay the scene from last weekend, when we were expecting friends to come for dinner, and he showed up at 5:30 after a full day of cross-country skiing with a friend and claimed to have "forgotten" that we were responsible for making a meal for four.

Or I think about the numerous times that I have come into the house, exhausted, at 7:00 after a full day of work and a meeting after school, and found him searching for music on the Internet instead of preparing a dinner for us both. On those days, I have silently walked into the kitchen and begun chopping vegetables or boiling water for spaghetti, and with every slice of my knife, every pot that I pulled from the cupboard, I grow angrier and angrier, until I could not even stand his presence in the same room. He might walk in and say something as innocent as "What can I do to help?" or even "Why don't you sit down and let me make dinner?" and I would absolutely explode with fury, shooting back at him, "Well, I'm starving and exhausted and I don't really feel like waiting around for you to finish your fucking Internet search so that I can eat something before nine o'clock!"

On such occasions I will be angry for thirty minutes, or maybe until I have eaten something. I will ruminate on the place of the woman in today's "modern" society. I will cook and clean, and all the while think about how I am falling into the same trap of housework that my own mother fell into. As I scrub the kitchen sink, I will hear her voice saying, "You have choices," and I will scowl at the concept of a choice. I will decide that my modern, liberal, open-minded boyfriend, having been raised by a mother who did everything in the home (in addition to having a job), will never notice or care if his girlfriend or wife takes over those same domestic responsibilities. He is capable of doing all of them, but if they get done for him, my thoughts go, he might never even realize that they needed doing in the first place.

But then slowly, as I finish picking up the dirty clothes from the floor, I will think about his day, will remember that he works long hours, too—and that he loves music, that finding new albums to record off our computer is a way for him to relax, to wind down. It will occur to me that maybe he was waiting for me to come home so that we could eat together; that he didn't know I would be arriving so late; that he was sincere, rather than just trying to avoid a fight, when he offered to cook for me. Perhaps I will remember that he had a meeting after school, too, and had probably arrived home only fifteen minutes before I did. Gradually, my anger will start to wane, and in its place will come guilt and confusion and sadness. I will imagine my own mother, coming in from a long day—or, worse, having never even left the work of the house—and wanting nothing more than to sit down and read the paper; and in a million years, her husband would never have offered to make her dinner, as my boyfriend has just done for me. The question in my mind then becomes, Why didn't I let him? Why, when he was standing right there, ready and willing, did I ignore the chance to pour myself a glass of wine and sit on the couch for twenty minutes while he prepared a meal for me? Why, instead, did I become so angry so fast?

The answer, sadly, surprisingly, self-defeatingly, is that I want to be angry. Or at least, I *choose* to be angry over the long list of alternate emotions waiting in line: guilt, sadness, the exhaustion of trying to change things, to figure it all out. I feel angry at the confusion of adoring my mother, of thinking she is a phenomenal woman who raised her children with grace and style, of thinking I would give anything to be like her . . . and at the same time, looking down on her for all the things she quietly accepted, and knowing that I want to be nothing like that. I feel angry at the confusion of wanting my own relationship to be balanced, to share all responsibilities equally, yet at the same time, wanting things done my way—with the tidiness and timeliness that I have inherited from my parents. I feel frustrated by the guilt that accompanies asking Paul to take the initiative to run the dishwasher, to do the laundry without shrinking my sweaters, to buy groceries that are healthy . . . to ask for what my mother never would have, to be what she would have considered a "nag." In wanting my home to be as well organized as my mother kept hers, I feel as though I must choose between doing everything myself and constantly asking Paul to do more.

I already know how to manage a household, not because I asked someone to teach me, but because I watched my mother and learned while I spent countless hours by her side (or on her hip) all those Saturdays when she worked from 7:00 A.M. to bedtime to keep our house running. I never asked for this knowledge. I never wanted the internal clock that tells me enough time has gone by that we really should change our sheets; never requested the awareness of how long it takes to make lasagna and thus the willingness to give up an afternoon so that dinner will be ready when the guests arrive. I never asked for anyone to teach me how to wash my silk shirts by hand. But, of course, as almost all girls do, I learned, and now I'm stuck with it. And no matter how much I sometimes wish I wasn't the one in my relationship who knows all this, I admit that I also sometimes feel proud of knowing it all, and proud that I do it all well.

Last weekend, Paul and I agreed to house-sit and baby-sit for neighbors of ours with four children. Almost immediately, I found myself taking over everything, rather than showing Paul how to do it. Though he asked me several times to show him how to run the fancy washing machine, I never did teach him. Instead, I did all the laundry myself, making the trip down the basement steps three or four times a day, furious that he was watching a movie with the kids while I was doing chores. When Keith, the six-year-old, needed breakfast, rather than mentioning it to Paul or asking him for help, I simply made pancakes for everyone, then fumed as we all ate them together. When Paul asked me what was the best way to clean a cast-iron skillet, I responded harshly to just leave it and I would take care of it myself. The weekend was a seemingly endless stream of moments when I angrily "did it myself" instead of showing him how. Every dish that he didn't notice I had picked up for him, every morsel of food he ate that I had cooked, every stair I descended that led to the clothes dryer, was another tick in my mental log of things to resent him for.

I returned home from the weekend of baby-sitting exhausted physically, mentally, and emotionally, commenting again and again how glad I was that we don't have kids or pets or even our own washing machine. But as my anger waned, I realized I was feeling something else, too: a sense of power and pride in knowing that I had been the supermom for the weekend. I was the one who had kept everything under control. It was I who'd made sure that the kids were picked up on time, took showers each night, ate a vegetable at dinner. I felt as though I could have done the whole thing myself. The package was complete: anger and pride.

. . .

So there it is. In trying to find a man as different as possible from my own father, in trying to avoid the life of an overworked housewife that I see my mother as having occupied for more than thirty years now, in choosing a boyfriend partly for his willingness and readiness to share the "woman's work," I am freely walking closer and closer to everything I had wanted to escape, enraged with every step I take. Somehow, some part of this cycle seems unavoidable, unchangeable. Paul will read what I've written here and ask me, so earnestly, "What can we do to solve this problem?" and already I know that I will shrug him off. "It's just me," I'll respond, "this is something I need to deal with."

Rather than trying to impart to him some of the domestic knowledge and sense of responsibility that I have, I will, I fear, go on being angry that he wasn't given it to begin with; angry that, unlike me, he was not closely observing, for his future, his own mother during the many hours she spent taking care of everyone in the family, and therefore now doesn't have the voice in his head telling him he *should* be constantly aware of tasks that need to be done, of meeting everyone else's needs before his own. And yet, side by side with this anger, will be the pride, the satisfaction of knowing that someday I could be an excellent mother, always available to my children and maintaining a well-kept home, all with a kid by my side or on my hip—like my own mother. I will, I fear, go on doing as much as I can, caught between pride and anger, furious at my exhaustion and Paul's inadequacy. Almost as if to entitle my anger, to justify or even fuel a frustration that's already there, I will—for now, at least—refuse any help from anyone, then bask in the fury of having too much to do and no time for myself. Recently, I have been thinking back to the years I spent as a kid living at home with my parents. Only now, when I have an apartment of my own and am responsible for my own meals and dishes and laundry and everything else, am I beginning to gain a more complete understanding of what my mother was doing between five or six or seven in the morning and bedtime. Owning a home, raising a family, maintaining sanity in a house—these are not small jobs, and my mother accomplished them all expertly, even after she added a career to the list. Though I wish she could have been more relaxed, that she and my father could have shared the chores in the house more equally, I'm beginning to understand why she didn't leave him. I'm beginning to see that she didn't just lie down and accept everything from the start, but that her role, her tasks, her *dissatisfaction,* came gradually, over a period of years. And along with whatever anger she felt beneath her cool exterior, there must have been, too, a tremendous sense of pride that came with knowing she was such an integral part of our family.

Whether I will follow her steps and have a family of my own I don't yet know. I do know that as I write these words and glance at my still-sleeping companion, I feel an odd mixture of frustration and love. Together we have a wonderful, open, trusting relationship, but sometimes I wonder if the hostility already in me, and my need to be angry at someone or something, could eventually destroy our bond. I suppose only time will tell. Unlike my mother, I don't have to go from my father's house to my husband's. And perhaps it's simply this time and space to think about the future and to love and live with and learn from whomever I please—time and space and freedom my mother never had—that she referred to when she said I have choices. At twenty-four, living in this day and age, I still have years to figure things out; to try to learn how to feel pride and even power without running myself ragged; to be with a man without being angry for the rest of my life. I hope I can.

Getting the Milk for Free

Veronica Chambers

THE TRUTH IS that I've never had many fantasies about marriage. The daughter of a brutal divorce, I never dreamed of being a bride. One long flowing white dress was the same as any other. The veil never seemed romantic; walking down the aisle, an engagement ring the size of Texas, a honeymoon on some secluded beach . . . none of them worked their way into my dreams. Even when I was as young as ten or eleven, I'd watch a TV show or movie with a blushing bride and a glowing groom and I'd be as jaded as an eighty-year-old three-time divorcée. "Wait till ya get home," a deep voice would growl from inside me. "That's when the shit will hit the fan." The year my own parents divorced, *Kramer vs. Kramer* came out. To say I took it as a sign is to put it lightly. I embraced it as a life lesson, along the lines of a Grimms' fairy tale. It was ugly, it was heartbreaking, it was utterly real.

. . .

My earliest and clearest memory is of a time when I was three years old. Our family was living in England in the military town of Peterborough. My father was in the air force. It was late at night and my mother, who was pregnant, was flopped across the bed wailing. My father appeared at the doorway and she started screaming at him. "Where have you been? Where have you been?" My father stomped across to the closet and pulled out a suitcase. He began to throw his clothes in, shouting expletives at my mother, who was screaming and crying and pounding the bed with her arms and legs. Then my father turned to me, as if seeing me for the first time, and said, "I'm leaving. Do you want to come with me or stay with her?" I could tell by the tone of his voice that there was only one right answer, so I said, "Come with you." My mother screamed louder, as if my words were bullets, arrows, stones. "I've got to go someplace right now," my father said. "I'll be back for you later." He took his suitcase and left.

Even writing this, I wonder about the veracity of my memory. I was only three, I know. But I remember it so clearly—perhaps because it was a scene that would be played out again and again. In the house on Beverly Road, in the blue dining room with its crystal chandelier that sparkled and made me feel that our family was finally rich (we weren't) and that we would all finally be happy (also untrue). In the house on Rutland Road, where the tub didn't work and my mother boiled hot water to bathe us when the pipes froze. In the brick building near Kings Highway, right across the street from the public school. Different houses, same scenario. My mother's tears. My father's temper. And always the dramatic exit, delivered with an ultimatum: Who did my little brother and I want to live with? Who did we love more? Were we coming or were we going? Again and again, my father forced us to betray our mother by uttering his name as the most loved. Then he betrayed us by walking out the door. By the time I was ten years old and he left for good, I was exhausted. "We're getting a divorce," he said. "At last," I thought.

After that, I remember a Sunday afternoon sitting in our backyard playing Barbies with a friend. "This is who Barbie marries," I said, grabbing Malibu Ken. "And this is who she marries after she divorces him," I said, reaching for a brunette Ken doll. My friend's mother, overhearing our conversation, was clearly disturbed. "Barbie doesn't have to get divorced," she said to me, in the soothing tones of an adult speaking to a child. "She will if she wants to be happy," I announced snappily.

In the years following my parents' divorce, I made several decisions about the life I would have as a grown-up woman. By the time I was twelve, I'd sworn myself to a couple of very firm vows. First, I would not have a baby before I was twenty-one, as was the norm in my family and my neighborhood. And second, I would live with a man before I agreed to marry him. In fact, I would live with him for many years, possibly ten. So by the time we got married, I would know him completely. Chances were good we would divorce anyway, but at least I'd enter into the Faustian bargain of marriage with both eyes open.

The first vow proved relatively easy to accomplish. The second has proven more complicated. In fact, it became something I struggled with for the next decade and a half.

. . .

I can't remember when I first heard the phrase "Why buy the cow when you can get the milk for free?" But I do know that it did not immediately offend me. I had already figured out that my virginity could be commodified. Some people urged me to "save it." Others cautioned me not to "give it away cheaply." Boys and later men made offers—both emotional and material—for the chance to deflower me. When I first heard the old saw about the cow and the milk, I wasn't rankled at the thought of being compared to a cow. I thought, "Well, this is interesting. Even sex after virginity has a price stamped on it."

Still, it seemed to me that living with a man was the best way to get to know him. And I so desperately wanted to know a man before I made a lifelong commitment to him. Friends of mine would speak about the compatibility of living habits. Are you messy or neat? Are you a day person or a night person? I wanted to live with a man because I feared that in the hours we spent apart, I might miss crucial information about his hidden dark side. As a person who will always choose to hear the bad news before the good, I wanted to know: Would he come home when he said he would? Would strange women call the house? After the initial rush of romance, would he tune in to the TV and tune me out? Slam his fist against the wall when he was frustrated? Slam his fist against me?

Immediately following my college graduation, it seemed that all of my closest girlfriends moved in with a man. As they shopped for furniture at

Ikea, hosted small dinner parties, and collaborated on Martha Stewart-esque projects from gardening to brewing their own beer, I watched with no small amount of envy. The desire to live with a man began to take on a different meaning for me. Now I wanted to do it not to inspect him, close up, for marriage material. Forget marriage. I wanted to do what my friends were doing. I wanted to play house.

A few years later, I was living in California when I met a man and fell madly in love. It was a long-distance relationship and I soon moved back home to New York to be with him. A struggling painter, he lived in a marginal neighborhood in a marginal building that I never once considered living in myself. I had a good job and found an apartment of my own, a sunny miniduplex on a pretty brownstone street not too far from where he lived.

. . .

At first, my boyfriend began spending weeknights at my house and weekends painting at his home. But soon enough, my house became our house. For one thing, it was well stocked. His apartment, on a good day, might have had a box of dry pasta and some stale cereal. For me, weekly visits to the local gourmet grocery store and four-star wine shop meant that my pad was regularly outfitted with wine and beer, meat and fish, fresh olives and fruit.

My boyfriend's place was the type of apartment you couldn't get truly clean if you tried. One step above a squatter's rest, it was located in a building in a row of factories. The windows were permanently caked with soot; the thrift-shop furniture was as tattered as a rag doll missing a leg and a significant part of her stuffing. There was a small television and stereo, but no cable TV. My boyfriend said that as an artist he didn't care about material possessions, but that didn't stop him from getting comfy on my Shabby Chic overstuffed couch and watching ESPN at my place on Sunday afternoons.

The customary dresser drawer that dating couples reserve in each other's house for clean underwear and a change of clothes turned into one of my apartment's two closets as he stuffed into it half of his wardrobe and a hefty pile of sketchbooks and painting supplies. My boyfriend began to receive most of his phone calls and all of his important mail at my place. For all intents and purposes, we were living together. But he never paid rent or contributed to the food bills or the utilities.

In retrospect, I can see how it might seem that I was blatantly being bamboozled. But the fact was that my boyfriend was very sweet and not the least bit conniving. He could barely pay the rent on his own apartment; his parents frequently chipped in to prevent eviction. So how, I asked myself, could I ask him to contribute to—much less split—my own sizable rent? I love him, I would remind myself. I want him to eat my food and spend each night with me. So I offered everything and asked for nothing and told myself that I was being the perfect girlfriend.

The truth is that I never knew how to ask him for what I wanted, for what was fair. The only thing I knew to do with a man was what I'd learned from my parents: to fight or not fight. I had no idea how to craft a partnership beyond that one basic thing. What's more, discussing finances or asking for help around the house seemed very minor compared to the Important Things. My boyfriend didn't hit me, he didn't yell at me. What more could I ask? The only thing that was taking a beating was my checking account.

Of course, after a while, it all came around; by underwriting our relationship so drastically, I wasn't giving my boyfriend a chance to be my partner, and I began to resent the imbalances. I tried to say so, sort of. But old habits die hard and I wasn't asking for changes very firmly. In turn, my boyfriend wasn't exactly making change easy. He reminded me that our living together, as it was, was all my idea. He said he wouldn't clean my apartment, because he had his own apartment/studio to worry about. He wouldn't pay for risotto and top-of-the-line Parmesan; at his apartment, he reminded me, he ate Kraft macaroni and cheese and that was just fine. He knew his limits, he went on. If I wanted to enjoy certain things, I had to pay for them.

So I did. I paid and paid and paid. For a cleaning woman and the groceries and the cable and our vacations, because I didn't want to eat at the Shark Bar alone or vacation in South Beach without him. The old saw about living together took on a decidedly different tone in our relationship. Not only was my boyfriend getting the milk for free, the cow came with room and board, Broadway tickets, and all-expenses-paid vacations. I don't mind saying now that that cow was producing gourmet cream.

. . .

It's been five years since that relationship ended, and in the time since, I've done an about-face on the subject of living together. I decided that I didn't want to live with a man unless we were getting married—unless we were officially engaged. Part of this, of course, came from analyzing and deconstructing what exactly happened during those years with my boyfriend. But another part I owe to a friend who fell in love with a guy we all adored. When I asked her why she didn't move in with him, she explained that she wouldn't until she was engaged. I was taken aback. Was she trying to manipulate him? Was this some twist on The Rules? As our conversation went on, it became clear that my friend's attitude was an interesting blend of old-fashioned values and modern feminist ideals. She was her own woman, with her own apartment, who paid her own bills. Why should she sacrifice that independence, she asked me, unless it was to build her life with another person? She wouldn't move in with her boyfriend unless they were soon-to-be-married because she didn't want to give up her autonomy except in exchange for a deep, lifelong commitment.

I began to think differently about living with a man (not to mention what I wanted and needed from a future boyfriend, but that's a whole other story). Living together was less a step on the way to marriage and more a sacrifice I would make in exchange for something else: something equally great but very different. The kind of relationship I wanted with the man I would live with had to be worth giving up all the richness of my single life. I considered my well-stocked fridge, my good snow boots and warm winter coats, the hundreds of books that surrounded me like postcards from exquisite worldly friends, the paintings I'd struggled to buy, in whose swirls I could lose myself for hours. All of it filled me with a sense of pride and deep contentment about the home I'd built for myself, every bit of it with money I'd earned by working hard. I realized, perhaps for the first time, that it was an accomplishment that I could take care of myself so well—especially since, unlike my ex-boyfriend, I'd never had parents who could help me out. And if my tastes ran toward the expensive—if I'd rather have good champagne than cheap beer, or gourmet Brie than Kraft mac and cheese—I'd earned the right to those tastes, not to mention the cash to pay for them, and I would have them proudly. And never again would I share everything else without asking for anything in return. In the name of love or anything else.

. . .

About a year ago, I met another man and again fell in love. He lived in Philadelphia in an airy, spacious brownstone; I lived in New York in a charming, sunny apartment with a working fireplace and a view (both worth their weight in Big Apple gold). From the beginning, we talked about how much we valued our homes and the time we were able to spend alone. Early on, we would often say how great it was that we lived in different cities. We could enjoy weekends together, but we could also enjoy our time alone. Then a funny thing happened; increasingly, we couldn't bear to be apart. I spent long afternoons reading on the couch in his living room. He spent more and more evenings settled in by my fireplace. We were two fiercely private people who found it very easy to share, perhaps because each of us respected how hard the other had worked to build a home of our own. Within a year, we were engaged. We sublet our homes and found a place in the tristate middle ground: New Jersey.

It's so early in our journey to build a life together, and the little girl in me is still wary of what the future may hold. But so far, this is what I have to report: we both buy the milk and we both buy the champagne. And I think we both feel that it's a pretty good deal.

Crossing to Safety

Jen Marshall

A WEEK AFTER I graduated from college, seven years ago, I moved in with my boyfriend, Doug. Like most college sweethearts attending the same school, we'd been practically inseparable. Doug was my first boyfriend, and it was bliss—until he graduated. I still had one more year to go. In order to avoid a campus that would be made immeasurably duller without him (the university was in central Pennsylvania, after all), I spent half of my senior year abroad. We wrote to each other almost every day, my letters describing kangaroos and rain forests, his chronicling job interviews and investigations into places he might want to live.

One day, a letter arrived from Doug that had not been written on the usual onionskin airmail stationery. The envelope and paper inside it were heavy and opaque with news. "I've found a job as an environmental engineer in western Massachusetts," he wrote. "I'm moving to a town called South Hadley. It's pretty and near mountains and lots of colleges. I think you would like it there." He had enclosed the promotional brochure for the apartment complex where, with the help of his mother, he'd found an apartment. "Welcome to Riverboat Village," it read. There were line drawings of one- and two-bedroom layouts, as well as some illustrations of trees and, of course, a river. A quote from a happy resident said it all: "Today, I saw a deer." I read Doug's letter with a mixture of trepidation and tentative elation. I had vaguely imagined myself working in book publishing or as an English professor after college. Could either career be pursued in South Hadley? I wasn't sure, but I did know that I wanted to be with Doug. And of these two desires, only one could be made a certainty with just a swish of my pen. Pushing hesitation aside, I wrote back to Doug and said I would love to live in South Hadley, Massachusetts.

. . .

A few months later, as I packed up my tiny pink and purple room at my parents' house in Connecticut, I felt as if I was on the verge of becoming a real adult. I'd read the mushy novels, seen all the right movies, and watched *Days of Our Lives* for almost eleven years, so I knew that Living Together was a major milestone in the progression of love. Aglow with anticipation, I didn't care that Riverboat Village had turned out to be a gray, faux-colonial-style complex with an abundance of squirrels and parking lots rather than deer. I didn't mind that Doug refused to throw out a plaster lamp shaped and painted to resemble a preschool version of himself as a peewee hockey player, or that the lamp was now atop a chest of drawers in what would soon be our bedroom. I glossed over the fact that the only job I could find was as a $5.50-an-hour clerk at a pseudo head shop. As for South Hadley, I told myself I would grow to appreciate its country charm. So what if there were no museums, no city sidewalks, no famous publishing houses where I could pursue my dream of editing the great American novel someday . . . not even, it seemed, an available peer group of women my own age? None of that would matter, because I had a boyfriend and we were moving in together.

All my life, I had been taught that a romance headed for Weddingville was the Holy Grail, the answer to every question. My adolescence had been a jumble of breathless conversations about boys and what they did and who they liked and how my nerdy friends and I could ever induce any of them to fall in love with us. Rather than rerouting this inane chatter into more productive channels, my parents reinforced it, wondering aloud if the reason why I didn't have a prom date was that I spent too much time alone, reading. Eventually, most of my friends found willing boys to kiss in the Burger King parking lot on Friday nights. But I didn't. Instead, I had nightmares that I was twenty-five and had still never been on a date. Matters weren't helped when, my senior year in high school, my dad "jokingly" wondered if I wasn't bringing home boys because I was a lesbian. When I assured him that I did like boys—they just didn't like *me,* so far—I saw in his face for the first time how relief can utterly transform someone's features. It's understandable that I came to believe that finding the right man was the central goal in life. And now that I had Doug, I expected that everything else would naturally fall into place.

. . .

At first, living with Doug was just as cozy as I'd envisioned it. We decorated our small apartment with charming garage sale finds. Weeknight dinners spontaneously evolved into candlelit occasions complete with heartfelt toasts and classical music, even though we were only eating tofu pups and beans. In short, we had lots of convivial fun before the dull puzzle of reality set in. First of all, we had to deal with the bathroom. Neither of us wanted to clean it. Or share it. And then there was the problem of how to make money matters fair, when his salary was four times mine. It was scary how powerless I felt just because I made less money than he did. I began to suspect that this whole living together thing was not as simple as it looked on TV.

Another issue was my job at the head shop. Selling fake tattoos and patchouli incense to pimply tenth graders was decidedly not what I'd gone to college for. Of course, lots of recent graduates have similar experiences and cheerfully work as ski instructors or lifeguards while they figure out whether or not to apply to law school. That's probably why I'd thought living an undecided, exploratory year would be easy. However, I should have remembered where I came from. When I was growing up, my family wasn't exactly rolling in cash. And so ever since the day it was legal for me to work, I'd been (in chronological succession) a baby-sitter, a cashier at a run-down grocery store, a waitress, a clerk at Caldor, and a chambermaid. Most of these jobs involved zippered polyester smocks, plastic visors, and constant humiliation. Richer kids would come by Caldor or the grocery store just to make fun of me. I went to college in part so I'd never, ever have to work at a job like that again. And yet here I was, college degree in hand, selling candles and roach clips.

Making matters worse was Doug's comparative success. Unlike me, he had found a real first job in the field of his choice. He came home from work every night full of stories about how interesting it was to have an office and like-minded coworkers. My employment tales usually concerned yet another shoplifting attempt on the Hacky Sack display. He had health insurance and a business card with his name printed on it. I had a locker and a bottle of Windex for wiping down the jewelry counter. Unbelievably to me now, I felt guilty rather than resentful when I compared his work with mine. "Maybe I'm not cut out to be anything but a clerk in a store," I thought to myself, "and this is what people mean when they say you can't make a silk purse out of a sow's ear." In a misguided attempt to make up for the equal money and analogous work experience that I wasn't contributing to our life together, I cooked complicated dinners and took on chores like reorganizing the laundry closet and sorting Doug's sock drawer by color and texture. At Christmas, I even hand-sewed a Victorian caroling costume for the little stuffed animal topping our tree. Before long, I resembled a housewife straight out of Hollywood's central casting, complete with secret sorrows just begging to be smothered by Valium.

One night, while preparing an especially punishing dinner, I accidentally placed a big, empty glass casserole dish on an extremely hot electric stove burner. I turned away before I realized my mistake and a half second later a terrifying *pop* filled the closet-sized kitchen. The dish had exploded, and every imaginable cranny was sprinkled with shards of glass—big French-fry-shaped chunks and little itty-bitty bug wing slivers and all sizes in between. Miraculously, I was not cut. I stared at the sparkling mess in disbelief. And the first thought that came into my head was that I should just walk away. Just leave it. Because the idea of having to painstakingly go over every inch of that kitchen made me want to get into bed and not come out until I lived someplace else, someplace where I would be interested in the life I was living.

After that, even when I did manage to make a meal without some minor domestic mishap sending me straight into the slough of despond, it was no guarantee I'd be civil to Doug when he came home from work at night. In fact, just the sound of his shoes on the carpeted stair leading to our apartment was enough to make me incoherent with anger and frustration. Doug always smiled when he walked through the door, happy to see me, and all I could think was "Is this it?" And this *was* it, apparently, and that made me so sad and at the same time so ashamed of my sadness, and the two feelings together choked me. I couldn't stop myself from starting stupid fights about everything from the temperature of the apartment to which music we listened to. Afterward, when we were in bed, silent, with our backs to each other, I would feel terrible and stay up half the night quizzing myself. What was my problem? I was living with a smart, sensitive, handsome man whom I wanted to marry someday! Why did I feel like a hornet trapped under a drinking glass, frantically dreaming of escape? Wasn't cohabitational bliss the jackpot I was supposed to spend my twenties desperately pursuing? And I had it now, at twenty-two, eight years ahead of schedule! How could I possibly be less than thrilled?

I doggedly made up my mind to try to be happier with the lot I'd lucked into. After all, you just didn't give up on a live-in honey like mine. Everybody knew that.

Step one in my South Hadley Self-Improvement Plan was landing a job at the neighborhood bookstore, which allowed me to quit the hideous head shop. Next, I learned to identify birds, since hobbies are known to relieve boredom and despair. I resolved to find beauty instead of emptiness in the farm fields surrounding us. I volunteered at the local family planning clinic so I could think about someone else's problems for a change. I even swallowed a multivitamin every day.

Although these measures had their small (and, later, much larger) benefits, they hardly addressed the real issues keeping me awake every night: Why wasn't living with Doug making me happy? Had I become some kind of weird western Massachusetts June Cleaver/Carol Brady hybrid despite my frantic efforts to the contrary? And if I had, was this what I would *stay*? Unchecked, my misery at home soon spilled over into other aspects of my life. At the bookstore, I growled at customers who reshelved biographies in with the gardening titles. I rarely felt hungry anymore. I dreaded seeing anyone other than a few close friends, because embarrassing questions might be asked about my postgraduation achievements. Hiding at Riverboat Village and reading obsessively became my chief occupations. Doug started to wonder if I wasn't a little insane. Maybe I was.

Finally, even I couldn't take my low mood any longer. I was sick of my "inexplicable" disappointment with life. Out of desperation, I decided to see a psychologist. Dr. Jerald. I had my concerns about him right away because he had a bookshelf full of military history titles in his office, but he was all my insurance would cover. Two sessions later, Dr. Jerald put me on an antidepressant. I liked the tiny white pills because they let me sleep like a normal person. But the prescription did little to restore my appetite or to dissolve my dissatisfaction with what my life had turned into and who and what I had become.

The break came when my best friend from college invited me to her apartment in New Jersey for a weekend visit. Part of that trip was an afternoon spent sight-seeing in Manhattan. I had only been to New York twice before: once with my grandmother to see *Cats* (for my twelfth birthday), and later, in college, when a kind professor drove a small group of students in so we could hear Sharon Olds read at the Academy of American Poets. Both times I remember feeling intensely and oddly comforted by every aspect of the city, as if it were my familiar home. Now, as my friend and I drove over the George Washington Bridge and into Manhattan, the same heady sense of crossing to safety came over me. Later in the day, while touring the Museum of Modern Art, I began to feel hungry for the first time in months. That night, I ate enough at dinner for two people my size.

. . .

When I told Dr. Jerald this, he blinked and sat up in his chair. "Hmm," he said. "Now, I don't know that we'll find this in any medical textbook, but your experience sounds like a geographical cure if ever I've heard of one. Let's talk about what it might be like if you were to move to New York." My stomach turned. Doug adored western Massachusetts and rural life right down to the last green leaf. That he would never move to a city was a certainty both frightening and—suddenly—thrilling. As I discussed my contradictory feelings with Dr. Jerald, possibilities that I hadn't previously considered began to appear. Maybe I wasn't ready to live with a boyfriend. And maybe that was just fine, and not a measure of how much I loved him. After all, as I'd found, living full-time with a romantic partner involved compromise on many levels. How could I unreservedly give large parts of myself to someone else when I hardly knew who I was or what I wanted to become? New York, exploring a publishing career, and time alone suddenly seemed obvious rather than ridiculous.

Still—even though I knew Doug didn't like cities and also that I needed to be on my own—I asked him to come to New York. In truth, I begged him. I was really scared to go there by myself. But any uneasiness I felt was soon replaced by fury. In his eloquent refusal, the love of my life let it slip that he didn't believe I'd make it in the big city. He reasoned that because I was constantly so depressed in South Hadley, there was no guaranteeing I'd be content in New York—or anywhere else, for that matter. Why should he relocate if there was every chance I'd still be unhappy and want to leave for yet another new place in six months? What if sadness was in my blood? I hated him for about a minute and then realized I could hardly blame him for how he felt. I had been miserable for the past year and a half. It was clear that if I wanted to try New York, I'd have to do it myself. And once we agreed, I felt oddly liberated. I would do this, and do it alone. Now I just had to find a job and a place to live.

It turned out to be easy. Because part of my job at the bookstore had been planning author events there, I'd met quite a few book publishing people from New York, and a call to one of them resulted in an interview almost immediately. That led to my first publishing job, as an assistant in a book publicity department. It paid $24,000 a year, a fortune compared to what I made at the bookstore. Then, just as I was beginning to panic about where I'd live, an old family friend of Doug's wandered into the store and told me she knew some young women just outside the city who might need a roommate. I moved to New York two weeks later, with Doug's blessing. Neither of us ever considered breaking up. I still loved him deeply, and I knew he felt the same way. Thus began our long-term, long-distance monogamy.

After a few months in New York, though, I wondered if I had done the right thing in keeping a hometown sweetie. City living was even more fun than I had ever imagined. How much better might it be if half of me wasn't constantly being pulled in another direction? It also didn't help that my new friends thought I was crazy not to date, especially since Doug and I weren't even engaged. Working in publicity for a major book publisher meant that I attended lots of swanky book parties with free food and electric-pink cocktails. Who knew what great guys I might meet? My glamorous, well-groomed boss would lean across her palatial desk and whisper, "No ring, no strings! Break up with him and be done with it! Wear more skirts. Go out every night. He's not the one for you." I'd listen, wondering if I should follow this honest-to-goodness sophisticated New Yorker's advice even though she'd never met or talked to Doug. I settled on a compromise: Go to the parties with an open mind, but still see my much-missed boyfriend every weekend. So that's what I did. And what I found was that the parties were invariably filled with nervous writers, tipsy editorial assistants bragging about their bosses, and loads of elegant, single women with fabulous handbags. Not one date prospect in sight. After a few of these excruciating evenings, I decided not to waste any more time thinking about dating other men. For one, it was dreadfully dull, and second, it wasn't at all why I came to New York.

Over the next year, I made more friends, found an apartment in Manhattan, and got a job with the publisher I'd always dreamed of working for. I was happy through and through. And then I decided that the one little thing I needed to make my joy complete was for Doug to move to New York. I thought about how much fun it would be to share the *New York Times* in the morning, to have someone who could carry home my heavier purchases from the Chelsea flea market. I'd also never have to go to other couples' dinner parties dateless again. So, conveniently forgetting that Doug was a card-carrying member of both the Massachusetts Audubon Society and the Appalachian Mountain Club, I began campaigning in earnest for him to come to the city. I shrieked persuasive little nothings into his ear like "If you really loved me, you'd move here!!" and "All the important things are in New York!" Not some of my more subtle moments, I now know. Even worse, when he refused to pack his bags and meet me in Manhattan, I told all of my friends that he was ruining my life.

But soon I started to notice something. Our relationship, which consisted of comforting phone calls and mostly wonderful weekend visits alternating between Manhattan and Massachusetts, afforded me something quite extraordinary: plenty of time to do exactly as I pleased. Having a long stretch of time all one's own in a city as worldly as New York is an indescribable luxury and the best gift I've ever given myself. Once I realized that, I stopped pestering Doug to move to New York and began to enjoy my double life to the hilt. Monday through Friday I devoted myself to publishing work, art classes, lectures, walks through Central Park, an ever-expanding list of good books, and lots of movies. Doug followed suit. While I mixed paint at the School of Visual Arts, he earned an M.B.A. and planned a solo hike across the New England portion of the Appalachian trail. If we still had been living together in Massachusetts while he did these things, I would have been chartreuse with envy. But now, with a life of my own to ground me, I only admired and loved him more.

Still, there was a price to pay for our unconventional arrangement. Most of our family and friends supported our long-distance romance, but they also wanted to know when I would be "done with New York" and moving back to Massachusetts. It was as if my independent life had an expiration date on it that everyone but me could see. Time to come home now, people were saying. Time to think about getting married. And if I couldn't consider those things, well, time to break up. Nobody was shy about offering an opinion, especially our parents. After one glass of wine, Doug's father was apt to say, "Well, Jen, the third year in New York is when you decide if you want to live there forever or if it's time to leave." My own dad preferred more crass pronouncements like "Time to shit or get off the pot." To my dismay, Doug's mother once hinted in her widely distributed family holiday newsletter that he and I were about to be engaged. Everyone asked when the wedding was, but almost no one asked if Doug planned to move to New York. It was infuriating how people expected me to radically amend and truncate my life so it would fit comfortably into his.

At first I responded to such opinions by nastily taking apart the profferer's own personal life. My favorite zinger went something like: "Well, I prefer to look at my situation as one that allows me to neatly avoid a disastrous first marriage. Too bad you didn't think of that." As time wore on, however, I changed my tactics considerably. Three years alone in a big city had forced me to develop and explore my own values and wishes, and eventually I understood that it didn't matter what other people thought. Aside from the minor annoyances that distance imposed upon us—outrageous phone bills, too much time spent in dim train stations—Doug and I were happier and more in love than we ever were when we lived together. And he wasn't any more anxious to shack up again than I was. So I let my mother sigh longingly over issues of *Modern Bride,* and my perhaps someday mother-in-law's church lady friends gossip about my unwillingness to conform to conventional relationship roles. They could waste their time if they wanted to, but they wouldn't waste mine anymore.

It's been five years since I moved to New York, and Doug and I, at thirty-one and twenty-nine respectively, are still content living apart. We never argue about things like who left the cap off of the toothpaste, and when friends in long-term, yet not long-distance, relationships complain to me about the seemingly natural waning of desire, I can only smile and shrug my shoulders. After a week or two of not seeing Doug, he looks pretty damn good to me in his boxer shorts. I sometimes recommend a little dash of distance to my frustrated friends, but they say I'm being unrealistic. Am I? Of course sometimes Doug and I miss each other during the week; of course we discuss living together again someday. We even talk about getting married and having children, possibly soon. And I'm excited about these possibilities. But given our history, I'd be lying if I said I didn't also worry a bit about how it will all shake out. My roommate (who also likes living separately from her longtime romantic partner) says that she and I have been spoiled by too many Saturday mornings of doing nothing but exactly what we want to do. We'll never be able to get married and have kids. Too many demands. She's joking, of course, but part of me sometimes wonders if she might be right.

Whenever I start to get too panicky about marriage one day eating up all but a crumb of my freedom, I remember a passage I love in *Elegy for Iris,* by John Bayley, who was married to the late novelist Iris Murdoch. Of the start of their long and much-celebrated marriage, he wrote: "Already we were beginning that strange and beneficent process in marriage by which a couple can, in the words of A. D. Hope, the Australian poet, 'move closer and closer apart.' The apartness is a part of the closeness, perhaps a recognition of it, certainly a pledge of complete understanding." As I read over these words, I think that Doug and I surely will have a little of Bayley's apartness that is a part of closeness in our own marriage one day (minus all the affairs Iris had, of course)—and that our relationship will be better for it. I imagine that there might even be a little outbuilding all my own behind any house we eventually live in. Who knows? But one thing I do know for sure: Neither of us is in any hurry to find out.

Moving In. Moving Out. Moving On.

Sarah Miller

I MET MIKE in Brooklyn, at a bar on Atlantic Avenue I'd never been to before and haven't since, at a birthday party for someone I didn't know and never saw again. I spent that evening trying unsuccessfully to work my way into his shifting line of sight and making halting, but constant, attempts to engage him in conversation. Whenever I addressed him, he would regard me with mild surprise: You're still at this? His responses were neutral and curt, with a possibly dismissive edge. I mentioned that in a week I was going to Europe for the first time. He replied, with cold politeness, *"Ah, Europe. How nice."* I immediately questioned my desire to go.

The more he half responded to me, the more sure I was that he had information about life that I desperately needed. I left the bar with the friend I had come with, and we headed up Atlantic Avenue. As we got into a taxi, I said, *"I'm going to marry that guy."*

At the time—almost four years ago now—I was twenty-eight years old and wrote a sex column for an occasionally inspired, largely banal, briefly defunct, and puzzlingly reincarnated men's magazine. It wasn't all that different from being a prostitute, except that I got to keep my clothes on and was paid with a corporate check instead of twenty-dollar bills. I wrote true stories about fucking and getting fucked. There were times when I thought what I wrote was funny. Mostly, I was ashamed. Each month, I presented an account of a sex and love life that was like some wild amusement park ride; in reality, both were the source of pain and endless disappointment. When I began the column, I was fairly insecure about how I behaved in my romantic life, and beginning to suspect that I acted out of not hedonistic but masochistic tendencies; by the time I had been a sex columnist for a year, I was completely disgusted with myself. How could someone who had told half a million strangers about the intimate details of her life ever be a wife, or a mother? I felt ruined, dirty, and totally unlovable. It occurred to me (as it may have occurred to Madonna when she began wearing plaid skirts, speaking in arched tones, and living in a traditional culture) that if someone would want to marry me, I might be redeemed, perhaps even re-virginated.

When most guys found out that I wrote about sex, they were very interested: There was a "Ho-ho, what have we here?" quality to their response. Mike, however, had given me an even, bored nod, and I saw just the slightest shadow pass over his eyes, as if he knew what I thought of myself, and that I was right to think it. I'd like to say it was an unconscious thought, but looking back, I think it was pretty much right there on the surface: I like hamburgers, I don't like winter, I think I should get another cat, I have to get married, because I'm a whore.

I had great difficulty pinning him down to a date, but finally, in May, he came over for dinner. He regarded my cheap aluminum pans suspiciously, saying they would give me ass cancer. He kept looking out the window, even though there was nothing to see but a wall. I had been thinking about him for months, and now that he was here, it felt weird and awkward. We stared at our food, and then pretended to regard my unexciting apartment with some special interest, and then gave each other these exaggerated wide-eyed looks: having fun, doing fine, how are you? I was determined that he not just walk out. I kissed him. It wasn't even a great kiss, but as it proceeded, I sensed that he had been seeking me as I had been seeking him. I felt a huge relief, the weight of wanting and yearning fall from me, and I felt him accept me, love me. We spent the night together, and became a couple. I spent the next week telling all my friends I was in love.

. . .

We had been together about a week. It was a hot afternoon. We sat on the couch in my dark, airless, overpriced apartment. He told me he was thinking of taking a job outside the city. *I'm being dumped,* I thought, feeling not merely defeated but terrified: what were the chances I could cavort my way through one more 1,200-word erotic farce bearing the total emptiness and misery of this rejection? Plus, I had been living with a friend and was about to move into my own place, and I couldn't stand the thought of being there all alone, in endless, terrifying silence. The place was huge, cheap, and needed a lot of work.

"I want to stay here," he was saying, *"but I just can't afford it."*

"Let's move in together," I said. He protested. He didn't want to be a pain, he was looking for a job right now, and for a while, he might not be able to pay full rent, he might not pay on time. *"I don't care,"* I told him, *"I just want you to have a nice place to live, a place where you can do your work."* He would sit down, crank out a book, sell the rights to Talk/Miramax, and we'd be rich. He would thank me in his book: "For S, who believed in me." He kept protesting. I had worked to get this apartment, he said, maybe I wanted it to myself. I looked lovingly into his eyes. *"Don't be silly,"* I said, *"it wouldn't mean anything to me if you weren't there with me."* I said, *"Don't you understand? Everything I have is yours."*

. . .

It's commonly believed that there's less pressure on a woman to be married these days than there used to be. If that's true, if things are better now than they were before, then they once must have been very bad indeed. I'm willing to buy that there's less pressure to actually walk down the aisle, but there's quite a lot of pressure not to be single, to be importantly attached to a man. I remember that around this time, a friend asked me if, when her boyfriend came back from a long trip, she should go to the airport to meet him. His flight came in at 6:00 A.M. I said that seemed a bit early for such gestures. *"But it's so romantic,"* she said, *"it's so romantic when people meet you at the airport."* I couldn't respond, because I was suddenly afraid I was going to cry. *"Don't you think it's romantic?"* she pressed. *"Who,"* I asked her, *"that I've gone out with would I have ever met at the airport? More important, who would have met me?"* She rolled her eyes as if I were being ridiculous, but I demanded to know. *"Who?"* I said. *"Who have I gone out with that would ever meet me at the airport?"* She didn't say anything. *"That's right,"* I said, ignoring her dilemma altogether now. *"There are some girls who've had a lifetime of boyfriends meeting them at the airport, and I'm not one of them." "I don't think that's how it works,"* she said. And I laughed, because to me, that's exactly how it works.

To me, there's a hierarchy among women: there are the ones most men like, the ones some men like, and the ones no one seems to like. When you start to get around marrying age, whatever stress you have been feeling in this department—probably since about the age of twelve—starts to come to a head. I've always thought of myself as somewhere between the middle and the top, and when I reached the age where engagement and wedding rings registered, it wasn't just a matter of noticing them, I read my entire fate around who was wearing them and who was not. I found myself engaging in some strange pseudoscience of worth: *She's so young and not all that pretty, maybe the guy she's marrying isn't so great . . . now that woman is so perfect, she looks nice, and smart, and of course she's beautiful, of course she's getting married . . . this woman is stunning, and what a great body, but barehanded . . . could she be a lesbian?* I realized, of course, that among the women I knew there wasn't this much rhyme or reason (though there was some) to who was attached and who wasn't. But I couldn't stop playing this game. Who was Chosen? Who was not?

It was with this sense of panic that I most fervently pursued Mike's moving in with me: so I could be a chosen one. Part of the reason I had been able to get this apartment was that I had promised to take care of two cats belonging to the previous tenants, my friends, while they spent the summer outside the city. But Mike was allergic, so I spent a better part of the week before I moved in getting myself out of this situation, at great inconvenience to my friends, to say nothing of an elderly, unwell aunt who suddenly ended up a pet owner. But I worked the phones, impervious to everyone else's schedule and agenda. *"Yes, I know you're leaving for India or Sweden or wherever in three days, but I'm sorry, and I honestly don't know what else I can do."* My friends were annoyed, not only because I was being a total asshole, but because it was painful to listen to me, insisting as I was that in a matter of days, my life had changed utterly.

Two and a half weeks after our first date, Mike and I were living together. My friend Melissa came over one Saturday while we were painting our living room. We were that special mixture of adorable and repulsive. We smiled, we laughed, we rinsed out each other's brushes and brought each other beers. Afterward, I walked my friend home. *"You guys are so in love,"* she said. *"I'm so jealous."* I know that I felt superior to her. I stopped in at the grocery store, and made my way homeward with produce bulging lushly out of the bags, basking in the glow of her envy, thinking, *These are my groceries, for my boyfriend, for our apartment.* A few days later, he asked me to marry him. I said yes.

Weeks later, it dawned on me that I hadn't thought about "moving in together" past the actual act of, well, moving in. I had fantasized about the shared purpose of tearing up floors, painting walls, and unpacking books and utensils. I had not thought very much about what we would say to each other when we were done. It took very little time to discover that the beauty and functionality of the structure we had assembled would in no way be mirrored by the life, and the relationship, lived inside it.

We started out the relationship with his owing me money, and this legacy, sadly, was to stick with us until the very end. At first, I was accommodating to a fault. I told him not to take a job if I didn't think it was good enough for him, secretly hoping, of course, that he would suck it up and take it anyway. I shielded him from the knowledge of certain expenses, and paid for things I wanted to do that he couldn't afford, saying that I didn't mind. And for a time, I didn't. After all, I believed he was only in a bad place because conditions had conspired against him, and once he was put into the right situation—a quiet place to work, a stable, pleasant place to live—he would flourish.

It's not at all surprising that in a lifetime of making poor judgments this was to be the feather in my are-you-a-stupid-idiot-or-what cap. This guy was smart, talented, and a good person. Unfortunately, he had absolutely no idea how to manage his life; if you'd given him the keys to the city, within five minutes, he would have dropped them into a sewer. I watched him nap, I watched him play video games, I watched him smoke pot. He did get a job, but he hated it, so much so that when he came home he only had enough energy to (say it with me!) nap, play video games, and smoke pot.

At first, I think, I was rather kind. I would patiently suggest that getting ahead in life involved limiting one's experiences with lethargy, intoxication, and joysticks. When I didn't see a noticeable change in his behavior, though, I started to seethe every time I saw him engaging in any non-revenue-producing activity. This is how our fight went: He would be unhappy, depressed, broke, or all three. I would suggest that he might have some responsibility for the state of his life and career. He would tell me I was cruel and that I enjoyed making him feel bad. I would insist this wasn't true and say that I did not consider getting someone to face the reality of his life to be cruel. *"You're kicking me when I'm down,"* he would say, *"I can't believe you're such an awful person."*

We must have had this fight fifty times. Every time it went exactly the same way, and every time I ended up conceding: Yes, I was an awful person, because only an awful person could kick someone when he was down. The truth—that committing to him had been a grave error—I could not admit, even to myself. So I would apologize, there would be tears, and we would carry on.

When two people who don't know each other decide to move in together, they must shift their ideas of what they hoped the person would be like to what the person actually is like. My fantasy about him was that with just a few small changes, just a little help and attention, his life would miraculously turn around. His fantasy about me was that because I had been generous, I had an endless store of patience and kindness.

. . .

I have thought since that it's a very bad idea for a man to borrow money from a woman he's dating, unless, of course, he wants to break up and is too chicken to do it outright. There are few things that make a man less attractive to women than financial instability. We can deal with men in therapy, we can deal with men crying, but I don't think gender equality will ever reach the point where we can deal with men broke. I realize that they don't want us to be broke, either, but when it comes to money, their desire, their requirements, are just not on the same scale as ours. Women might lose credibility as people when we are struggling financially, but it doesn't interfere with our identity as women. It does not make us less sexually attractive. When the situation is reversed—when the man is the one struggling—this is not the case. One of the many lessons I learned in my relationship with Mike is that I will never, ever go out with a man who isn't naturally adept at making a decent living. I don't care if I sound chauvinistic and retro—I might even think that of myself from time to time. But I will never change the way I feel about this.

I'm not saying that women should never provide financial help or support to their husbands and boyfriends, or that most women mind paying the rent or making the mortgage payment on the odd bad month. All I wanted to know, with Mike, was that if the tables were turned, I could rely on him—and I had no reason to trust this would happen. How could I? Granted, I hadn't known him long, but where was there any evidence that he had the ability to take care of himself, much less me? And what if I got pregnant and had a baby and needed to take care of it, income-free, for a while? The very idea that he would want to have sex with me but would have been at a total loss dealing with possible consequences—even if that were helping me pay for an abortion—repulsed me.

"You think you own me," he would scream, *"you think you own my time because I owe you money."* By the time our arguments degenerated to this

state, I hated him and I hated myself. We had imagined that a mutual desire to love and be loved, combined with appropriately domestic surroundings, would generate a beautiful relationship. Instead, we were waking up to a stupid, clichéd, and contemptible impasse. He wanted me to prove his worth as a man by believing in him; I wanted him to prove my worth as a woman by becoming, for me, the confident, successful, coolly aloof and knowing man I'd first taken him for and still wished him to be.

When we'd started dating, we'd asked each other every night before we went to bed if there was anything one of us wanted to say to the other, any unfinished business from the day to discuss. By now, of course, our "unfinished business" was much too complicated and ugly to resolve in the five or ten minutes before bed. We were hardly going to brush our teeth, huddle under the covers, and talk about how we based our relationship on urgency and dependence, and made a sick pact to call it love.

Invariably, I was asked, *"How is everything going with your boyfriend?"* And since I could not bring myself to reply, *"Everything sucks. I am in an awful, unwinnable situation brought about by abject neediness and harebrained immaturity,"* I would instead say something like, *"Sometimes I wonder if we're really right for each other."*

"Oh, everyone always thinks that," I would be reassured. *"No relationship is perfect."* I knew that when people said this, they were referring to the nature of intimacy, to the fact that you can't expect to be head over heels in love, or even at all in love, with your partner at any given second. I also knew that if I'd had the courage to relay the misery of my situation in any detail, I'd have been confronted with more pointed advice. My strict adherence to only the most vague reports of my dissatisfaction meant I was able to wrap myself in the warm blanket of banal counsel: we were just like any other couple having problems, and it was true because everyone said so.

In my worst moments of panic, I would find myself walking the streets or sitting on the subway furiously cataloging my virtues. Some of them were serious, general stuff about having good character and personality; others were more shallow, like I had nice sheets and nice shoes and my parents were pleasant, healthy, and financially stable. I won't embarrass myself with more proof of why I am a shining, brilliant individual. The point is, now that I was actually *going* to be married (as opposed to seeing marriage as a big goal to be achieved), I realized how much I wanted and needed from a husband; so many qualities, both general and specific, just had to be there for me to consent to, in effect, give myself away. For life. For life! It was beginning to dawn on me what I'd pledged to this man, and to realize that although my needs were extensive, they were not unreasonable, and I had the collateral to make certain demands. Before, I had always wondered, *"Who would want to marry me?"* Now, in the face of it actually happening, this had shifted 180 degrees, to *"Who will get to marry me?"*

All these ruminations sent me into a tailspin of guilt. After all, we had made promises to each other; plans were in the works, expectations set, congratulations and cards and good wishes arriving daily. Plus, there were times when we got along (like when we were playing a game or watching television, or out drinking—when there was any sort of mediating force that would mean we were not merely facing each other, in all our naked humanity), so maybe things weren't all that bad. As the days passed, I almost always managed to stay about ten paces in front of absolute horror and dread.

Then, one night, we were meeting each other on a street corner. I'd had one of those humiliating days writers have from time to time—the days that we spend wondering which should dismay us more, our poverty or lack of talent. All I wanted to do was sit down and relax with a sympathetic, understanding friend, preferably one who would pay for my drinks. As soon as I picked Mike out of the crowd, I knew that that person wasn't him. Here was a real person walking toward me, his needs and problems and issues and limitations coming head-on at mine. I was sick of being there for him. I was sick of us pretending that the eagerness with which we'd come at each other was the result of any force more powerful than the fear of being alone, my fear of not being "chosen." I knew that

I would never again be able to talk myself into thinking that everything was fine. That night, I told him we were through.

He was furious at me, and I had no interest in listening to him detail the reasons why. I already knew that I had done something cruel. So I packed a bag and moved to a friend's house, telling Mike he had a month to find another place to live. I never saw him again.

. . .

About a week before my thirtieth birthday, after Mike was long gone, I came back to the apartment we'd shared. I stood there in the doorway for a second, taking in the depressing remains of this ridiculously foolish endeavor: the dust, the half-painted walls, the floor scratched where furniture had been angrily removed. Then I walked into the apartment, shut the door, and locked it behind me.

I would live there alone for the next two years. I would eventually quit writing the sex column and, gratefully, begin writing about the lives of people other than myself. I started to notice wedding rings with more reasonable eyes. There wasn't anything special about the women who had them, and there wasn't anything noticeably malformed about the women who didn't.

I'm thirty-two now. For the most part I still want a husband, and children, but I've become strangely unconcerned about when that's all going to happen. I imagine that at some point I will meet someone I want to marry who will also want to marry me. We will get married and have kids, and then I will have other problems.

Sometimes, alone in my apartment at night, I can't believe how precious the stillness is. I think of all the people in the world who would kill for the privacy, the space, and the silence that so terrified me four years ago. It's strange that it took this rather miserable human experiment to make me appreciate being single. I wish I could have gotten here some other way. But I didn't.

Papa Don't Preach

Kerry Herlihy

EVEN THOUGH MY inner Catholic is begging me to go straight to a confessional and then forget this whole thing, I can't shake wanting to tell the truth to the world. Maybe it's recently having turned thirty, maybe something else altogether, but anyway, here goes: I have been with married men. Yes, in the biblical sense. Yes, with more than one (no, not at the same time). Go ahead and say what you're thinking so we can get on with the story: *Slut. Homewrecker. Pathetic. Dumb. Can't-get-your-own-dick kind of girl.* Maybe some of you are saying softly, "You go, girl." Wait until I tell you the rest. I got pregnant by, and had a baby with, one of those married men. No, he didn't leave her for me. No, that wasn't my plan in the first place. Yes, I am happy.

But I get ahead of myself. Maybe now you're thinking, *Why haven't I seen her on the circuit—Ricki, Jerry, Maury, Montel?* They all would give their eyeteeth for a piece of me. Truth is, I am content to be on this dirt road in Maine, living with my parents and daughter—six months old as I write this—taking walks by the ocean. Sound bizarrely wholesome? Do you wonder how a girl like me got in a story like this? I think there are lots of girls like me doing things I have done but they are afraid to tell anyone. So I'm here to confess to everyone, and to set my record straight.

I never planned on being a coveter. It wasn't as if I was reading *Penthouse* while my friends read *Seventeen.* I dreamed of growing up and being one of those walk-down-the-aisle-in-a-white-dress kind of girls. I had boys I pictured having forever with. But when I grew up, it seemed that every time I got into the relationships that had that potential—to make me what most women dream of becoming, a serious girlfriend, a wife—I felt unable to be myself. And when I got quiet, I realized I felt downright unhappy. I felt as if I were playing a leading-lady role when I really longed to be the crazy gal pal with the mysterious late-night houseguests. Perhaps I just never met "the one." But I knew I wanted something different than that sort of new old story. You know the one: Meet boy. Date boy. Fuck boy. Fall in love with boy. Get engaged to boy. Marry boy. Have babies with boy. Go back to work and try to juggle boy, baby, and life. Repeat baby part if desired.

So, about ten years ago, right after college, I started to choose what some would call strange bedfellows. An older man here, a woman there, peppered with acceptable boys now and again. Those stories usually went something like this: Meet boy or girl. Simultaneously fuck and fall in love with boy or girl. Convince self boy or girl is sexual soul mate. Hang out for a couple of months with boy or girl. Have epiphany about boy or girl. Move away or break up with boy or girl. Keep boy or girl on recycled sex list for several years. Repeat cycle when heart is mended. Truth is, I loved being in love. I loved the beginnings, the heat, the drama, the intrigue. I loved the passion. It was that edge that kept me going back into the field just one more time.

For the record, married men were not part of the repertoire until recently. And there were only two. Also, the first one was not entirely my fault. I was moonlighting from my regular teaching gig, as a waitress, to earn some extra cash. This man—we'll call him Cheffy—tempted and tantalized me with his crabcakes, risotto, and the coup de grace . . . baked figs with Gorgonzola. This fig bliss in combination with his large meaty portions made my fall from virtue inevitable. I thought it romantic when he told his wife he had to drive cross-country and find himself. In reality, he just drove across the Brooklyn Bridge to my apartment, where we smoked pot naked and planned our future life together when we moved to New Orleans. He would work in some hip Creole restaurant and I would write my novel. After a week, I confidently sent him back to his wife to pack up his things and tie up the loose ends of his five-year marriage. One week went by. I was calm. I went to yoga three times and patiently awaited my love. Two weeks passed and I hiked up the yoga to five times a week and began chanting the mantra "Thy will, not my will, be done." At three weeks, I went over to my friend Morty's house, sore from trying to wrench myself into heart-healing poses. Morty knew the Zen mama was dangerously close to spiraling into a cosmic meltdown. He said, as I was mumbling *om shanti,* "I don't think he's going to leave her."

At first, I laughed. I mean, the trip he took last week with her had been planned for months. And the couple's therapy? Well, he wanted an amicable breakup. He said he loved me. He cried when he left me. For God's sake, he baked me figs. Does that sound like a man on the verge of patching up his marriage to someone else? Apparently so. Two days later, Cheffy called me, hysterically crying, to let me know he couldn't do it, even though I was his soul mate, even though I had taught him what real love is; he just could not hurt his wife like that. I think her six-figure income made him feel her hurt a little deeper. After several middle-of-the-night knocks on the door where I found Cheffy looking for consolation pussy, I cut him off and out of my now ruined life.

I cried for three days under my covers until my boss called and ordered me back to work. I focused on bouncing back, more out of pride than anything else. I had been duped by the oldest boy trick in the book, and I could not bear the whispered "I told you so's" I thought I heard at every turn. I picked up the pieces and my credit card and shopped back my womanly dignity. I started dating again. I think it was the hunky salsa dancer who finally healed up my Cheffy wounds for good. I swore off married men to my forgiving sister friends and reentered the acceptable-single-girl track.

I stayed on the wagon for a year. Not even a trace of a married man could be found anywhere in my closets. But I was lured by an offer that seemed like divine intervention. I was, a year after Cheffy, in love with a Texas cowgirl who was running hot and cold, keeping me on the edge of moving south of the Brooklyn border. I decided I needed a distraction to cure me. Enter, stage left, an absolutely gorgeous six-foot-tall black married man we'll call Michael, who had a white-girl fantasy with my name written all over the part. By chance, I had a little jungle fever of my own that made me look twice. Well, in reality I would have looked twice no matter what his color, because he was that cute.

Now, I know what you're thinking: *Did you lose your entire mind or just the part with any sense in it?* However, I thought I was a changed woman. I had learned some very important lessons from Cheffy:

1. Never try to make a husband your husband.
2. Never take him seriously when he complains about his wife.
3. Never wait around for him to call.
4. Never believe that you are the answer to all his problems.

Finally and most important:

5. You most certainly will not die without him.

With that wisdom tucked in my G-string, I listened to Michael proposition me with a one-night stand. He said he was the perfect candidate to distract me from my girl troubles. He said I could tape a picture on his head and call out whatever name I wanted. He also assured me he would not linger around for small talk or snacks. With that, I acquiesced. I liked the cut-and-dried nature of the offer, one that many single guys would be terrified to suggest, thinking women always want snuggles and commitment. In this case, I looked at it as being like therapy but cheaper. My sister friends would see it as an empowering, millennium-girl thing to do, right?

Just in case, I told no one.

We agreed to meet at my place after work one Friday night. We had a window of a couple of hours before my roommate got home. I was so nervous I drank two shots of tequila before he arrived. I don't know whether it was the tequila or him or to make sure the cowgirl rode into the sunset, but I went back for another session the next week. Soon my one-night stand had stretched into months and we were on a three-times-a-week routine. My fate down the slippery slope was picking up speed, but I didn't care. I had a lover who made house calls, brought dinner, cleaned up, brought me to several toe-curling orgasms, and then went home. I thought I had finally figured out how to do the married man after all. And this married man was perfect, because he and his wife had an agreement of sorts. They both were allowed the latitude of extramarital affairs as long as it was discreet. Now, I couldn't know for sure if this agreement was as clear-cut as he explained it to me. However, I felt that it let me off the hook in a karmic kind of way. And because I wanted Michael to keep coming around, I asked no more questions. Of course, my roommate was not speaking to me and my other friends were waiting for my heart to break again. But no matter. I was happy and in love in a temporary kind of way.

We continued to get down in serious sin until one day the line was drawn. Or should I say, two lines were drawn. Yes, Virginia, I was pregnant. At first, I panicked. I could see no way out of this dilemma without getting crucified by someone. Having a married man's baby? The line would be around the corner. Nation of Islam, white supremacists, women of all colors, anyone happily monogamous, my family . . . just about everyone I could imagine would disapprove.

But having an abortion at this stage of the game didn't make sense to me. I was thirty years old, with a maternal instinct and a belief in divine timing. I called Michael, who talked to me for an hour until my hands stopped shaking, making sure I didn't let the Irish Catholic demons run rampant over my already fragile state. He was sweet, calm, and supportive. He thought I wouldn't be crazy enough to give up my life of independence to have a kid. We hung up, and I did what I usually do when I have a life crisis: hula-hoop. I gyrated for two hours before I arrived at my answer. I was going to have a baby. I knew on paper it was absolutely insane. I had no savings, no permanent housing, no conventional partner, and a predilection for changing my mind in the face of huge decisions. But some deep, nonrational, and truthful place in me knew it was not only the right thing to do, it was also what I wanted. Perhaps, in some weird way, it fulfilled the traditional girl in me. At any rate, I sat down with Michael the next day and told him my decision. He nodded and said he understood this decision and supported it. I think he still thought I'd change my mind. I gave him the option to walk away from the whole situation and never see me again—or the baby. I really had made the decision to do this on my own. However, I knew him well enough to suspect he might stick around.

As I tell it now, it would be easier to say I didn't know how it happened, I didn't know he was married, I didn't know how to use a condom. But the truth is, I had known that my actions had a script that could go in a million directions. And I chose this script. Being a victim of circumstance, while a popular option for the masses, would have been a real downer for me.

The time came to tell my parents. I dreaded it; let's face it, when is it ever fun to tell your parents you are having the baby of a married man? After the obligatory hysteria, my mom was happy she was going to be a grandmother, by hook or by crook. I cried for ten minutes before I could tell my father, who was so relieved I wasn't about to die in the next thirty days that he simply said not to worry, he'd be there if I needed anything.

I went back to my life, working full-time teaching teenagers and adults to read and hanging out in my loft in Brooklyn. I tried to imagine my future life. As the months passed, I kept checking in with myself during my baby yoga classes and found myself remarkably calm. Don't get me wrong, I had my moments on the lunatic fringe. However, most days, I dressed in miniskirts and tight tank tops and felt sexier than I ever had. Michael and I continued to be happily involved.

I ran into Cheffy when I was about five months pregnant. He was with his daughter and pregnant wife. He wouldn't look me in the eye and I resisted my desire to come clean. Instead, I silently thanked my lucky stars the universe had kept me from him, figs or no figs.

I decided, when I could feel my daughter move inside me, that I needed to take a break from New York and move to Maine with my parents. Eight and a half months gone, I left Michael and my life in New York. He kissed my face and my belly and said, "We did good baby." I cried so hard I thought I might send myself into labor. But as I drove out of Brooklyn in the U-Haul, I knew I had done the right thing. I also knew that as unhip as it was to move back in with my parents, they would take care of me, even if I lost my serene glow.

I delivered my daughter alone with my midwife while my family waited outside. Michael was in New York, at my request. For all his support, the choice still felt like mine and I wanted her arrival to be something sacred between her and me.

Since my daughter arrived, I feel as if my life has focused in on her details: Eyelashes growing, laughs getting louder and longer, eyes that cannot wait to see me each morning. These are the milestones and I continue to be amazed at how much she rocks my world. I feel like my New York edges are, for the time being, softened. My leather pants hang in the closet next to her snowsuit. My dildo gathers dust in the garage. All things considered, I feel I have glided into motherhood without many bumps—yes, with the help of my parents; yes, without a husband by my side; yes, without a long-term plan for the future; and yes, with, I'm sure, the condemnation of many; but so far, it's making me happy. I got a letter from a friend yesterday who told me I was the most peaceful person she knew. She says this surprises her. I think she, like most people, expected me to rise to the drama my circumstances seemed to beckon for. Most days I choose peace over drama because it just feels better.

As for Michael, we continue to extend our one-night stand into an unconventional love story that somehow works. He calls each day and occasionally visits but mostly loves us from a distance. I have moments when I want him to be there for happily ever after. But I remember that when I chose to have my daughter, I chose him as well, married and all. For now, it's enough. When my daughter gets old enough, I'll tell her how much I loved Michael. He may even be there to tell his side of the story, too.

I have started those yoga poses again to try and ease the knots of questions that are popping up these days. How will I ever leave my daughter with a stranger? What if I can't find a job that pays enough? What if I'm only good at beginnings? I realize my choice to be a mother has left my life suspiciously close to that of the traditional-girl path I shunned, minus a husband to help. But the route to get here feels more genuine, more me, for all its drama and unanswered questions. So I make a phone call, edit my résumé, e-mail a real estate broker, and remember that sometimes increments work just as well as leaps.

I know myself well enough not to say "Never again." I can't imagine having time for illicit affairs now, but crying under my covers two years ago, I couldn't imagine it either. Perhaps I'll be the quintessential girl of the new millennium who, after years of juggling children, job, sex, and scandalizing partners, finally figures out how to do it all. If so, I'll let you know.

Memoirs of an Ex-Bride

Looking Back. Looking Ahead.

Daphne Merkin

Here's a little fact that might help you understand what I have only recently come to think of as my somewhat phobic views on the subject of matrimony: Although I still have two boxes of wedding photos bearing the discreet insignia of the photographer ("Fred Marcus, New York") on the covers, I never went on to have my wedding album made. Not then, in the months immediately following the event; not ever, despite the thousand-dollar deposit that my mother paid. I suppose you could attribute this lack of follow-through to a kind of paralyzing malaise that takes hold of me when it comes to documenting my own life, filled as it has been with what seems to be a disproportionate amount of decisions that began in anxiety and ended in unhappiness. My impulse at such occasions has always been to avert my gaze, the better to blur the reality of whatever is about to be preserved on film. I do know I made more than one appointment over the next twelve months to go to the photographer's studio to select photos, which suggests that I must have had some faint intention to memorialize the event with an album. But one year became two years, and then somewhere along the way I remember hearing that Mr. Marcus had died, leaving the business to his son. Which shouldn't have mattered, except that by this time I was thinking about divorce.

So, yes, I suppose you could attribute my failure to get my wedding album made to my chronic ambivalence about all decisions undertaken—big and small. But I attribute my inertia to something more basic, if vaguely related, which is the strong possibility that I was never meant to be married in the first place. Oh, I imagine once upon a time I had an honest-to-goodness Marriage Fantasy, just as I had a Wedding Fantasy, in which I featured as a tiny-waisted Barbie doll-bride, standing on top of a lacy white cake: true love anointed in a swirl of buttercream frosting and candied violets. These frilly expectations are, after all, culturally driven and socially reinforced; little girls were bred to dream Wife Dreams in those years and as far as I can tell still are, give or take a few adjustments. I wasn't any different, except in this one respect: I simply couldn't conjure up the image of a man—the groom, the husband-person, the Ken-like figure—standing next to me up on that cake. It's a significant omission, I'd say, and one that suggests that, hard as I tried, *real* marriage never figured into my vision of a grown-up life, even then, when I was a girl, caught up in sugarplum dreams.

To tell you the truth, I'm not sure I've ever really grasped the point of marriage, except as a ceremonial abstraction, a crucial developmental step that only gay people and misfits failed to take. The whole hallowed institution made no sense to me even at the penultimate moment when I was standing under the flower-bedecked *chuppa* in my parents' living room, dressed in contraindicated virginal white, my makeup too orange and my smile too forced, on the brink of becoming A Wife unless someone had the presence of mind to stop me. Alas, I was not the doe-eyed Elaine Robinson from *The Graduate,* and there was no Benjamin Braddock to dramatically break down the church door and scoop me up and away from my fate. There never is, I suppose, except in the movies.

. . .

Let other former brides revel in their misty-eyed memories, paging through leather-bound wedding albums the better to recall the glorious day. I have my two proletarian boxes of snapshots, stuck away on a shelf, to be hauled out when the mood strikes or my daughter wants to study them again. And even though I look back mostly in horror, that's not to say there aren't some photos that call up nostalgic memories: of my two favorite nieces, for instance, who had flown in from Israel with their parents for the occasion. There they are, standing up in their pretty smock dresses, their excitement palpable and their hands linked for sustenance, piping out a song my sister wrote for them—the younger fading off shyly while her older sister sallied on until the end. The lyrics, full of tender wishes, were set to a Hebrew melody; listening to it, I remember wishing I could be the storybook bride they wanted me to be. And there are the flowers: an undeniable triumph, courtesy of Ronaldo Maia, an Upper East Side florist who specializes in "less is more" arrangements at a "more is more" price.

But even now, twelve years and one divorce later, the painful recollections are more vivid to me than those few festive images caught in the camera's eye. I hated my dress, for starters—which was, as I would come to realize too late, remarkably unflattering, with a swath of extra fabric ending in a bunny-rabbit bobtail flourish on the back, right below the waistline. I'm not sure what delusional notion of myself led me to choose it, except that my judgment was clearly off from soup to nuts. Chosen from Kleinfeld's mythic bridal emporium in Brooklyn with the help of a friend whose fashion sense I thought I trusted, the dress was designed by Carolina Herrera, who had designed Caroline Kennedy's dress when she got married. But Caroline Kennedy was reed-thin and Herrera was a friend of her mother's. The designer didn't know me or my family from the Joneses and certainly could not have had anyone of my physical order—more voluptuous than delicate—in mind when she devised this unwieldy concoction. Then again, I can't envision anyone who would have looked good in that dress, except perhaps Elton John.

. . .

And here I am, getting married. . . . I can still remember the state of rictus-like terror in which I walked down the stairs in my parents' apartment on that Sunday evening in December, no doubt looking accurately joyless. In the living room and dining room, the sixty-odd guests were seated on gilded folding chairs on either side of the makeshift aisle, awaiting my triumphal entrance. It should've felt homey, but it felt alien instead. Why had I decided to go up against the accepted tribal way of doing things by opting for this kind of intimate, small-scale gathering? It was elegant, to be sure, but weirdly understated, especially for someone of my background. Most of my friends as well as several of my siblings had gotten hitched at lavish hotel affairs with groaning smorgasbords, hundreds of guests, and lots of floor space on which to dance the requisite *"mitzvah tenzel."* It seemed to me that I was impersonating someone whose life had followed a well-laid-out course but with whom I had nothing in common: a debutante type, say, whose name was Muffie and whose expectations were blue-chip. I, in contrast, had few expectations, blue-chip or otherwise. I wasn't a much-loved and loving daughter who had decided to get married in the bosom of her supportive family, wearing jewels that dated back to the *Mayflower*. I was, rather, the daughter of tough-minded, wholly unsentimental Orthodox Jews who had escaped Hitler's Germany with their lives and not much else. What's more, I had published an autobiographical novel a few years earlier in which I had evoked an emotionally scarring childhood as one of six siblings. Why, then, had I decided to take this giant step forward in the very home in which I had experienced so much past misery?

. . .

Why, indeed. This brings me back to what is perhaps the strangest aspect of this strange story, which has to do with the bizarre circumstances in which the original decision to get married was reached. It wasn't really my decision, you see, and it wasn't made in tandem with the man who was to become my husband. This particular conjugal venture came about because of a group consultation between my mother, my shrink, and myself, wherein it was decided that (a) I should get married and (b) I should get married quickly—as soon as possible—because it would give me less time to ruminate and change my mind. (I had done this once already, having broken off my engagement to my husband-to-be only to get reinvolved some months later.) When I look back on it, I'm not even certain that my future spouse and I had arrived at a definite conclusion on the subject of marrying each other before this meeting took place, but his interest seems to have been taken for granted. As for my own hyperventilating level of ambivalence, surely I'd settle down into relative bliss once the glass had been broken and the *mazel tov*s rendered. I remember my shrink and mother nodding their heads in sage agreement about the certainty that I would never get divorced. I was too "loyal" for that, the shrink said. Absolutely, my mother concurred. By which I think they both meant that I was too indecisive—not to mention too afraid of change—to ever unmake so large a decision. Little did they know.

The simple truth was this: I couldn't decide to get married on my own cognizance, in the ordinary fashion, because I wasn't *ready* to plight my troth. I don't think I had ever felt ready to marry—or at least not in the way I assume a lot of other women do, out of a sustained and propulsive instinct. It wasn't as though I was content with my single-woman status: I was thirty-four, no spring chicken, and everyone in sight had gotten married already. But although I had fallen in love (or some approximation thereof) before, and had known my share of besotted suitors, I had never met the man whose wife I ardently wished to be; never caught someone's eyes across a crowded room, like Maria and Tony in *West Side Story,* and realized in an instant that this was the other half of my whole. Oh, there had been the globe-trotting Brit who proposed on our first date, and sent an enormous bouquet of white lilies the next day; I can still remember the lush scent of the flowers filling my apartment. But I hung back, overcome by hesitations in the face of his noisy enthusiasm, and he eventually went on to other diversions. In hindsight, it seems to me that I could have done worse than marry him—given my profound and ongoing reluctance to marry anyone, I mean.

As for the marriage I did enter into, you must realize by now that it was doomed from the start. I had imagined that my abiding sense of panic would go away once the deed was done, but it only increased. I cried on my wedding night, stuck with my new life partner in an elegant but cold suite in a hotel that was renowned for its power breakfasts, within hailing distance of my parents' apartment.

You could, I suppose, put a charitable spin on my tears and say they were just the overflow from a buildup of nervous excitement, a case of wedding-night jitters. But let's face it: I wasn't a mail-order bride, come face-to-face at last with a flesh-and-blood man I had known only through letters. I had been living with this person on and off for six years, in which time I had become acquainted with every mole on his body. Still, we had kept two apartments—Mine and His—and in retrospect, it seems to me that what I hadn't sufficiently taken into account was how dependent I had become on the elbow room our flexible premarital arrangement had provided, allowing for all the comforts of domesticity without any of the restraints. I had, for instance, been in the habit of going to work-related parties and dinners by myself more often than not, and there were usually one or two nights a week when we slept apart in our own apartments. Without being entirely conscious of it, I think I strived to unlink myself as much as possible from the confinement of coupledom. Now I was feeling utterly trapped, as though someone had stuck me in a closet together with my husband and thrown away the key. All the air was instantly cut off, and worse yet, I couldn't find the light. How was I to locate myself, wedged up against another person in such tight quarters?

It didn't take long for me to reach the conclusion that the me who had once been—independent, driven, solitary, intellectual, if also slightly compulsive and depression-prone—no longer existed. It seemed to me that my sense of identity, which had never been that firm to begin with, was fragmenting before my very eyes. This alarming insight presented itself with startling clarity one day shortly after the wedding. I was lying on a beach chair in Maui, engrossed in a book on the borderline personality (trying to determine, among other things, if I was one and whether that might help explain the sustained panic attack the act of getting married had induced in me) while my husband was off scuba diving. We were a freshly married couple on our honeymoon simulating a freshly married couple on their honeymoon—or so it appeared to me when I looked up from my reading for a moment and gazed into the claustrophobic vista that stretched ahead of me. My husband and I had been fighting bitterly ever since we had landed in this paradisaical spot, and all I wanted was to turn the clock back, to a time before I had committed myself to this enterprise. I felt like a character in a Polanski or Bergman film, living out a waking nightmare.

Why, come to think of it, hadn't I been warned of this—the loss of identity, the potential claustrophobia, the feeling of being utterly trapped—by those who had gone before me, afloat in yards of tulle and demurely holding their bouquets? By my mother, for God's sake, or my shrink, who, in retrospect, had joined forces only to set me up? Or was it impossible to relay the information once you got "inside" precisely because the whole belief system behind the institution of marriage was predicated on artifice? Looking back, it seems to me now that I was suffering from an acute case of what I will call Stepford Wife syndrome: I had become an unreal figure in an unreal arrangement. I may have looked and talked like my premarital self, but inside, in my own panicky imagination, I had mutated into a passive, will-less Wife. By mere virtue of getting married, I had become an apron-wearing, man-pleasing, dinner-serving robotic replacement of myself. I didn't own an apron, as it happened, and it was my husband who usually made dinner, but in such cases the facts are hardly the point. The point was that I couldn't catch my breath. I stuck it out in that suffocating state for as long as I could bear it—longer, really—and then I made a run for it.

. . .

This is not a story about the wonderful freedom to be found outside of marriage or the wisdom-imbuing catharsis that is the light at the end of the tunnel of divorce. Above and beyond the lingering whiff of failure that divorce brings in its wake, it has little to recommend it: not the legal hassles, the painful division of accumulated goods, the never-quite-satisfactory custody arrangement, the squabbling over money. As for the sobering reality of life outside of marriage, it is first and foremost lonely, often sexless (unless you got divorced because you were already hooked on someone other than your spouse), and if you have a child, frequently guilt-inducing. To this very day, I know that nothing would make my daughter happier than my getting remarried to her father. Although she is too sophisticated to express this wish out loud the way she used to when she was little, I have never lost the sense of having let her down.

And yet, if I don't fully understand how I corralled the courage—the necessary suspension of disbelief—to marry in the first place, I can't begin to fathom how I had the guts to leave in the second. Never mind that great wits down the ages have invariably had something withering to say about the monotony and antierotic effect of the matrimonial state. When all is said and done, marriage remains the only practicable game in town for most of us—the standard of interrelational skill against which we measure ourselves. (Although I'd like to take a moment to advance my own private theory that marriage may well require *less* maturity rather than more—that the less childish you are the more the idea of being a couple seems like a flimsy defense against the inevitability of existential loneliness.) I can't speak for men, but it seems to me that very few heterosexual women really believe that marriage isn't for them, or remain unmarried out of conviction. Sure, there may be other, more glamorous or merely eccentric possibilities to be had, but few of us have the wherewithal to try and actually inhabit these alternative scenarios other than in our heads. Whenever I hear about a love triangle or ménage à trois, my first thought is that somebody is going to come out a loser.

Finally, there's the fact that once you're divorced, everyone else suddenly seems to be married—safely tucked in for the night in their tidy Noah's Ark of coupledom—while you're out in the lonely forest scavenging for a warm body to huddle up against. Both sex and solitude become more burdensome after divorce, requiring new psychological accommodation and different strategies. And none of this gets easier with the passing of time: people tend to respond to young, still-unmarried women with their own romantic curiosity piqued, envisioning all sorts of possibilities, whereas once you've been married and divorced, no one warms to the role of matchmaker or cheerleader with quite the same enthusiasm. Women, especially, are mostly left to their own devices—when they're not seen as outright threats to the status quo, that is, suggesting a social rawness that isn't easy to integrate into parent-teacher conferences or dinner parties. It doesn't help that divorced women seem to be a dime a dozen, while divorced men get treated like precious commodities.

No, having tried it both ways, I'm here to tell you that in many ways—in fact, overall—it's easier to be married. I don't just mean that you live longer (which applies to men more than women in any case) but that you live with less strain on the nerve endings. It's no wonder that even though more than half the marriages in this country end in divorce, most divorced people choose to get married again. I've even noticed that it's easier to criticize marriage when you're married; you sound wisely disillusioned rather than simply bitter. When I told a married friend I was writing this piece, for example, she immediately pronounced: "I only know unhappy couples." (I didn't dare inquire whether she meant to include herself in this acid remark.)

So where does this leave me? Although I haven't remarried, I haven't ruled out the hope that the marital experiment might yield a better result the second time around. But eight years after my divorce, I have also begun to entertain the possibility that I am too skittish a creature for the sustained and up-close domestic arrangement that is marriage—that I may be one of those people who is more equipped to handle the risks of loneliness than those of intimacy. Perhaps my failure to have a wedding album made was a positive statement in disguise, telling me that my real destiny lay elsewhere—out in the open where life is more vulnerable but also more unpredictable, less "easy," perhaps, but also more intriguing. Whatever happens, I'm sure of one thing: if the occasion to be a bride should arise again, I plan to play myself rather than Muffie. Next time around, if there is one, I hope to get hitched not in an atmosphere of pale Waspy reticence, but in one of high-pitched ethnic celebration. And who knows but that I might yet possess the genuine article—an actual wedding album—to have and to hold.

For Better and Worse

All tragedies are finished by a death,
All comedies are ended by a marriage.

—"Don Juan," Canto I, Stanza 216
George Noel Gordon, Lord Byron

I Do. Not.

Why I Won't Marry

Catherine Newman

Of course nobody thinks to ask me and Michael—my partner of eleven years and the father of our two-year-old son—why we're not married until we're all at a *wedding,* which is kind of awkward, at best. "Um, maybe because marriage is a tool of the *patriarchy?*" I could say, and smile and take another bite of poached salmon and wink across the table at the bride and groom. But I don't, because I love weddings, and I'm in a borrowed stone-colored outfit, and I probably cried when the bride kissed her parents at the altar and I've just read my special passage from Rumi or Rainer Maria Rilke, and I'm buzzed and happy and eating the entrée I checked off on the reply card months ago. And Michael's terribly handsome in his blazer, and he's probably touching my linen-encased thigh under the table, moony and drunk off of other people's vows. But somebody's father or uncle always has to lean over, all shiny and loose with champagne, and ruin it. "So, how come you two aren't doing this?" he might ask, with a hand gesture that takes in the bride, the cake, the open bar. My best bet is to stall elaborately over a mouthful of fish. There are so many reasons, and they're all only partly true and shot through with contradiction, and I can't say any of them out loud—not here, anyway.

Because marriage is about handing the woman off, like a baton, from her father to her husband. Also known as "traffic in women," this is how men have historically solidified their economic connections to other men (think *empires;* think *in-laws*) and guaranteed the continuation of their Seed. The woman has always, of course, been deeply valued for her own sake, hence the *dowry* that required her family to bribe another family with lots of money and cattle and embroidered pillow shams to take her off their hands. Thank goodness we're so much more evolved now! Except, of course, for the embarrassing detail of the bride's family shelling out the ten or fifty thousand dollars for the wedding itself. And the awkward transfer of the veiled woman, father to son-in-law, at the altar. Wives can bear a disconcerting resemblance to objects. Back in the sixteenth century, adultery was a crime of theft (like making off with your neighbor's snowblower), since wives were no less, or more, than personal property. Thank goodness we're so much more evolved now! Except at a very Catholic wedding we attended recently where the bride was handed a lit candle, which she used to light a candle for her husband. She then had to blow out the first candle, which was supposed to represent her naughty old independent self—the same lucky self that had now been absorbed, and extinguished, by her husband. Hooray for modernity.

. . .

Because the Religious Right and their Defense of Marriage Act use marriage as a vehicle for homophobic legislation. Marriage is, of course, a supremely natural and God-given institution and a naturally and God-givenly straight one. But *just in case,* we'd better treat it like it's a fragile and gasping little injured bird, and we'll make it illegal for gay people to even visit a town where there's a bridal boutique. As long as they don't tell us they're gay, though, they can still serve as our Wedding Coordinators, because, let's face it, they really do understand fabrics and color. That's the political version. There's another, less noble version: *Because I'd feel like a real A-hole if I put on a beaded cream bodice and vowed myself away in front of all our gay friends—smiling and polite in their dark silk shirts or gossiping wickedly about our choice of canapés—who cannot themselves marry.* Not that they would all deign to get married, even if they could (see above). But what they're snubbing should certainly be a viable option.

. . .

Because I could, myself, have ended up with a woman. Into my mid-twenties, I spent some time in love and in bed with women—a handful of astonishing romances that left me with a lot of steamy memories and a crew cut. You can imagine my horror, then, when I surreptitiously bedded and fell in love with Michael, who played hockey (ice, roller, *and* video) and was relentlessly cheerful. A handsome, athletic, doting guy: not my ideal specimen for a life partner, but there it was. I persist in the knowledge that women are, way more often than not, sexier, funnier, kinder, and more interesting than men. All of my friends certainly are. Do I still think of myself as bisexual? If a tree falls in the forest but you're inside reading *Spotted Yellow Frogs* for the fourth time in five minutes, do you give a shit? If you have ever lived with a two-year-old, then you know that Grappling With Your Sexuality does not tend to make it onto the roster of daily activity goals, like brushing your teeth or not locking the baby in the car with your keys. My mind, it is not such a vibrant organ these days. I can squint past the clogging mass of words like "nasal aspirator" and "glycerin suppositories" and just barely make out the dim shape of a memory of sexual identity, but that's about it. Pulling the crispy skin off of a roast chicken and eating it right there in the kitchen, before the bird even makes it to the table—now *that's* a sensual act worth defending. Especially these days, when our bed is more like a museum of Cheerios artifacts than a place of sexual worship. But it does seem weaselly to participate in a privilege—specifically, marriage—that I would have been denied if I had ended up engaged in a different kind of relationship. Or, really, just a different configuration of wild-thing hydraulics, which is all we're actually talking about here. (I do love the idea that the Law has nothing better to do than referee the naked Hokey Pokey: "No, no—you put *that* in. No! No! Not in *there*! Yes, we know it happens to *fit* there, but that's not where it belongs.")

. . .

Because we don't believe in monogamy. At least in theory. Can it possibly be that climbing onto the same exact person for fifty years maximizes the erotic potential of our brief fling here on earth? Especially back in the early days, when I identified more physically and politically as bisexual (*Bisexual People Speak Out!* is a book I had, which makes me want to write, for kids, something more mundanely exuberant like *Bisexual People Buy Bananas!*), it seemed cruel and unusual that one should have to give up so much in order to commit to a man. Open, honest nonmonogamy seemed like the ideal solution. Abstractly, it sounded righteous and right. But in real life, nonmonogamy can sound more like your partner's lover revving a motorcycle right outside your bedroom window, which is just a total bummer. It can look, more or less, like a trampy, selfish bout of sleeping around, talking about it, and hurting everybody's feelings. Beliefs, even strongly held ones, can be somewhat aloof from the world where people actually *feel* things. We are too well trained in the grammar of possession and jealousy, too mired in the blurring of sex and love, to simply turn our backs on convention; we are poorly insulated from the sharp pokes of heartsoreness and humiliation.

And, it turns out, that *third* person inevitably has feelings, too, of all things! Feelings you can't control, not even by chanting "I'll never leave my boyfriend" over and over like a mantra. That third person might even be likely, in fact, to have *extra* feelings, the kind that find expression only in phoning compulsively throughout the night or popping by after supper with an ice pick. Michael and I were ultimately so strained by a few rounds of nondomestic toad-in-the-hole that we gave it up. (A friend of mine who is a famously radical theorist of sexuality once said, tiredly, "Maybe sex just doesn't even *matter* that much.") But we still believe in honesty over the sticky lies of the motel room; we still believe in imagination over living by the available scripts; and we believe, I hope, in treating each other's desires with respect and compassion. We still believe in the *principle* of nonmonogamy, even if we don't have the energy to do it.

. . .

Because I will not be possessed. Michael holds everything that comes into his life—our son, a peeled orange, a bath towel, me—as if it is as fragile and fleeting as a soap bubble; he has the lightest, most beautiful touch. And yet—and this is the worst, brattiest kind of contradiction—I wish sometimes that he would demand that I marry him, that he would despair so poetically and much about his great love for me that he would have to possess me entirely. (Sometimes, because we share a decade of inside jokes about ourselves, Michael slits his eyes at me over lunch and snarls, "I *must* have you this instant," with his bare foot pressing around in my lap and the baby grinning gamely from his high chair.) Michael is not, how shall I say it, the most passionate tool in the shed. We were recently leafing through our photo album, and there's this glorious picture of me, forty weeks pregnant, which he took himself, and I'm naked and radiant with the gold of the sunset illuminating my huge, ripe belly, two days before the harrowing and miraculous birth of our baby, and Michael says only, about a half-full plastic bottle in the foreground, "Oh, honey, remember how you made that fruit punch? Yum."

You know that kind of romance where your hair is always all matted in the back and you get rug burns on your elbows, and you stay awake all night chain-smoking and watching each other breathe? Everyone has at least one of these. ("Mmmm, the hot dog man," my friend Megan sighed over her passionate interlude with a snack vendor.) Michael's more likely to hop up after sex and say, amiably, "Want a bowl of Golden Grahams? I'm having one." So he would, for instance, never punch someone out over me, like my beautiful and spindly high school boyfriend who once, on the subway, shook his bony, lunatic fist in the face of an innocent bystander and growled, "You staring at my woman?"

But even though I catch myself longing for it sometimes, the truth is that extremes of passion have unnerved me. The people who write poems about your forearm hairs glistening in the moonlight are the same ones who, later, throw beer bottles through your kitchen window from the street and call drunk and weepy every New Year's Eve. They're the same ones who don't always seem to actually *know* you that well—who say baffling, wrong things like, "I just really love how *calm* you are," which send you reeling out to the bookstore to skim *The Complete Idiot's Guide to Zen Meditation*. The best life partner might, I think, be the one who sees you as you are and loves that person—the person who is boring and anxious or blotchy from a weekly scrub mask—not the imaginary one who is poetic and broodingly smart and sexy and ecstatic all the time. The best life partner is exactly the sort of person who doesn't crave possession.

. . .

Because not being married means we get to keep choosing each other. Can married people do this? Of course they can (although one married friend described this as the difference between, in our case, choosing to stay together and, in hers, choosing not to divorce). For us, there's something psychically liberating about that little bit of unmarried space that allows us to move forward, to come toward each other, over and over again. Michael knows me deeply—he sees me truly—and, astonishingly, keeps deciding to stay with me. He can walk into the bathroom while I'm tweezing the hairs on my chin, wrap his arms around my waist, and smile gently at me into the mirror, instead of shouting, "Step right up, folks! See the incredible Bearded Lady!" which is what I would surely do in his place. When I'm not completely infuriated over his occasional bouts of remoteness, or overwhelmed by the frantic dullness that can suck the life out of making a home together, I look at Michael and breathe a huge sigh of relief. I would choose him again this second: his strong shoulders from rocking our baby to sleep every afternoon; his utter lack of unkindness; the way he finds the things I've lost—keys, my cardigan—and then returns them to me as gifts, all wrapped up in fancy paper and ribbons. If you believe, and I do, that people are secretly their truest selves in the middle of the night, then my truest self might be, "Are you going to snore like that until I put a bullet in my head?" Michael's is, "Oh, sweetheart, can't you sleep?" while he pats the smooth cool of his chest for me to crawl onto. I would choose that again in a heartbeat.

. . .

Because we have a kid together. So, um, scratch that last paragraph, because I am stuck with Michael forever. What more permanent soul binding can there be than the sharing of a child? This is the real till-death-do-us-part. We could still split up, of course, but only if the benefits seemed distinctly greater than, say, the awkwardness of showing up separately at all the same bar mitzvahs and eighth-grade performances of *Our Town;* and still, we would be ultimately connected. When we were in the hospital, with the baby just born and the three of us in love in our matching plastic ID bracelets like a little nuclear gang, a yearning flitted through me for all of us to have the same last name; I really got it, for a minute—that desire for a united front. (Instead, the baby has my last name. Don't try this unless you want to spend the rest of your life with everybody getting all panicked and sweaty and saying, "Oh, that's so *fascinating*!" about it, as if your kid has an extra limb sprouting from his forehead.) But we are that, anyway—a united front—with or without a shared name or the deed to our relationship. The difference between us and a married couple, apart from some nuances of tax paying and title wielding (Mrs. Michael J. Millner? Who could that possibly be, besides his drag-queen persona?), is slender indeed.

. . .

Because we already have rings, is what we always end up saying, and we hold up our hands as proof of commitment. "We got them on our seventh anniversary—seven years is common-law marriage in California." Common-law marriage? That and three-fifty will get you a latte at Starbucks. We don't even know what it means. But for somebody's father or uncle at a wedding, it tends to settle the issue more often than not. Nobody has to know that we fought like the dickens while we were *getting* the rings—that Michael, instead of gazing at me committedly, was humming a Coors Light jingle (he doesn't even *drink* beer), which enraged me inexplicably much. So much that, in the end, instead of the intimate, beachside vows we had planned, there was merely a "Take your stupid ring!" accompanied by the peevish flinging of velvet boxes.

But I do wear his ring. He is the father of my child. I take Michael in contradiction and in mayhem. In grief and in delight. To cherish, dismay, and split burritos with. For good company and daily comfort. For the tornado of rage and for love. I take him. I do.

Killing the Puritan Within

Kate Christensen

On our first date, my now-husband, Jon, and I ate Russian food and drank vodka on the boardwalk in Brighton Beach, then rode the roller coaster at Coney Island. Already, I was wildly attracted to him. He was the man I'd been looking for, the boy next door in a motorcycle jacket. I felt comfortable with him, sexy and open and funny. Late that night, we went out for a nightcap. As we drank together at a rickety table, I told him that I was a Puritan. It was a challenge and a warning.

Undaunted, he nudged my foot with his and said, "Well, I'll have to do something about that."

Before then, I'd had a series of long-term live-in relationships with withholding, critical men who earned my respect by confirming my worst opinions of myself. Always, instead of leaving, I dug in my heels and tried to "understand" them—to give them what they wanted, accept them as they were. My failure to do this was my own fault, I figured; I needed to try even harder. (The last one, whom I'd dated for close to five years, lived with for four, and almost married just before I met Jon, had told me that reading my fiction writing was like having a sharp stick shoved up his sphincter.) Every time, inevitably, things fell apart, but then I'd just move on to the next bad choice.

To my astonishment and joy, Jon made it clear from the start that he adored me—even my worst, weakest, most self-doubting and unachieved qualities. We understood each other right away, deeply and thoroughly. Though on the surface we're extremely different (he's a painter and a musician, I'm a writer; he's Jewish, I'm a WASP; he spent his entire childhood in Pittsburgh, my family moved every couple of years), we soon realized how much we have in common: We're both firstborn children of divorced parents; both of us had dorky, lonely, tormented adolescences; we're equally anxious and moody, ambitious and secretly rebellious and overtly responsible. Instantly, we fell into a lovestruck swoon that nauseated our friends and thrilled my mother, who'd been afraid I would marry the stick-up-his-sphincter guy. She recognized right away who Jon was, and why I loved him.

But though I relished all of this, it also terrified me. There was nothing for me to feel bad about here, no familiar angst or withholding, nothing to make me hate myself. What was this sweetness and light, this warmth, this acceptance? In the world of men, I had no experience with pure joy, and I deeply mistrusted it.

I was afraid most of all of myself—terrified of choosing wrongly again, losing myself, giving up my newfound, hard-won independence. I established strict, self-protective rules, to which Jon cheerfully acquiesced ("We can't see each other every night; our work comes before anything else; the minute this turns bad, we'll end it," and so on). Several times, I announced that I just couldn't be in another relationship so soon; I had to learn to trust myself before I could trust any man. He understood, he assured me, but it seemed to him that I'd just bring these same fears to the next man I was with, so why didn't I stay with him a while longer and try to work them out? I couldn't help smiling. And when I told my mother how freaked out I was about falling in love again before I'd had time to be alone, she pointed out that I had always been alone until now, even when I'd lived with men. What was wrong with letting myself love and be loved for a change, she said, and although (or maybe because) she'd been through three wrenching, painful divorces, I listened to her, and over time, my anxiety abated enough for me to throw myself headlong into our wild, romantic, decadent courtship without worrying that I'd be punished somehow for it later.

Two years after our first date, on my thirty-fourth birthday—at the outdoor restaurant on the boardwalk in Brighton Beach where we'd gone on our first date—Jon asked me to marry him. I accepted, in tears. Ten weeks later, we had a big, complicated wedding we'd planned and organized together in an almost seamless meshing of taste and teamwork that, we thought, boded extremely well for our future together. Afterward, he carried me over the threshold of our hotel room and lay me on the bed in my wedding dress. "My wife," he whispered. It was the sexiest thing anyone had ever said to me. The next day, we drove out of Brooklyn, heading south—toward New Orleans, our honeymoon, our new married life.

. . .

The transition from dream to nightmare, the plummet from the heaven that had been our courtship straight down, was immediate and shocking. As we approached the end of the Verrazano-Narrows Bridge, Jon barked at me—the very first time he had ever talked to me this way—"Which way do I go?"

"Which way?" I repeated, dazed; I don't have a driver's license, and at that time I had no concept of New York City highways, or any highways for that matter.

"Look at the map!" he said. "Quick! Which way do I go?"

Cringing, I unfolded the map, turned it right side up and looked ineffectually at it just as we swept past our exit. Jon pulled the car over.

"Look," he said, jabbing the map with his forefinger. "We're right here. Don't you know how to read a map?"

"Yes," I lied in a choked voice. "But not if you yell at me."

Of course, this exchange both was and was not about the map. We were both freaking out. How were we going to navigate this new marriage together? Was I going to ride along while Jon did all the work? Was he going to blow up whenever I didn't hop to fast enough? We sat there for a moment, trying to get our bearings, external and internal. We had missed our exit. Worse, we had turned into two strangers, married ones. It was as if an evil fairy-tale witch had cast a spell on us and turned us into clichés: a dithering, smoldering wife, a barking, critical husband.

The rabbi who married us had had, when we'd first met with him, quite a few things to say to us about marriage. We'd come to ask him to do our wedding and, not realizing premarital counseling was part of the package, had showed up for our appointment in his tiny, stuffy office without having had any coffee or breakfast yet, half hungover on wine, thinking we'd breeze in and out. Instead, the rabbi droned on and on—about the "oneness" of it all, about the key to a happy marriage, about going out to restaurants with his own wife. We nudged each other in silent commiseration. Why was he telling us all this? He was wasting his time and ours.

Yet, in spite of our arrogance and hangovers, we both somehow heard and remembered many of the things he advised. Two in particular stand out. "The most important thing in marriage," he said, several times, "is to want to please your spouse more than you want to please yourself; desiring the other's happiness more than you desire your own is the key to a happy marriage.

"Second," he went on, "you've got to figure out together whether you want children and how many. If you can do those two things, you'll be all right. But they're the hardest things."

We drove away laughing. He had no idea who he was dealing with. Us, problems? Ha.

• • •

Like most of the girls I knew when I was growing up, I'd always assumed I'd marry the perfect man. But for me, the man himself wasn't an important element in my fantasies of the future; he existed in my imagination as a flawless but shadowy alter ego, a male version of myself who would read my mind, meet all my needs, and have none of his own. My mother had divorced my father, and later divorced her second and third husbands, but I always expected that I would naturally learn from her mistakes and choose the right man as soon as I was ready to settle down. What dominated my fantasies was the great life this barely there, perfectly amenable, mind-reading husband and I would have: We'd live in the country, somewhere cultured but bucolic, in a Victorian house with window seats and working fireplaces. I would be thin and muscular from daily exercising and a stringently low-fat diet. Our children would read, practice their musical instruments, climb trees. In an airy room under the eaves, I'd write somber, brilliant novels in peace and solitude. Our frequent dinner parties would end with passionate sex and intimate conversation with my Perfect Husband, whoever he turned out to be. He was the least important part of the whole shebang. It was really all about me.

Naïve and absurd though it may have been, I brought this fantasy into my marriage, almost unchanged from my childhood expectations. I thought we would begin our adult lives now that we were married. My childhood vision would finally be realized. So when we got back from our honeymoon and moved in together, this map overlay fell upon the bedrock of my daily life with Jon. A loud voice in my head told me it was time to live that ideal life in that perfect house, complete with that other, perfect husband—that other, perfect version of me.

Thus, very soon, and not surprisingly, despair and frustration set in. Here I was in ugly, treeless, industrial Brooklyn with a freaked-out new husband, flaking sprinkler pipes on the ceiling, trucks roaring by. We watched *Star Trek* every night—something we'd never done during our twice-a-week courtship dates, when we'd been too busy eating, drinking, and having sex to do anything else. I had to admit that I loved *Star Trek,* but guiltily, the way I loved steak. Speaking of which, instead of cooking all those healthy meals I'd anticipated in marriage—or even continuing to subsist on the ascetic, budget-conscious fare I'd dined on before I met Jon and, even after, on nights when we hadn't eaten together—we ate out all the time now. We routinely had wine or drinks with dinner, and soon I'd put a few pounds on my formerly stick-thin frame. I was horrified, even though Jon assured me that I actually looked better. In fact, he always encouraged all my sensual, pleasure-seeking appetites; he had no truck with the puritanical backlashes of renunciation and self-recrimination that would hit me every so often.

But in the back of my mind, I wondered constantly: When would we grow up? When would our real life start? I was working on my first novel, but nothing I did seemed particularly somber or brilliant; it was just my own voice, unspooling on the screen. What was worse, in between the great dinners, the *Star Trek,* the fun nights out, Jon and I fought as we never had before—hotly and irrationally, over things that seemed silly but, in retrospect, weren't any sillier than the things most newly-married-and-cohabitating couples fight about. He was cutting wood with a loud power saw when I got home, and didn't want to stop his work just because I longed for peace and quiet after a hard day; I let bits of food go down the kitchen sink, which clogged up the pipes he'd worked so hard to install. He piled his mail on the kitchen table; I let the trash overflow the can without tying up the bag. Incensed at being criticized, we defended ourselves: "I've always been like this. I can't believe this bothers you." Neither of us could give in or fold or crumble. We were too proud to show any weakness to each other and too stiff-necked to admit we were scared.

It didn't help that, in our mid-thirties, we were both fairly set in our ways. The differences between us that had fascinated and excited us during our courtship now seemed insurmountable, terrible, frightening. I mourned both the single person I'd left behind and the married person I couldn't seem to become. I would wake up in the middle of the night and stare up at the bedroom ceiling, thinking, "What the hell have I done?" On my walks during the day I passed my old apartment, the place where I'd lived for most of our courtship—a huge, lovely, cheap, high-ceilinged paradise, or so it seemed now. I'd moved into Jon's loft because it was bigger, more convenient, dirt cheap, but now I'd look up at the bay windows of my old bedroom and yearn bitterly for my single life again, for the days of our courtship, when I had Jon but still, I felt, had myself. I had lost that self now, despite all my vows not to—lost the self I considered my best one.

. . .

My metamorphosis from an independent, up-for-anything, passionate girlfriend into a needy, angry wife reminded me constantly, painfully, of my mother. Between her first and second marriages, as a single mother of three small kids in the 1970s, she had seemed like a goddess to me—an invincible Wonder Woman who hosted raucous poker games but also enforced a comforting schedule, practiced her cello, made us dinner, and took us shoe shopping. She invented amazing bedtime stories, found time to watch the plays we put on, stayed up with us when we had nightmares—all without help from any other adult, and while earning her Ph.D. in psychology. On her tiny graduate stipend (there was no child support from our long-vanished father), she managed, through strict budgeting and denying herself luxuries, to provide us with books, music lessons, dance classes, creative Christmas presents. We were poor, but so was everyone else we knew, and we didn't feel our poverty because my mother didn't let us. There were no men around, so we looked to her for leadership, strength, and authority, and she always came through.

Then she met a handsome blond architect at a concert, and after that, everything changed. We left the comparative wilds of backroads Tempe for a middle-class Phoenix suburb: a sprawling air-conditioned house, a new school, an "ordinary" life. I was eleven then, stringent and judgmental and preadolescent, and I felt no affinity for this man who'd suddenly appeared in our lives. To make things worse, my mother suddenly seemed unhappy, distant, preoccupied most of the time. This may have been mostly because she was now working sixty hours a week at her first postgraduate job instead of going to classes and writing her thesis at home, but either way, I attributed the change to the unwanted presence of my new stepfather. She'd been happy and free without him, and all ours. Now, in some grown-up way I didn't understand, she wasn't there anymore. But she wasn't anywhere better either, it seemed to me, and I couldn't understand why she'd allowed this to happen.

In our old house, my mother's bedroom had been the place where we watched *The Carol Burnett Show* and *Sonny and Cher,* where we piled into bed with her on Saturday mornings, where, on nights when she went out, we'd watch her brush her long dark hair and strap on her high-heeled sandals, swooning over her gorgeousness. Before she left (she conducted her sex and dating life offstage), I'd throw my arms around her and kiss her over and over. I adored her. I loved her room, a sanctuary where I was always welcome.

In complete contrast, I hated the bedroom she shared with my stepfather in this new house, with its water bed, its faint smell of stale incense, its unhidden copy of *The Joy of Sex.* My mother had a whole secret life in that room, a life I knew about only peripherally but that repulsed me to my core. In the evenings sometimes they'd go in there for a while and then come out, smelling of pot smoke and giggling. On Saturday mornings they slept late, the door now closed to us—not that I wanted to be in there anymore anyway. And during the week she came home late from work, often angry and tense. If this was what being a wife—withdrawn, decadent, no longer completely there—did to a person, I would never succumb to it. At least, not in the ways my mother had.

. . .

Poor Jon. In our early years of marriage, I was as hard on him as I was on myself. Nothing was right unless it was perfect—and nothing was, of course: after all, how many brand-new marriages are? So I lashed out at him with accusations and harsh demands, and afterward, I subsided into equally harsh, self-castigating remorse. Meanwhile, for all his supposed and real flaws, for all my anger and criticism and our frequent knock-down fights about minutiae, Jon had begun supporting both of us on the money he made as a building contractor—physically grueling, mind-numbing work he loathed—so that I could quit my own hated secretarial job and write full-time. Between our fights, he read every draft of my first novel and reassured me over and over when I doubted myself (which was all the time). He believed in me so much I couldn't let him down, and so I kept going until the novel was done. At the same time, he built us a new bedroom so I could have his old one for a writing studio, soundproofed his studio so his practicing wouldn't bother me, refurbished the deck outside our bedroom window for a garden and a place to sit outdoors. Looking back, I think, *What more could I have asked for?*

We played music together in Jon's studio, as unselfconscious as kids—instruments strewn everywhere, candles lit, drinking tequila or mezcal. I had never truly enjoyed playing the viola before—all those years of lessons and practicing, of feeling competitive, inadequate—and now, for the first time in my life, music became a communal, transcendently fun experience for me. We went on trips—Mexico, Israel, Australia, Amsterdam—and immersed ourselves in foreign food, music, bars, hotels, landscapes. In New York, we heard music, went to dinner parties and movies and bars, slept late, worked in our studios all day.

But still. The voice in my head, my Inner Puritan, kept telling me in no uncertain terms that this life was not the one it had planned for me, and that a marriage like this—with sex and food and decadence, as well as a lot of stress and conflict—was way too much like my mother's marriages, and was doomed to fail the same way hers all had. This voice made me resent and feel guilty about the very things I most loved, made it impossible for me to be happy in that plentiful and passionate life.

. . .

The worst was still to come. It started as a small schism: At the beginning of our marriage, whenever I broached the subject of children and Jon looked at me askance and changed the subject, I thought, *He'll come around, he's not ready yet, I'll convince him, we'll do it soon.* Having children was inextricably bound up with my ideal life. The way we were living then seemed neither legitimate nor worthwhile.

Then, a year and a half after our wedding, my agent sold my first novel in a two-book deal that gave me an income for that year and the next. Six months later, when my closest friend became pregnant with her second child, I realized I was ready to have children. I announced this decision to Jon.

To my amazement, he replied that he didn't really think he wanted kids. Not now, and maybe not ever.

I was floored. I couldn't imagine not wanting to have children. I'd wanted them all my life, and I'd always assumed I'd have them when I was ready. Now I suddenly longed for their warm little bodies in my arms, imagined telling them stories, singing them songs, kissing them good night. I was meant to be a mother; it was who I was in the fantasy. Also, fights aside, Jon had never denied me anything I truly wanted before—and I had never asked him before for anything I wanted so absolutely. I began to ask again, and then again. I saw him as nothing but an obstacle in my way, something to get around. To plow over, if need be.

My desire for kids was real, but I was imposing it on Jon: it didn't arise organically from either the reality of our marriage or our feelings for each other. In fact, it wasn't even really something I saw doing with Jon, particularly. I had, I confess, always imagined my children as just that, *my* children, not ours. After all, my mother had raised us mostly alone, and I had learned from watching her that a mother didn't have to give up her work or her private life to have kids, and that she could do it without a man's help. I presented this argument to Jon, full of righteousness and urgency.

He countered that he didn't want the responsibility of children—didn't want his whole life to be centered around bottle and diaper schedules, didn't want to be restricted by bedtimes and school times and the availability of baby-sitters. Now, we were unencumbered and unburdened, free to do the work we wanted—and already, there were barely enough hours in the day to get it all done. Why give this up, why curtail our freedom? He loved our life the way it was.

I didn't care. I wanted children. He could argue until he was blue and gasping, but I wasn't budging.

It was around this time that the rabbi's advice came back again to bite us in the ass. Desire the other one's happiness more than your own? Figure out the children issue? We had laughed, rolled our eyes. Now we were failing miserably.

But no matter how difficult things had become between us or how insoluble our problems seemed, I still loved Jon, and I knew he loved me. And much as I sometimes mourned for my old single life, I couldn't imagine living without him now. We shared the desire, if not the absolute need, to stay together. We were determined not to repeat our parents' mistakes, not to get divorced. Both of us felt as if we would do whatever it took to work it out.

So we went to see a therapist. During our first session, after we'd given her a good look at the sorry state we were in, she said bluntly, "You two are polarized. Each of you has taken an opposing position about having kids, and you're stuck. Kate can't feel or express any doubts about having children, and Jon can't feel or express any desire for them. But if you allowed yourselves to move toward the middle together, you might discover that you're equally ambivalent. You might even find that you agree."

We stared at her. Just like that, as if she had turned on a light, the whole thing was illuminated—not just the Kid Issue, but the root of our whole problem. From the moment we'd crossed the Verrazano Bridge after our wedding, we had retreated to opposite sides of the boxing ring, glaring, arms folded, thinking only of landing the first blow, getting our licks in, winning. We'd become two opponents trying to destroy each other, rather than a team protecting and shielding each other.

We drove home in dazed silence. At a stoplight, we looked at each other as if we were seeing clearly for the first time in two years. And then, over the next few days, tentatively at first, we started talking, a conversation that went on and on. Yes, I admitted, sometimes I was afraid of having a baby. Yes, Jon confessed, of course he thought about how great it might be to have one. We had one more session with the therapist. That was three years ago.

Since then, we haven't stopped hashing out whether or not to have a child, though at the moment—as in most moments—we are in agreement about not having one. Still, we've fought, argued, switched sides, played devil's advocate; we came into the center of the ring from our respective corners and talked a lot about who we were and what we wanted and why we were with each other and what mattered most to us, separately and together. We figured out how to fight without blowing up, getting embroiled or paralyzed, lashing out, or saying things we'd regret later. We began the process of healing and cementing our bond, of fighting on the same side. And through all this turmoil and struggling, our real marriage emerged, naked and flawed, from the swamp of our separate, incompatible expectations and preconceptions and fears.

These days, we're still in the same loft in the same industrial neighborhood in Brooklyn, with the same rusty pipes and trucks going by; Jon's still the opinionated, all-too-real husband he always was, and I'm still the same demanding, moody wife. Our marriage goes through that waxing and waning—of affection and passion, of feeling bonded (or not), of agreeing and disagreeing—that I now think is inherent and necessary to any good, honest marriage, at least one where both partners have strong ideas and active minds. But the voice in my head is mostly quiet these days: I no longer expect more than this—from myself, from my marriage, from Jon. Maybe we'll change our minds about having a child, maybe not, and someday, hopefully soon, we'll move to a new apartment or house. But for now, we have everything we need.

There's a Jewish saying I love: "Drink to celebrate fullness, not to fill emptiness." I think of this whenever it hits me that someday either Jon or I will die first, and we'll lose each other. Along with piercing sadness, this realization gives me an odd kind of peace and joy I've never known before. It implies that we'll be together to the end, and meanwhile, all we've got at any given moment is whatever the moment holds. Life's too short for perfection.

Houseguest Hell

My Home Is Not Your Home

Chitra Divakaruni

After months of rain and fog, I woke this morning to a brilliant cloudless sky. Jays were chattering in the bushes, the Niles lilies were exploding in blues and whites all over my garden, and the Japanese maple had unfurled every one of its delicious green leaves, landing us squarely in the middle of spring. Anyone else would have been delighted. But I experienced a sinking sensation in the region of my heart. Because spring meant that the houseguests would soon be arriving.

Each year, sure as the swallows of Capistrano, houseguests swoop down on us in flockfuls. (Correction: on me. My husband, who escapes to the office each morning, has to deal with them only at the dinner table. I, who work full-time from home as a novelist and journalist, am a twenty-four-hour captive.) Houseguest season begins in late spring and can last, depending on my luck, until the end of summer, by which time I am a physical and emotional wreck. (I used to think that I was subjected to this particular torture because I live in the desirable San Francisco area, but my friend Surekha from Poughkeepsie assures me that she suffers the same fate.) Since I am of Indian origin, so are most of my guests. Many of them are also relatives. A deadly combination, this, houseguests who are relatives—especially if they are arriving directly from India. Because this means they require Maximum Maintenance.

Maintenance begins in the morning with tea. Not your instant drip-bag kind, but brewed properly, Like-We-Do-at-Home. (Make note of this phrase; it will appear again.) Houseguest tea is boiled on the stove with milk, sugar, ginger, and cardamom. Yes, it does taste delicious, but have you ever tried cleaning out the pot afterward? My guests have not, because in India they have servants to do this—and here they have me.

Along with tea comes breakfast, cooked hot. (Like-We-Do-at-Home.) Preferably something Indian, like idlis or pooris. The rice and lentil mix for idlis has to be soaked overnight, then ground and steamed. Poori dough has to be made ahead, rolled out, and fried. Both require accompaniments—a chutney or a curry—and leave you with a sinkful of dirty dishes. You're getting the idea.

After breakfast, we gird our loins for the real work: sight-seeing and shopping. I love the beauties of the Bay Area, but circling the Golden Gate Bridge parking lot for the 563rd time as I search vainly for a spot is beginning to lose its charm. And here's another confession: I have a low threshold for shopping pain. Malls make me hyperventilate with anxiety. I have no clue as to where the brand names that roll so effortlessly off the tongues of my guests are to be found. ("You mean you don't know where the nearest Macy's outlet is?!" my guests exclaim incredulously. "How about Neiman Marcus? Surely you've been to Saks? Or at least to the Gap-Lane-Bryant-Fashion-Plaza-Men's-Wearhouse-Miller's Outlet?" They smile their compassion. "Don't worry. By the time we leave, you'll know it all.") We reach home at the end of the day, staggering under pyramids of boxes and bags. We kick off our shoes and collapse on the couch. Then someone says, "Ah, wouldn't it be nice to have a hot cup of tea."

Guess who gets up and makes it? And fixes a four-course dinner, with dessert afterward. (Like-We-Do-at-Home.) And loads the dishes in the dishwasher. And mops the kitchen floor. And makes sure the bathroom is stocked with clean towels, soaps, shampoos, toothpastes, deodorizers, and Q-tips. And soaks the rice and lentils for tomorrow morning's idlis, so that they'll be ready in time for our trip to the Napa Valley. All the while wondering how on earth she's going to find time to complete her *other* work, the creative, income-producing kind.

Guess who's spitting mad by the time she gets into bed, where her husband's waiting with amorous inclinations. (Because he has entertained the guests with jokes over dinner and helped clear the table afterward, he thinks he's done his bit and is entitled to some fun and games.) Guess who's so furious she pulls the quilt over her head, because she knows that otherwise she'll start a quarrel, and maybe burst into tears, and then he'll say, "There you go again." He'll say, "It's your own fault. You don't have to do all this for them."

You're probably thinking the same thing.

Why is it that I feel impelled to behave this way? Why can't I just show my guests where the Special K and Lipton's tea bags are? Why can't I point them to the bus that would take them to the mall, or drop them at the BART station with instructions to phone me when they get back from the city? Why can't I order pizza for dinner and ice cream for dessert? Why can't I insist that my husband take them sight-seeing over the weekend while I put up my feet and relax with a good book?

I ask myself these questions over and over, trying to find a satisfactory answer that will help me understand my unconscious needs. Perhaps it's because—despite the books I've published and the writing awards I've won—I still feel that a big chunk of my identity as a woman is tied up in how well I manage my home. Guests, when they come into my house, become part of this responsibility. It's my job to be their caretaker. And in some paradoxical way, even as I complain bitterly because my husband isn't participating, I don't want him to encroach into my realm. I asked Alice, my Caucasian friend, if she feels the same kind of obligation to her guests, or if this is an Eastern thing. She says that whenever she has houseguests, she, too, has to battle with the anxiety of having everything be perfect. ("Or what will they say after they've left?") And unlike other aspects of her life that people may comment on, criticism of her home and home habits tends to hit a particularly vulnerable, private spot. "We women still see ourselves as the Number One Homemaker in the family," she comments. "Our sense of success hinges upon it." Even when we have a nine-to-five job (or in the case of Alice, a senior executive at her company, a nine-to-nine job)? "Especially then," Alice says. "We overcompensate out of some kind of genetically programmed guilt." She thinks for a moment. "But I'm getting better. All last week, when my second cousin and her family were visiting, we ate salads and takeout dinners."

Hearing this, I'm filled with admiration and new resolve. Takeout dinners it will be for me, too! But then I think of how my second cousin and her family would react to such a menu. ("Rabbit fodder? Food in cardboard boxes? Is this why we came all the way to America? Why, at Home we'd never treat a guest this way!") Perhaps part of the problem lies in my memories of my mother, a genuinely hospitable person who has always enjoyed having our large extended family—her side as well as my father's—come to visit. True, she did have a maid to help with cooking and cleaning; also true, since my father supported the family financially, it was understood that her job was to take care of the house—and the guests who came into it. Still, the visits created a lot of extra work for her. Any dish that required true skill she made herself, to be sure it came out perfectly. I still remember how she would stay awake late at night, after her household duties were done, shredding coconut and boiling it with jaggery to make narus for the guests to snack on. Or in the afternoons, instead of taking her usual nap, she'd be up on the terrace laying the quilts out in the sun, so they'd smell good for the guests. But she was able to imbue these chores with a smiling sense of holiday that is somehow beyond my capacities. Unlike me, my mother was not distressed by the upsetting of her daily routine. I am not sure if this is because of her superior mental poise or because her routine was so different from mine, which bristles with imminent pub dates, demanding editors and agents, and hectic book tours—all a result, I realize, of my own ambition. Maybe my mother enjoyed getting away from the humdrum existence of husband-children-cooking-helping-with-homework to go for a jaunt to Victoria Memorial or a visit to the Kali temple. At night after dinner, she stayed up chatting for hours with the visiting women, listening to stories of faraway villages where scandals and disasters and miracles seemed to occur as a matter of routine.

Or perhaps the source of my mother's pleasure in guests and my discomfort with them lies in a fundamental value difference between my birth culture and the one that I've adopted. For while Americans value privacy almost to the point of obsession, it is a concept that hardly even exists in India. Take, for example, our respective sleeping arrangements when guests come to stay. In my home, guests have their own bedroom (one that I have gone to great trouble and expense to decorate appropriately, with items that impress but can't easily be broken by their children). And when they enter it at the end of the day, I heave a great sigh of relief and go to my bedroom and shut my door. And lock it. And God help anyone who comes knocking on it before morning.

In India, however, we had no guest room. Most families didn't. When we had guests, several big beds would be made on the floor. All the children slept on one, usually in a room where a grandparent could keep a benevolent eye on them. The men slept in the drawing room, and the women congregated on pallets in one of the bedrooms, talking and laughing late into the night. I remember how exciting it was when I finally was considered old enough to graduate from the children's room and join my mother in the whispery, moonlit half-dark filled with the smell of jasmine from the garlands the women wore in their hair. What a rite of passage! I have nothing similar to pass on to my children.

Here, then, is the real source of my frustration. I see the traditional Indian way of hospitality in some ways as more gracious and mature and loving, where the guest is seen as "God come to visit." But I haven't figured out how to make this concept an appropriate and meaningful part of my own feminist lifestyle. I cannot replicate my mother's life. Even if I wanted to, it would never work. Our situations are very different, and our roles. I've spent much of my life battling the ideas of males-as-superiors and women-as-servers, which were realities she had to accept. Perhaps in the process my voice has grown strident. We all have to pay for the things we believe in. Her way was to give and give. Mine is not.

My mother was allowed no boundaries, no borders to separate what was hers from what belonged to the family, the community, the society—and so she never thought to do so, and thus could embrace her houseguests for the treat they were and for the delicacies they offered, without a hint of defensiveness. I, by contrast, have fought to gain my boundaries and borders—the ones I so need to create the space for my work—and now must fight to protect them. My mother was taught to acquiesce. I must learn how to say no without feeling that I'm betraying her. I must learn to refuse to give what people want from me when I feel it's unreasonable—but to do so with love.

I've started practicing already. I do it each morning in front of the bathroom mirror, trying to get my smile just right. "No, Susheela auntie, I can't make another trip to the grocery tonight, even though we've run out of buttermilk. How about we drink some of this nice mango juice instead?" Or, "I remember how fond you are of chicken tandoori, Uncle Mohan. Well, tonight I'm taking you to Raja's Diner—it's their house specialty." From time to time, I take deep yogic breaths. From time to time, I employ what one of the *Don't Sweat the Small Stuff* books advises: I imagine the people I'm dealing with as infants, or as people who are 100 years old. I'm making great strides. Here's one of the latest additions to my repetoire: "This is the Grey Line Tours terminal, Janak and Uma. I've booked you on their Napa tour. I hear it's quite lovely. I'll be back at eight P.M. to pick you up." By the time next houseguest season arrives, I'm going to be a pro, ready to greet the spring and its accompanying barbarian hordes with firm charm—just that much more firm than We-Do-at-Home.

A Man in the Heart

Hazel McClay

THIS IS ABOUT sex. It is also about love. I have never had the pleasure of confusing the two.

Until recently, I had the first—sometimes in spades—without the second. Some of it was very, very good, spontaneous, even ecstatic. A lot of it was rotten. Rotten as in leaden, or submissive, a chore to dread before the fact, a memory to regret after. Ecstatic as in the stuff of romance novels, what with the quivering and the melting and the heedless abandon. The stuff that, if you've never felt it, is hard to believe is real.

It is real, of course. It does happen, if you're lucky. But can it last? And if not, should it matter when you're choosing a relationship that may be for life?

. . .

One of my longest-standing and most passionate relationships began when I was twenty-five—over a decade ago. Nick was terribly handsome, funny, full of interesting moods. After a few months together and without an ounce of deliberation or hesitation, we moved in together.

Each time one of us went away, it meant we got to reunite, and for a while, the reunion involved tearing away each other's clothes and doing it on the kitchen table, in the woods, wherever we could steal a private moment, pronto.

I loved Nick, but I can't say I loved him completely, because for me, something was always missing. I did not feel known by him. Somehow, instead of seeing what was there, he projected things onto me that were not. My Catholic upbringing, for instance, became for him a shadowy past of mysterious rituals. To me, of course, it was nothing of the kind, more funny than strange, but no less important for that. My mundane life mattered to me. For Nick, it was not enough. Instead, I suspect it was his misreadings of me that fueled his desire. He got it wrong, but those wrong ideas compelled him. I represented something to him—less a person than a concept, an ideal. I felt it was a miracle that someone as appealing as Nick adored me, and I was grateful. But how do you converse with someone who adores you? How do you live together, managing the mundane details that must be managed every day?

Nick thought that he could win my love, and he tried, but instead I won. I disabused him of that mystifying, romantic view of me. He began to view the details of my past, my present, our life together, as indeed mundane. I liked this version of events less. In fact, it was quietly horrifying.

Maybe as a result, my passion for him waned. I loved to look at him while he was sleeping, but when he was awake, I seldom felt like fooling around. Asleep, he was the same man I had fallen for. Awake, he was the man who had replaced him—a man I was fond of, to be sure, but also one who knew me too well, though still not well enough. We'd demystified ourselves in lots of ways—besides sharing a bed, we shared a bathroom, a refrigerator, a phone. In another relationship, this might not have mattered. With Nick, in our ease, we no longer had the mystery of our early passion, when everything was new and exciting, and we hadn't replaced that mystery with some new intimacy or closeness that was comparatively satisfying. The relationship foundered, and the sex died—or maybe vice versa.

Yet in the wake of my disappearing passion for Nick, a new, surprising tenderness for him grew. We had never held hands, never displayed affection in public, but in our final months together, on an evening walk or somewhere as mundane as the grocery store, I'd slip my hand around the crook of his elbow, pull myself in next to him, and hold on tight. I could have stayed like that for hours.

Perhaps that tenderness was merely the sweet melancholy of autumn, the gorgeous season that settles so lightly, so briefly before the inevitable death to follow. Whatever it was, soon after it set in, we parted.

In the ensuing years, I searched and sifted through other men for something as good as the early passion I had with Nick, or as tender as the feeling that followed in its wake. I found little passion, and the only tenderness I could ever muster was a kind of pity, when the man mistook the sex for something else. I kept at it anyway. Sometimes the sex was pretty good, and it bought companionship, but my companions were men I neither admired nor felt compelled by. Like Nick, these men considered me a mystery; I didn't find myself mysterious in the least. They said they didn't know what I wanted; I found my wants distressingly simple.

What I wanted, in a nutshell, was to be understood. Even as life challenged my romantic hopes and notions, I began to see myself as living in a kind of fairy tale, as something akin to the youngest sister in *Beauty and the Beast*. It was not her beauty that we held in common, but a desire she makes known to her father at the story's start, a desire that sets all the story's subsequent events in motion. Departing on a long voyage, the father asks his three daughters what they'd like him to bring back. The older sisters both ask for luxuries, pearls or jewels, the youngest for a blue rose. Although it seems the simplest of requests, such a rose proves far more difficult to find. In fact, nearly impossible.

It seemed to me that my notion of love was not unlike the blue rose: simple and impossible. As I waited, nearly a decade went by, but unlike Beauty I did not wait patiently or sweetly. I was lonely as the devil, and to blunt that feeling, I got laid. I broke several hearts, and secretly blamed the men for being fools, then began to blame myself instead.

Time and again, I entered into liaisons that, if I'd been honest with myself, I'd have known from the get-go would never work. I let the men draw near, then batted them away, not especially surprised when the batting piqued their interest. When I broke up it was always with a show of kindness and regret, gracious like an actress on the stage, but not *truly* gracious. I did not care about these men. I was bored and jaded. They had become something to do.

I had lost my dream and, in so doing, my dignity. But if I couldn't have the dream, I at least wanted my dignity back. And so I decided to stop having sex with men unless the most unlikely of events transpired: unless I fell in love.

I do not equate dignity with chastity. In many cases, the two are unrelated. But in my case, I had come to see sex as a weapon I did not understand well enough to use responsibly. And so I stopped.

My dealings with exes—with many of whom the relationship had festered on and off for months—became firm, no-nonsense, humane, and blessedly brief. I warmed to the prospect of spending my time more gainfully—of taking up reading again, a pastime I'd loved as a child but seemed to have more or less given up in adulthood, of riding my bike, of making more money, of gathering berries in the woods.

I'd like to say this productive period went on for a while, but it did not, and for the best possible reason, the only acceptable one, according to my terms. Three months into my vow, a few months shy of thirty-five, I fell in love.

. . .

I remember the moment it happened.

I had moved to the West Coast a month before. Charlie and I met shortly after my arrival, and right away I respected him and liked him but, at first, nothing more.

Meanwhile, the little house I rented was just five miles from the ocean, but I'd always feared the ocean and had been avoiding it. One Sunday I ran into him at the Laundromat, and we decided to take my dog to the beach.

If you have ever been to the northern coast of Oregon, particularly in the rainy season (i.e., most of the year), you know the sort of beaches there: wide miles of sand, uninterrupted by rocks, buildings, or people. It was the windy month of March, blowing enough that day to lift the top layer of sand, carry it gently past us, and set it down again in long, gorgeous patterns. There were huge, ancient pieces of driftwood tossed up near the dunes, rotting ever so slowly into the sand. Not another human in sight.

We started down the beach and Charlie threw up the hood on his hunter green sweatshirt. It reminded me of the ones my brothers wore when we were kids, the ones I wore myself. The wind made his nose red and runny. He didn't have a handkerchief and neither did I. As we strolled along, he sniffed more and more violently.

We were discussing the existence of God, one of the simplest questions on earth, and to me, one of the most harrowing. I was talking about different people's ideas of God, what this group thought or that group, occasionally turning my head to study the sea, when Charlie fixed a steady look on me.

"And what do *you* think?" he asked.

It was one of the most intimate questions I've ever faced. I didn't answer, but I pretended to, trying to shift the topic away from me. He listened patiently, carefully, but when I finished, he repeated his question.

"And what do *you* think?"

I looked up and down the beach, everywhere but at him. I could not believe it. Here was a man I couldn't fool. I'd met my match.

Charlie asked me a third time. I told him what I thought. The wind blew, his nose ran, and I fell in love. We continued down the beach.

We started spending time together, and then more. I loved every minute of it.

You fall in love with somebody for big reasons, but they manifest themselves in the small things, and pretty soon you can't tell if you love the quirks because they're his, or you love him because of the quirks. Of course, Charlie was smart, sensitive, and funny enough to make me laugh out loud a dozen times a day. Less generic was his fascination with humanity. Charlie keeps a pair of binoculars on his desk so he can watch the folks who come and go on the city street below his office window. If we go to a restaurant, he takes the seat against the wall so he can track everyone in the room. And he's forever striking up conversations with strangers. Some of these strangers are delightful; some are crazy. Sometimes I wish Charlie would act a little more like most people—that is, that he could just ignore the delivery guy, or the little old lady in the cracker aisle, and we could get on with our day. But getting people's stories *is* Charlie's day. It's one of the things he lives for. And I love to watch as he draws out these strangers' stories, as they bloom under the warmth of Charlie's kind attention. That's just one of his quirks I fell in love with.

Eventually, to my great good luck, Charlie fell in love with me, too. I brought him home, introduced him to my family, my friends.

"He's a keeper," everyone said, a thing no one had ever said to me before, not even about Nick. "He's perfect for you."

They were right in so many ways—still are—and I am happy with him. Deeply happy. I walk down the street with my hand tucked around his elbow, and this tenderness feels less like autumn and more like eternity, because this tenderness was there from the start.

There's only one thing missing. I'll give you one guess.

This man has never wrapped me in his arms, never covered my mouth with his and kissed me until I gasped for breath. I have never forgotten where I was when we made love, or not cared. We do not tear off each other's clothes. We do not make love often, never have, and, I suspect, never will.

It's not that sex with him is bad. He satisfies me physically, more or less, and that's more than I can say for most of the sexual partners I've had. It's just that I don't crave it. The passion that I had for Nick, at least until it faded, is simply missing from this relationship.

I have thought long and hard about why this might be. Part of it could be simply physical, chemical. Unlike with Nick, I did not fall in love with Charlie's body, but with his soul, his spirit, his mind. And while one might argue that true passion does involve all those things (soul, spirit, mind, and so on), one could counter that whatever love is ultimately "about," the reality of sex is two bodies slapping together, two sets of eyes and lips locking on each other, and if the chemistry isn't there—the smells, the tastes, the heavy breathing and sweaty palms—regardless of what other important ingredients are, the sex can never be ecstatic.

Here's another possibility. Knowing each other as well as Charlie and I do—having the emotional and intellectual connection I felt when I fell in love with him and continue to feel (the very thing my relationship with Nick lacked)—precludes another element that sometimes fosters great sex, which is the need and desire to get closer to someone: to understand him or her, to push deeper, probe harder, pun both intended and not. This is what it was at the beginning with Nick: Once the chemical rush had attracted us to each other, there was almost a desperate urge to know him and have him know me—one that, naturally, I felt closer to achieving when we had sex. This might also explain why I felt so disappointed each time the sex ended—because it hadn't worked. Once I realized that sex was not really making him know me any better, perhaps I gave up, which ended my desperation and maybe my passion for him as well.

With Charlie, by contrast, I already feel known and understood. And comfortable. "You're like brother and sister," my friends say, and sometimes, even though I think it's intended as a compliment, of sorts, it gives me pause.

We *are* a lot alike. We talk alike, love the same stuff, hate the same stuff, laugh at the same stuff, eavesdrop on the same conversations. We even have the same eyeglasses (though not the same prescription, lucky for him), purchased before we met. But most couples don't aspire to be like siblings, and we are no exception. Driving together the other day, he turned to me. "I don't want us to be like brother and sister," he said.

I paused, wondered: *Is he worried about the same thing I am?* I looked at him and smiled.

"Neither do I," I said.

Can a couple be *too* harmonious? *Too* best of friends? Does our kind of intimacy preclude another kind, the mystery between the sheets, on the desk, out in the shed? Charlie and I don't "need" sex to connect, and since sex was not what attracted me to him in the first place, I don't really crave it. This doesn't mean it doesn't feel nice to hug him, or to sleep next to him, or to feel his warm naked body against mine. It just means that I get enough from him without this, and often I'm just as happy to sleep in my pj's and go to bed with a book. Is this a problem? Depends how you look at it.

. . .

Here's the thing. Evidence—my own as well as what I read, what I see (not on TV, but in life), what my friends say—suggests that long-term passion is a rare thing, and that even short-term passions don't always make for the happiest or healthiest relationships. This is very disappointing but probably makes sense if you believe, as I do, that passionate sex is not about intimacy but about something more raw, shocking, forbidden. (Contrary to popular belief, this may be particularly true for women, whose level of attraction seems to be more subject to a given situation and its psychology than most men's.)

The point is, perhaps the very thing I'm missing with Charlie doesn't exist for long anyway. This is not to say I don't believe there are married couples who have great sex for most or all of their married lives. I do, but—at least judging from the ones I know who are honest enough to talk about it—these couples are few and far between, especially once children (which I definitely hope to have) come into the picture. And even then, great married sex rarely seems to involve the romance-novel stuff—the quivering, the melting, the physical passion. What's more, the few married couples I know who do have passionate sex after the first couple of years (or the first kid) fuel their passion with anger. I guess anger is fine in a marriage, if you don't mind living with it. But I don't think I'd be very happy living with it until death did us part. Charlie and I rarely fight, because we rarely disagree, and when we do, we resolve things peacefully, gently—no yelling, no storming out of houses, no days of raging silently and not speaking, no screaming "Fuck you" in a way that makes us then need to reconnect in bed the next day or week. Perhaps this lack of fighting is our sameness manifesting in a different way, but if so, it's a way I welcome. Perhaps, then, I simply got what I picked: I traded the volatility of what seems to accompany long-lived (if sporadic) marital passion for something more important to me. But then, in my life, I've always been more interested in love than in passion—perhaps because, until now, love has always been the scarcer commodity.

Again—friends and books and common sense notwithstanding—I'm still not convinced that a woman has to choose between sexual passion and the kind of love I feel today. I'm not even convinced this woman has to. It may be that if I kept searching I'd find a man with whom I felt both, even without the fights and the fuck-you's. And maybe the passion wouldn't wane with familiarity, or even with a kid or two in the house. Maybe we'd live happily ever after making passionate love twice or thrice a week, the stuff of storybook endings come to real life.

Maybe, and maybe not. But after almost two years with Charlie, I choose him—perhaps, if he chooses me back, for the rest of my life. And if that means giving up stellar sex with someone else—so be it.

One might suppose I make this choice because I'm thirty-six and worn out by the hunt. Yes and no. At twenty-two, and twenty-eight, and even thirty-one, I did harbor certain notions about love that I no longer do, because I learned a few things the hard way. For instance, no matter how much a man fascinates you, if you can't relax around him, or can't speak your mind, it isn't going to work for very long—great sex or no. And no matter how many poems he writes you, no matter how well he kisses, no matter how often he says he adores you, if he happens to add, in the next breath, "if you'd just change this one thing . . . ," forget it.

Then there are the notions of love I still harbor. I want to build my life with one man, to live with that man the rest of my life. In order to manage that, I need to love him an awful lot, and I need to feel he loves me *and* knows me, both. Charlie fits that bill. That makes the choice easy—not perfect, not without its occasional worries, but easy nonetheless. I'm not willing to give him up, or to jeopardize what we have by sleeping with another man. That's my bottom line: I may have compromised, but I didn't settle.

Which is not to say that I don't miss sexual passion, or that I won't continue to as time goes on. I do, and I will. Sooner or later, I'll probably be tempted to cheat. I'm not looking forward to that time. Sex is unpredictable. It cannot be trusted. But at those times, I will remind myself of some important things.

First, I will remember what my life was like before I met Charlie, and I will compare it—oh so unfavorably—to my life now.

Second, I will remind myself that, historically, marrying for passion is a relatively new phenomenon—one that just happens to correspond with the rising divorce rate (at last check, it was, what, over 50 percent?). Really, it's mostly since the sexual revolution that women have come to believe passion is a requirement or a right of marriage—and look where it's gotten us (straight to divorce court). If you don't believe me on this, ask your grandmother what she married for (and if she says passion, if it lasted—and if so, what she gave up for it). As one well-known writer recently put it, "the longing for passion is a sort of low-grade virus circulating among us."

Finally, I will look at the kinds of passion Charlie and I do have, and how deeply important they are to me. A passion for high jinks and laughter, for music and the open road. For truth. For courage. Integrity. Imagination. And each other.

Sometimes, when Charlie and I finish making love, I find myself crying—tears of gratitude, because I'm lying with him and not someone else. This is something that has never happened to me before. And it means more to me than a hundred breathless fucks.

Why I Hate That My Mother Was Right (Well . . . About Most Things)

Turning into Elizabeth Taylor

Karen Karbo

LAST THANKSGIVING I went to a party with my new guy. Dinner was being served later than is customary and in the evening my ex-husband dropped off our nine-year-old daughter, Fiona. Every year Fiona has two dinners: earlier with her father's family, later with me. We hope these double dinners are not so much setting her up for an eating disorder as showing her that even divorced people can have holiday traditions. Someone knew my ex-husband and invited him in for a drink. Another guest, an archgossip whom I hadn't seen since my ex and I were still married, glimpsed him in the kitchen, scotch in hand, standing next to the new guy, scotch also in hand, who is considerably younger than my ex and, it must be said, looks not unlike him; both are five ten and stocky, with large, mournful eyes, goatees, and floppy hair that parts in the middle. The archgossip grabbed one of my best friends by the arm and stage-whispered into her ear, "That's gotta be strange, the husband and the boyfriend, right there, side by side." My friend said, "Oh no, that's her ex-husband. There's been another husband between him and the boyfriend, so it's perfectly fine." Everyone laughed. Including me.

Of all the things I imagined I'd be when I grew up, a woman with a personal life that cracked people up was not on the list. I was relieved to be wearing all black, and too much jewelry; at least I was dressed the part. As one friend said, when I told her it looked as if my second marriage wasn't going to work either, "Well, if you're going to be Elizabeth Taylor, ya gotta have the rocks."

This is a mystery to me, how I turned into Elizabeth Taylor. How I left first one husband, then the next, over the course of seven years. I'm not sufficiently beautiful, rich, famous, or kooky. I was a Girl Scout until eighth grade. I never cut a class and didn't smoke pot until I was in college. I want to be married (not that badly, apparently).

In fact, I was trained to view marriage as life's greatest achievement—training that ended abruptly one bright day in March 1975 when my mother, aged forty-six, slipped into a coma. She had brain cancer. I was sixteen and still a virgin at the time, the whole panoply of unrequited love, underwhelming sex, and marital mishegaas ahead of me.

Because my mother is now long dead, I maintain the illusion that if I had just listened to her, I would have a perfect husband. (That there is no such thing, and I know it, is immaterial.) The frustrating part is that I felt as if I was listening but just didn't get it—not unlike in high school French class, where Madame Dutton, who was a Scot raised in Italy, would hold forth in an accent that even the A students like me couldn't understand. For I came late to teenage rebellion; I had just gotten the hang of eye rolling when my mother's headaches started. I was ready to shock her with the f-word about the time she started chemo. I didn't have the luxury of telling her she was full of shit, only to come around decades later and realize she may have had a point. Her death was like that of the only witness and possible accomplice in a murder mystery, lying on the floor, expiring moments before revealing the secret that would solve the case. I had sixteen years of my mother's hokey aphorisms, but no explanation.

Before I get to the things my mother said—the things about which she turned out to be more or less right—may I just ask where did she get off? When it came to love, men, and marriage, my mother knew it all. Did she know *intuitively* that if you say something with enough authority it always sounds true? My mother was not afraid to traffic in clichés. After all, as she told me, a cliché wouldn't have become a cliché in the first place unless it were true. She held forth in a way none of us living in the postmodern age have the nerve to do, unless we are enthusiastic members of a fundamentalist religion or have read too many books by John Gray. What were her credentials, other than being the mother? I'm the mother now, and I feel the ambivalence of life deep in my calcium-fortified bones. My mother had never been to college or out of the country. She'd had one job for one year before she met and married my father. Still, she pontificated from her post at the gold-and-white Formica breakfast bar. She wore floral blouses and polyester capris. She always had a glass of Coors Brew 102 in a woman-shaped beer glass and a mentholated Salem perched on the edge of one of those massive glass ashtrays from the 1970s that could have been a murder weapon. The cigarette filter was imprinted with her signature Orange Peel lipstick.

My mother said if I wanted a boy to love me, I had to make him do everything. Make him call me, come to the door, open the door for me, pull out my chair. Make him pay the tab. Always. "Dutch treat is a crime against nature," she once said. When she said this, I was fourteen, going on my first date. I didn't pay attention to the Dutch treat portion of her exhortation, but I did think a lot about what a crime against nature might be. As I recall, the only thing I could come up with was littering.

Making the boy do everything was related to playing hard to get, to which she also subscribed. Her rule of thumb on how to play hard to get? The more interested you are in a boy, the less interested you act. And then, once you get the boyfriend, "However much space he claims to need? You need twice that much." I remember her telling me this one night when she was at the kitchen sink peeling carrots, wearing her yellow rubber dishwashing gloves. My mother was a redhead, with skin so sensitive that contact with the most benign vegetables gave her hives. She was wearing shorts. I stared at the blue veins behind her knees. How could this be? I loved Billy Mohr in the seventh grade, and when he didn't act interested in me (which was all the time), it didn't make me like him more, it only made me like myself less.

It was all academic, anyway, like discussing how one might live successfully on Mars. Setting aside for a moment the fact that I had no idea how to make any boy do anything, the only boys I was supposed to want to work my mother's mojo on were boys who were "appropriate." To be appropriate, a boy needed to be (a) older than me (easy; I'd skipped first grade, everyone was older than me); (b) taller than me (this narrowed the field; at thirteen I was already five nine); (c) smarter than me (a conundrum: there were no boys in my class who were both taller and smarter); and most important, (d) able to drag me up the rungs of the socioeconomic ladder by my smooth hair, straightened every other night on empty Sunkist orange juice cans. For my mother was a proto–Material Girl. My mother wondered what love had to do with it long before Tina realized she'd be better off without Ike. My mother had married up, and was damn proud of it.

My mother also said, "Never forget, it's as easy to love a rich man as it is a poor man." I didn't know any boys who were older, taller, and smarter; now they also had to be richer? Where were all these mythical boys? I remember thinking in college,that falling in love was not a whole lot different from a drinking game we played with cards, where the winner of each hand got to add a special rule. If you broke the rule, you had to drink. The goal, of course, was to add so many dumb rules that the more everyone drank, the less they could remember them and the drunker they got.

My mother introduced most of her rules for getting a boy to like you during the years I had my ear pressed against the radio, where all I heard, day in, day out, was that love, love, love was all I needed. That love was a heat wave. That it had no pride, and was an itchin' in my heart that would eventually tear me apart. The songs on the radio made sense to me. This was the way it felt when I was making out in the pool cabana with my first boyfriend and it was suddenly as if I'd wet my pants.

The pool cabana boyfriend was younger, my same height, and just as smart. He was not the richest boy I knew. The richest boy I knew was the one-year-older brother of a girl in my grade, a boy with a discolored tooth who worked in the paint department at Sears and had gotten a girl named Misty pregnant. I felt sure my mother wouldn't approve of him. She appeared to approve of the pool cabana boyfriend, not because he was rich but because his family had what she called "real" money. His father was a vice president of Standard Oil. They'd just come from a place called Darien, Connecticut, noted for its rich people. They drove an old brown Chevy we called the Taco Wagon, and bought their clothes at JCPenney, where the "real" rich people shopped. I loved the pool cabana boyfriend throughout high school and into college, until the day he came out of the closet to me at a restaurant on Melrose when we were both nineteen. I remember watching my tears drop into my French onion soup au gratin. He was taller than I was by then.

Anyway, the pool cabana boyfriend didn't factor into my mother's plans for me. She was not interested in my having a real boyfriend, which would inevitably lead to messy struggles with attachment, intimacy, sex, possible pregnancy, and eventual heartbreak. She simply wanted me to practice catching one, and whoever came down the pike was good enough, like a pickup game of basketball. After all, you can practice your skyhook against anyone with two hands and a pair of sneakers.

After the pool cabana boy, no other boys came down the pike for a while, which frustrated my mother. What was wrong with me that I didn't have any suitors? She used words like that: suitors. It didn't help matters that men liked my mother. Boys liked my mother. My mother had one extraordinary gift: she was able to find something interesting in just about anyone. She was classist, racist, and sexist, and yet she numbered among her close friends several gay men; Hallie, the African-American woman who took care of me for about a year before I started school; and a Hispanic divorcée and mother of three whom she met at the Laundromat. I used to come home from swim practice and find three of the pool cabana boy's friends sitting around the breakfast bar, talking with my mother. When I got home, they often left, the party now over. What was wrong with me? I wish I could report that I was one of those bucktoothed, knobby-kneed geeks who grew up to be both beautiful and monumentally cool, like Uma Thurman. I was tall, but I looked all right in my yellow velour bikini, the kind with gold rings on the side. As my mother liked to point out, I had friends who were far less pretty than I who had more boyfriends. I was a disappointment. No one was interested. My mother didn't know why, which was alarming in its own way, since my mother knew everything else.

The bit of domestic economic wisdom that troubled me most was the one about the cow and the milk. Why buy the cow when you can get the milk for free? I didn't know who the *you* in the sentence was. Who was she talking to? And what milk? And why would I want to buy a cow? Wasn't owning a cow a lot of work, just to get something sold at every corner market? It took me years to figure out that I was the cow and the milk was sex and that the person doing the metaphorical purchasing was the rich man who was older, taller, and smarter, the one I was going to find easy to love.

Once, a year or so before she died, my mother caught me in the den in the clutches of the pool cabana boyfriend. She gave me a stern lecture. "Boys only want one thing," my mother said. I said, "Yeah, I know, milk."

. . .

Nutty as the things my mother said might sound, I've obsessed about them for decades now. I'm unable to put what sounds like quaint nonsense into the larger context of the times, or to refract it through the prism of adulthood. Her wisdom remains a dumb bug encased in the amber of my adolescence.

Anyway—and perhaps needless to say—I wound up ignoring all of it. After her death, in college, I dated a few sons of wealthy men, guys who had access to the family yacht and routinely spent winter breaks in Aspen. They weren't simply dull; the few dates I had with each of them were absolute clock-watchers. I couldn't wait to get back to my sorority house and watch *Saturday Night Live* in my nightgown.

For the most part, the guys I attracted—and certainly the ones who attracted me—were the sort who could barely support themselves, much less me. They were not bad boys in any glamorous, Kurt Cobain sense;

the worst that could be said about them was that they were terrible with money. They had strange things in common: they were all dreamers who liked dogs and eating huge bowls of ice cream late at night. Unlike my father, they were talkers. And listeners. They found what I had to say interesting. Like the pool cabana boyfriend, with whom, in high school, I started a tie-dyed shirt business, they were compatriots, they were buddies. None of them were older, taller, smarter, or richer, but all of them made me laugh. Once, I asked my soon-to-be-ex-second-husband why he married his ex-wife, who seemed, to me, to be unpleasant in every way. "She laughed at my jokes," he answered. Now he'll probably be saying that same thing to some new chick about me. My mother is spinning in her grave.

I did not marry up. No one in America likes to talk about class, and I'm no different. I'm fighting the urge to say I married horizontally; in truth, I married down. My first husband's father sold cars. My second husband's father installed telephones. Both of their mothers worked, while my mother stayed at home and made beef Stroganoff and belonged to a women's club. My father had Investments. We dressed up for Thanksgiving dinner and never put salad dressing bottles on the table. I married men who were, from a class perspective, beneath me.

This was not so noticeable with my first husband (four months younger, one inch taller, as smart in some things, not in others), whom I met in graduate school. He's an independent filmmaker, and the fact that he's a used car salesman's kid gives him some street cred. When we split, he behaved well. We divorced without an attorney, shed tears in private, did not hurl the crockery. We didn't argue about the CD player or the dogs (both of which he kept). My mother, who had nothing to say to me about how one goes about divorcing, would not have complained.

My second husband (six years younger, three inches taller, smart but without a college degree), a man I chose—yes—because he was a cuddle bum, would wake me up in the middle of the night to tell me he loved me, and never needed to be persuaded to rub my feet. Unfortunately, that was about all he liked to do, aside from playing computer games. In this marriage, I learned that if a man thinks you can do it yourself, he'll let you do it yourself.

This marriage ending was both a heartbreak and a revelation. Perhaps this is what my mother was talking about when she advised me to let the boy do everything. You didn't let him do these things because you *couldn't* (I remember saying to her once, "I have two arms, I can't open the door?"), but because once you started doing things for yourself, he'd stop—not just opening the door for you, but picking up his dirty boxers, clearing his plate off the table, or making a living. You would find out the hard way the awful truth: the human male is not unlike the male lion.

You know those documentaries that always show the lions reclining on a mound and surveying the terrain? Those would be the males. Meanwhile, the females in the pride are out hunting, stalking, and killing the antelope, while the males sit around preening and roaring and waiting for the food, which the females drag back and place before them, waiting to eat until they're done. I have a handful of friends who are lionesses: they make six figures, mother overachieving children, maintain a nice house, stay fit, do the taxes, and are married to struggling sculptors or painters or "short-story writers" who are also allegedly househusbands but do far less than even the most lethargic, bathrobe-wearing, bonbon-eating, *Oprah*-watching housewife.

Near the end of our marriage, the cuddle bum, who had been working one day a week driving for UPS, had surgery in his neck to fuse a vertebra, and after the doctor cleared him to go back to work, he simply didn't. I was supporting my daughter, for whom I have joint custody with my first ex-husband, as well as the cuddle bum's two children from his prior two marriages, as well as the C.B. himself, all with my writing. Supporting anyone, let alone a family of five, by writing is like relying on a lemonade stand for income.

In return, my soon-to-be-ex would get up in the morning, get the children off to school, sweep the kitchen floor, then, at about 9:30 A.M., call it a day. He'd retire to the computer, where he'd play online until midnight. I worked ten-hour days, paid the bills, shopped, cleaned, helped the kids with their homework, chauffeured them to their dentist's appointments and tae kwon do lessons, cooked, policed them as they did their chores, got them to bed at a reasonable hour. I was both "the man," who worked from sunup to sundown, and "the woman," whose work was never done. How had that happened? Forget giving away the milk; I'd gone and given away the whole damn cow.

The class difference has never been more apparent than during our breakup. We argued, we shrieked, we wept, we carried on. Once, he hollered, "Woman! Shut your trap!" *Woman, shut your trap?* This was so preposterous, it ended the argument then and there. I giggled and couldn't stop. *Woman, shut your trap?* I'd never heard such a thing. But the thing was, I sort of liked it. I thought it was passionate. Until the night the cuddle bum decided to pin me to the bed, hard enough to pierce the back of my head with the post of my earring. I felt the hot syrup of my own blood trickling down the back of my neck.

The cuddle bum moved out the next day. Mom, you were right. If I had fallen in love with the rich man who was older, taller, and smarter, this probably wouldn't have happened. Or it would have. He would have bored me. I would not have laughed, nor had my feet rubbed, and I would have found a way to make the marriage not work anyway. The problem is—and this is a problem my mother never acknowledged, or if she did, she never did to me—the problem is that falling for a man is not like buying a car, where you can decide on the model, then pick and choose your options.

I have a recurring fantasy about having lunches with my mother where she turns over all the cards, where, after she orders her salad with the blue cheese on the side, she confesses things I've had to find out the hard way. Maybe she acknowledges that love is complicated, that in fact it's one of life's great mysteries and that all her rules about what to do—and how and when and with whom—were really frightened attempts to harness passion. Maybe she quotes the rapper Ice-T (since this a fantasy, why not?): passion makes the world go round, but love makes it a safer place. I was her only child, and she wanted that safe place for me.

Maybe she tells me that the second women started making real money, there was no real reason for marriage; that while it's a thrill to make money, it's never a thrill to fold the laundry, and that she folded the laundry because she had to fold the laundry, the same way my soon-to-be-ex-stepson has to pick up the dog poop every Saturday, in order to get an allowance. Maybe she admits that she was just winging it all along. And that for a daughter who is not just the cow with the milk but also the farmer with the money to buy it, she had no advice at all.

How We Became Strangers

Jill Bialosky

I SAT IN an outdoor café to lunch with an old friend I hadn't seen in nearly a year, between our work schedules, children, and writing lives. It was spring. The pond was beginning to thaw. The daffodils were in bloom. Triangles and rectangles of pale yellows lay in patchwork style around trees and in the islands in the middle of the streets. Their perky cheerful crowns reminded me of how dreary and endless the winter had been. A teenage girl with a series of pierces in her earlobe tucked her hand in the back of her boyfriend's pocket as they waited for a table, and I remembered the boy who slipped his hands into the pockets of my hiphuggers and asked "Do you want to?" before we lay down in the grass. At the table next to us, a couple hovered over their cappuccinos in an intense conversation. I noticed the woman had taken off her slingback sandal and was rubbing her bare foot against the calf of the man across from her. My friend and I conversed nonstop about the books we read and the films we saw. We moaned about how tired we were, between making cupcakes for the class picnic, expense reports to finish, a novel that needed to be turned in. The long, lavish lunch was like a luxury, a brief intermission from our lives. We gossiped about mutual friends and fantasized about trips to Italy and France. During dips in our conversation, I found myself looking at the teenage couple, now seated at a table, their chairs side by side. They kissed. The boy with the lean body underneath a V-neck sweater put his hand underneath the back of his girlfriend's shirt. Our conversation moved to our children, kindergartens, tantrums, bed-wets. We talked about our mothers and sisters. At the end of the lunch, my friend looked into my eyes as if she were peering into the farthest reaches of my soul and asked me about my marriage. "Are you guys having sex?" she asked, bluntly. And this image blossomed in my head of D.'s face covered in pox marks, more poxes bursting from his body, as he lay on our couch, miserable and not talking, quarantined in our bedroom like a leper, having caught chicken pox from our son. I wanted to burst out laughing.

. . .

It was not the picture I visualized twelve years ago when I thought about D. from the sixth floor of my office window, talking with him long-distance, when the sound of his voice made my body nervous and tingly. I had dated my share of intellectual men, but none of them were men I could imagine being the father of my child. When, inevitably at a dinner party, the conversation came around to how we'd met, ours was the storybook story that made people smile. We discovered each other at my ten-year high school reunion. D. was a jock and I was a flower child. In high school our lives barely intersected.

D. was athletic, boyish, possessed of a wry, dry, and sometimes angry humor. Both of us were middle children in our families, and watching and listening to how he interacted with his family, I saw much of myself. We were both listeners and mediators. We were do-gooders and ambitious. Both of us were motivated by this compulsion to make up for crimes we hadn't committed. He was going to law school in the Midwest. I was a poet working as an editorial assistant at a publishing house in New York. We visited each other every weekend we could manage. To this day we thank People's Express Airlines for those thirty-nine-dollar airfares that made it possible for us to sustain the long stretches where I thought I'd go insane if I didn't see the shape of his body leaning against the wall outside the airline gate waiting for me as I deplaned. Once during one of our weekend trysts D. drove me to the airport and, just as the plane was about to board, convinced me to take the next flight. We sat in two seats facing the runway mad with the inexplicable euphoria two people in love inhabit until the next flight began to board and D. tempted me to call in sick the next day and stay another night. When we were apart during the week, I fell asleep at night curled into the Princess phone while we talked long-distance. In the morning, his was the first voice I heard as I reached for the phone and cradled it next to my goose-down pillow. Once we moved in together, into my studio apartment just large enough for a pull-out couch, our days and nights were fueled by adventure.

We sat in bars and drank gimlets. We maxed out our credit cards over romantic dinners and weekends in front of fireplaces at crumpled-down and elegant bed-and-breakfasts throughout New England. We slept late. We awoke watching the moon slip into the sheet of the new light of morning. Or we didn't sleep at all. We went skiing, ice-skating, and to the movies any night we pleased. He pressed up against me in dark alleys. I gave him blow jobs as he drove on one of our weekend treks. We made out in taxicabs. There was a kind of volatile tension wired through our relationship that set my body on fire feeling his arm rest against mine in the dark cavern of a movie theater.

. . .

I remember waking to the pull of desire, in the landscape we shared, the morning we decided we wanted to have a baby. The night before, we had argued coming home from a New Year's Eve party in the midst of a bludgeoning snowstorm. Unable to hail a cab, we walked from one side of the city to the other screaming at each other, convinced our marriage had ended. In the early years of our relationship our fights were passionate. They were the kind where one of us stormed out the door, or slept on the couch. The kind where I'd be embarrassed, the next morning, running into our next-door neighbor in the elevator. Fights where I fell apart in the middle of a restaurant, tears falling in puddles in my too-expensive salmon mousse. It was the intense warfare couples engage in to negotiate their commitment. What woman doesn't think when she looks at her man dressed in his boxer shorts picking his toenails in front of the Mets game, "*This* is the guy I decide to end the quest for?" And what man,

I imagined, doesn't wonder as he tries to shave in the bathroom surrounded by drying Wonderbras and panty hose, under the strain of a mortgage and car payments, if he'd have been better off a bachelor. What did we fight about that night of the New Year? It began when, after trying to hail a cab for nearly an hour, I balked at the idea of riding the subway at four in the morning, and my husband retaliated with one of his famous "Who do you think you are, Queen Elizabeth?" remarks. By the time we made it home we were cold and tired and wet, but it was New Year's, already the dawn of the new day, and in our one-bedroom brownstone with the kitchenette the size of a closet, into the third year of our entry-level jobs, life was good, and D. was sexy in his white T-shirt and damp curls. We slept and we awoke. We were groggy and hungover and our bodies touched. We were burning like a patch of dry summer grass I once watched turn to flames as I held a thick glass close to the ground.

. . .

And then there were three.

. . .

No one prepared me for what it would mean to have a baby in the house. I remember the first day we brought L. home. Was it possible that I would ever sleep again? Truth be told, I didn't want to sleep. I wanted to perch beside my child's bassinet like an owl on a limb of a tree to make sure he was still breathing. I loved to study the perfect shape of his head. The way he crinkled up his fingers, shorter than the end of a Q-tip; the size and shape of every yawn. He was like an extension of my body. The first time I was away from him—I left the house for a half hour to get my hair cut, one block away, for the impending barbaric festival of his bris—I was so anxious, I left the salon, hair still wet, forgoing the blow-dry, and ran home. The panic attack was the same kind of anxious feeling that went through my body when I was waiting for D. to call before we got married. Instead of my husband rubbing up against my body at night, I awoke now to my son's hands gripping a clump of my hair or digging into a roll of my flesh. My body served only one purpose. It had become a vessel from which to sustain this child.

I kissed him all over as he lay on his changing table bare naked while he kicked his legs and screamed for more. I rubbed his back as he squirmed and tossed and fussed himself to sleep. I cradled him in my arms like a football and walked him from one end of the hall to the other and back in the early hours of the night. I wiped his vomit off my shoulders, let him bite down hard on each one of my fingers to ease his teething. I nibbled on his fat, pudgy legs. I bit his cheeks. I kissed his lips, his little button nose, his eyelids, his tummy. His little penis sprayed me when I opened his diaper. I took Desitin, rubbed it on my fingers, and squeezed it between the crack in his buttocks. I tasted his formula off the little drops I shook on my wrist before I let him drink from his bottle. I ate bites of his Gerber spinach to make sure it wasn't spoiled before it went in his mouth. I knew the kind of cry he made when he hadn't had a poop. I knew the color and shape of his bowel movements, what to do if he had diarrhea. I rubbed his little tummy when it was cramped with gas. I called him goose and boo and bandito ban dox and dolly and my little tulip. When he was sick I lay in his bed all night, putting cold washcloths on his burning-hot skin to take down the fever, and catching his vomit in a little bowl. I pried open his lips with my fingers to get Tylenol down his throat. I kissed his forehead and let him snuggle against my chest. I sang him lullabies when he couldn't sleep at night, made up stories. I kissed him all the time. I was so tired. I taught him how to kiss like an Eskimo. I rubbed my eyelashes on his cheek in imitation of a butterfly. He was mine. His body. He was all mine. Sexual desire vanished inside this intense kind of bliss. What more was there to crave when every part of myself was devoted to this child? Is desire fueled by being needed and wanted? About being the center of one's universe? If so, this child had become the axis around which all my thoughts, needs, and energies revolved.

And D. was also drunk on this new passion. He loved to take naps with our son perched on his chest like a cat. He chased him all around the house and screamed "Gotcha!" and when our son said do it again, Daddy, he said, "I'm going to get you, I'm going to get you," and he did it again, and again and again. We tied towels around our neck and pretended we were Batman and jumped from one bed to another while this child wailed with laughter. We listened to music from *The Lion King* and *Beauty and the Beast* in our car until I found myself humming the tunes at work. We drifted in the land of this little boy. We read him stories, took him for walks in his Snugli or in his stroller, took him to the beach, for long walks in snowstorms. We spent dinners staring at this child.

And in many ways our relationship deepened now that we had this child to take care of and protect. We had plans now, and they were plans together, for all three of us. We upped our workloads to save for a down payment on an apartment. The day we signed the papers for our first mortgage I called D. hysterical, fearful of the debt we had incurred. But we managed. When my first book of poems was sold and D. set up his own law office we toasted with champagne and takeout. We were doing the big things now, the real things, living the future we dreamed. But something was different, too. When our son entered our lives, our attention drifted to the practicalities of raising a child and having a two-career household. There was no time to lie in bed all morning having intense conversations and daydreaming about our futures. We were no longer the passionate, sex-starved young lovers we used to be. We were parents now, with someone else equally or more important to take care of than ourselves.

. . .

And then one day, this little boy was six years old. He was walking, he was running and climbing and jumping and talking so much we couldn't shut him up. He still came in our bed at night and wedged his body between the two of us, stretched out his arms and asserted his kingdom, kicking and thrashing. He had demands. "Read to me," he ordered. "I want juice. I don't want that," and *crash,* his plate of macaroni and cheese and carrot sticks went crashing to the floor. "Let's go to the park, the beach, *Rugrats in Paris,* I want this, Mommy, can I have that? How come the sky is blue, Mommy? What were you like when you were a little kid? Mom, come," when I was in the middle of cooking dinner, or stealing away for fifteen minutes on a weekend to find the thread in a paragraph of the novel I was working on. When I was at home, after a day at the office, where a slew of other people made their demands, there was no room for thoughts in my head, let alone any reason to make me feel sexy, to make me feel like I was a woman men once desired. I was filling bathtubs, rubbing in shampoo, putting calamine lotion on bug bites, making dinner, trying to think up answers to my kid's inquisitive questions. I fell asleep sometimes at nine o'clock squished into my son's twin bed still in my T-shirt and stretch pants.

. . .

Was it little wonder that now that the boy, the beautiful, lovely intruder in our marriage, was off to school, choosing his play dates, reading to himself, and now that there was this little window in my life, this little peek . . . was it *any* wonder, really, that I found it wasn't, to my alarm, my husband's attention that I craved? I found myself longingly staring at teenagers in love, couples squished together like statues, a man and woman leaning into each other on a subway train. The man I married got up in the morning, as tired as I. He went into the bathroom, brushed his teeth, shaved, put on his suit and tie, and walked out the door. He had conversations with people I didn't know. Long lunches working out the intricacies involved in a deal or negotiation. When he came home at night, usually after our son was in bed, I was too tired to ask him about his day, and he was too wrapped up in anxieties about the office to ask me about mine. I was curled into the couch with a manuscript or asleep. He stayed in the living room watching the Knicks or talked to one of his clients on the phone. Sometimes we made love, usually on a Saturday night or Sunday, but it was short and uninspired, and was more the kind of lovemaking where you are checking in to make sure someone is at home. I still desired my husband—sometimes watching him read my son a story, or pitch a baseball to him in the backyard, my stomach did somersaults—but a little faucet had turned off inside my body. My veins were cold. I didn't want to be touched.

Talking with other women who were in the same stages of their lives as I was, I realized that the lack of sexual desire I was experiencing was more common than I had known. We had entered this new precipice, and for many of us we were walking in the dark. It wasn't until much later that I began to see that I had entered a phase in my marriage that was about reinforcing a commitment to what we had built. I realized for the first time, really, what it meant to be in it for the long haul, and that part of that commitment had to do with understanding how passion changes.

But then, when I was deep into feeling the loss of my sex-charged youthfulness, I wanted the man whom I now knew everything about, whom I had ransacked with questions until he told me about every girl he kissed, every fight he had with his mother . . . I wanted him to be transformed back into someone new again, someone with whom I could start over from scratch—someone who again wanted to pore over me as if I were some kind of intricate, complicated puzzle, rather than the bitch I had become, the one who was furious when the bills weren't paid, the one who nearly had a breakdown upon discovering at midnight that there was no milk in the refrigerator, the one who was lonely putting her son to bed every night and had no qualms about making that loneliness known, who complained that we worked too hard and still didn't have enough money, who freaked out if toys were scattered all over the floor. I wanted the thrill of new young love to take me out of myself, so that I could transcend what had become the daily routine of my life. I thought of those teenagers groping each other unabashedly in the café, and I wanted to feel that freedom again, and that pulse quickening inside my body.

. . .

I took the subway home from the long lunch with my girlfriend with the picture of those teenage lovers in my head. I climbed up the long stairway from the underground of the subway and thought to myself, *This is my life,*

I am an unhappy, bored, anxious wife. I knew that on paper I was the luckiest woman alive. I had a great kid, an interesting job, a promising writing life, and a responsible, sexy husband. But somewhere during the six years that we were focused on our child, D. and I had lost the thread, the tensile, raw, electrical wire I thrived on. Like almost every other woman I knew in similar circumstances—raising young children, juggling a career and motherhood and the complicated demands of marriage—I asked myself a question I never imagined I would think about: If I did not intimately disengage from my husband, would I be giving myself over to a boring, commonplace life?

Clearly, now that our child was no longer a toddler and we were in a new phase, I was having a midlife crisis, only I didn't want to believe I was old enough to be in one. I thought of the single friends I knew in their forties. They had freedom, they dated, but they had that hungry, desperate look in their eyes, and I thought, *I don't want that life.* But another part of me was afraid that if I retreated to the quiet secure room of my marriage, I was destined to be ordinary. I had wanted to get married, but I realized now that I had never wanted to be a "wife." I associated the word with the dissatisfied, unrealized, and depressed Stepford wives of my mother's generation. I wanted to be a mother and a lover, but I didn't want the intensity of the passion I shared with my husband to settle or dissipate; I wanted it to go on endlessly.

Instead I was dull and angry and bored. I was angry that my husband did not realize how much I was moving away from him, and that he wasn't trying to win me back. I was furious that he wasn't interested in my life. I was afraid that if I became engaged in his life that meant that my own hard-won independence and autonomy were over and that I would never be desired again. Being desired had given me power, and a strong sense of self. I feared what would happen without it. And D. was furious. Where was the compassionate, affectionate, and caring woman he had married? In my anger I had built up a fortress banning him from the house of love. During the six years since our son had entered the picture, both of us had grown and changed. Now it sometimes felt as if the only thing that connected us was our child. We had become strangers inhabiting the same house.

And now that we were strangers to each other, I fantasized about other men. My friends confessed they did, too . . . come to think of it, what married woman doesn't? But I fantasized and felt guilty. Sometimes I flirted, but mostly I fantasized. Suddenly the city seemed alive with possibility, and I imagined I could sample these men as if I were at a wine tasting, trying to find the bottle I desired most.

This is how it can happen, I told myself, and in my mind I mapped out an intricate affair because now that my husband and I were strangers it was as if I didn't have a husband. I was a free girl again, one who woke up in the morning and took delight in what she was wearing and in the feel of a man's eyes as she walked down the street. In my mind I created this wonderful, exotic life. It was as if I were on holiday from my marriage, on a grand vacation, when I was alone with myself, free in my own thoughts.

And then one evening D. came home from work and delivered a bombshell. He blurted it out over our cheese and pepper pizza and glasses of red wine. A colleague of his, a guy he'd known for a while, a guy he'd thought had a solid marriage, whom we had repeatedly socialized with as couples, had just told D. his wife wanted a divorce. I was terrified. It was as if the fantasy life I was living had leapt out of my head and manifested itself in our friend's wife. "Why?" I asked. "He thinks she's seeing someone else," I heard D. say. And suddenly I thought about losing D., and I felt queasy with fear. I saw that all those weeks imagining an affair, I was tiptoeing across a minefield. I tried to picture what it would be like without my husband. I saw an empty, lonely house, in spite of my full life with my child. For months I had been remote and secretive with D. I felt ashamed. I looked at the stranger who was my husband, and I saw the man I fell in love with. The one I watched agonizing over the goddamn bar exam now had built his own practice. Our friends envied the kind of attentive, loving father he had become. In his eyes I saw the two sturdy pillars in which I propped myself up: he had given me the security and safety and love to become a mother, to go after my dreams as a writer.

D.'s love and kindness had made me a better person. I thought about waking up in the morning without him and felt the chill of an empty existence. . . . And for what? It wasn't even sex that I wanted from a lover. It was the intoxication of being newly known. I had wanted to imagine that someone else could fall in love with me, but now, looking at my husband in his Speedo gym shorts and bleached-out T-shirt, what I saw was that the man I was married to was the person I wanted to have the affair with. I wanted him to wrestle me to the ground, to say he couldn't live without me. I wanted to see the world again anew through his eyes. I hadn't known that my husband could be the fantasy. That while I was in my head building new boyfriends out of snow, the man I had married turned other women on. All I had to do was walk out of my head and begin to talk to the man who sat beside me the nights we managed to make dinner.

For all my extravagant, wild, reckless imaginings, I had already chosen the eternal one. Now, what we needed to do was to figure out how to reinvent our marriage and become reacquainted with the new person each of us had become. I felt guilty for my imagined affair, even though I had committed no act of infidelity. But I knew also that my imagination and longings were central to leading an authentic life. All I needed to do was let my arm reach out so that my husband could run his fingers up and down the veins on the underside, and we'd be there, I'd feel it again, as if I were at the airport gate waiting to see his shining face picking mine out from the crowd. He was still there. I had to peel back the layers we had built around each other, all those years when we were desperately in love with our son and had lost each other, until I reached the exposed heart.

Erotics 102

Staying Bad. Staying Married.

Cynthia Kling

Recently at a party I found myself listening to a group of middle-aged women talk about when they'd discovered their erotic selves. For one, it was a college relationship with a sweet, willing, and curious boy; another had embarked on a series of experiments in her twenties—testing bisexuality, aggressiveness, and hetero sluttiness to see where she fit on the bell curve. My erotic education, I was embarrassed to admit, came much later.

Which isn't to say that I was some sort of chilly virginal type. I'd had tons of relationships in college (some lasting less than twenty-four hours), then run around in my twenties because it was the 1970s and I believed I "had a right" to sleep with whomever I wanted (and, to be frank, I realized that sex with an almost-stranger was always hotter than sex with someone I'd seen flossing for the last couple of months). My friends were women who went to prisons and showed the inmates how to look at their vaginas in hand mirrors, who slept with the Puerto Rican super to show they weren't racist. They organized masturbation circles and examined every dank crook of their bodies. I dabbled, not quite as bold as they but taking it all in, learning everything I could.

Nearing thirty, I married a tall, handsome lefty politico I'll call J. We could have just lived together (everybody else did), but the truth is that I secretly wanted the marriage, the white dress and all it conferred, because it seemed much easier to become the wife of somebody and squish into his limelight than to try to decide what to do with my own life. I had tossed around "creatively" for several years—waitressing, selling furniture, organizing political events—but I hadn't managed to launch myself yet, and I was getting a little nervous. Gloria Steinem and Germaine Greer exhorted us girls to get good jobs, demand equal pay, and take over the world. But no one told me how to begin. Or that unless you were brilliant, you needed a well-placed cousin to get the grubby little assistant's job at the places that would lead you to powerful, take-over-the-world careers.

The marriage worked, for a while. J. and I were lefty show dogs: committed to the cause, friends with Alger Hiss and the staff of *The Nation* magazine, and passionate about each other. J. worked at a Third World press service smuggling in news from Haiti, Cuba, Nicaragua, the Philippines, etc., while I worked as an assistant in advertising (a job gotten through a connection of his). Mine was seen as an acceptable sellout because someone had to earn the money for rent—and I could keep an eye out for the evil doings of the corporate world.

After a couple of years, though, claustrophobia set in. I had signed up to assist J.'s cause, but I really wasn't cut out to be the assistant. And now that I'd put him on a pedestal, I resented him up there, bossing me around. It didn't help that we weren't having sex anymore—and hadn't been for quite a long time. Even before I'd begun to resent him, we'd sit in front of the TV watching wars on the news and getting quietly drunk so that there would be no possibility of even contemplating doing it. During those first years I secretly wondered where all of the sexual desire had gone. In retrospect, I think the end of our sex life came less from the failure of our marriage than from the failure, or at least oversight, of my supposedly sexually progressive and enlightened friends. Back then, no one ever sat me down and said, "Honey, you should know that when you settle down, eventually the pure animal rutting feeling stops rising out of your depths, and that's when you need to use your brain to take over and bring it back."

. . .

The marriage ended after five years, at a coffee shop in Mexico, for all of the obvious reasons. My girlfriends came back in droves to help me shoulder on. They found out about J.'s little affair. (He became the villain. No need to inquire any further.) They told me to move his stuff out of our place, to recheck the small print on the mortgage agreement to see what I owned, while my mother politely whispered that it was time to start dating again. They made big plans for me: I could start again, get this right next time around.

The first intelligent thing I think I ever did was to stop listening to them. Women complain that men boss them around and tell them what to do, but what about all that female coercion? The oppressive solidarity of the smart-girl set? I finally let myself fall down into that muck of feelings and try to figure out my own next move. I threw away the answering machine and "became impossible," according to my sisters. For about a year I sat on my blue velvet couch drinking vodka and knitting. Then I met Mr. X.

Mr. X. was a painter: impetuous, broke, brilliant. Most important, he already had a wife. We were bad—and that was exactly what I needed: a relationship so off the map, so secret, that it gave me the freedom and courage to explore in ways that I never could have in my marriage because I was so busy being a wife—the helpmate, the supporter, the household finance manager (Hillary Clinton eating glazed doughnuts with candidate Bill at some truck stop in Arkansas). Mr. X. desired me simply for who I was, not for what I could do or provide out there in the big wide world. The mistress has no social responsibilities. There are no friends, no dry cleaning to pick up, no in-laws to rein in, no kids' birthday parties, no school bills—none of the complications that keep a marriage together.

Was it all sex? Is it ever all sex? (The biggest problem I'd had with my one-night stands in the 1970s was the emotional involvement.) But for the most part, it was just the two of us in some little room somewhere. All we had was who we were in that moment; we were nakedly ourselves with our dreams and wants and lusts. For me, this was very powerful indeed.

And then, when he wasn't around, I pined a bit, but just for the drama. Because the truth was that I had the time, emotional energy, and courage to start to put together a life that might meet my heart's desires. Reader, I know that this is not the conventional understanding of the mistress: the sad, backstreet woman yearning for her man, alone on family holidays. But given the stereotype, did you ever wonder why Katharine Hepburn, Georgia O'Keeffe, Coco Chanel, Lillian Ross, and Veronica Geng all took this route? These were women with things to do in their spare time besides pine. Or, perhaps more accurately, women who *preferred* a little pining to the claustrophobia of marriage. After all, how else would they have had the time (and material) to create their wonderful work?

We choose our husbands, unconsciously or consciously, for what they can provide for us—unless we're total fools. Women "choose" their married men as well—only the list of requirements for this partner comes from a different region of the brain. Katharine Hepburn had four big affairs in her life. All of the men were married, and all very helpful to her at different stages in her career—a well-known playwright, an agent, a big producer, and a leading man. Coincidence? I don't think so.

In other words, ultimately there is an exchange in this relationship beyond that of bodily fluids. Sometimes it's money; just as often it is something else—at least, it was for me. When I met Mr. X. I secretly wanted to be a writer. He was a wild, crazy, and well-respected artist and he anointed me a member of the club of people who believe that they can create: not support it, sell it, manage it, or marry it, but actually *do* it. He showed me how to access my creativity, and then to hold on to and respect my own ideas right through to the end.

I started writing when I was with him. That was huge. It involved throwing away old notions about being too stupid and not knowing how to spell;

it involved freakouts and anxiety attacks. I couldn't possibly have cordoned off this psychic space for my own ugly, awkward transformation when I was a wife—at least not in the marriage I had created with J.—because the transformation took every selfish drop of energy I had.

But there's more. When Mr. X. came to visit he taught me that this creative brainpower didn't belong just to the page; it belonged in the bedroom as well. In the imagination, as in dreams, there are no rules, no sense of the inappropriate. But there is one law: follow what excites you. It could be the littlest hook—red lipstick, artfully placed on a nipple. It can verge on the ridiculous. The first time I teetered out naked but for a pair of black high heels, I almost cracked my front tooth. This was okay. This was the point. Risk is good. I learned to use my creativity to enhance what was happening during our lovemaking.

One day I picked up the phone and a woman's voice said, "If you come near my husband again, I'll shoot you." Mr. X.'s wife had come to claim him. Our relationship was over, as I'd always known it would be one day. But I had learned some lessons that I'd never give up—about self-respect, keeping my own counsel, unleashing my power, and using my imagination.

. . .

I forgave my friends for all of their whispering and snide comments about how destructive and inappropriate this relationship had been. They were trying to grow up, too, only they took their lessons from Gloria Steinem, Andrea Dworkin, and the brave women suing *Newsweek* for sexual discrimination. Fine for them, but for me, those "role models" were just another bunch of women telling me the rules of the day. I began haunting bookstores looking for a different kind of role model—transgressors who'd disregarded the chorus of the day and emerged victorious. The biographies of Hepburn, Chanel, and O'Keeffe proved instructive. I also took delight in even more ancient transgressors, like Theodora, a streetwalker of the Ottoman Empire who so bewitched the caliph that she got him to marry her. (Imagine Prince Charles marching down the aisle with

Divine Brown, Hugh Grant's notorious backseat-blow-job gal.) The caliph's empire was invaded a few years later. As he and his soldiers started to flee, Theodora convinced them to stick around and fight. (After what she'd been through in those catacombs, the battle probably seemed clean and easy.) Theodora was triumphant, the battle was won, and the couple ruled happily for the next several decades. And the caliph probably thanked his lucky stars that he'd chosen such a shrewdy.

Eventually, I started dating again. But I swore I'd never remarry, because I understood that the wife archetype held too much sway over me. She was by turns selfless and generous . . . and controlling, bitchy, secretly resentful as hell. Marriage, I feared, would turn me right back into her again.

Then I met Philip, a sexy, smart nut who took my heart. But maybe even more important, he didn't seem to want to pull a Pygmalion on me. Every other man I'd ever seriously "dated" had wanted to mold me: knock out a few bits of my personality—my rapacious curiosity, my tendency toward wheeling and dealing, my periodic need to disappear—or remove some other trait that didn't fit in with his understanding of who I was. Philip seemed to appreciate my schizophrenic personality, to actually enjoy watching me go from gypsy to hermit overnight.

The idea that I could be myself, in all my infuriating ways, was new and welcome indeed. But there was one problem: Philip wanted to get married. In fact, for a year he plagued me. I started to reconsider. Maybe it could work; after all, it had been a year now and he still wasn't suggesting improvements. I decided to try marriage again, consoling myself with the idea of another round of wedding presents. I wore an orange dress down the aisle this time.

The day after our wedding, the monster returned. Taking stock of what he'd done, my new husband turned to me, panicked, and said, "What am I going to do with all of my flirting energy now?" I thought fast. "You're number two of four or five men that I plan to marry," I said. "Stay interesting or you'll be out." He smiled—ahhh, the hunt wasn't over. She wasn't totally captured yet.

Now, what I had said about staying interesting was quite true; but it was also true that I was the one helping him discover a way out of his anxiety. I had slipped back into being the helpy wife without even thinking about it. Remember that *Reader's Digest* series "I Am Joey's Spleen," or "Stomach," or "Liver"? That day, I became my husband's extra brain.

And I confess that ever since—going on ten years now—I have, in spite of my reluctance, accepted this fate. It is my job to figure out the trivial for him. I am also his social organizer, shrink, professional finding service, and dresser. In exchange, he is my policeman and bodyguard out there in the world. I have ceded to this protective exchange because it can make life easier, because I have come to see what I get out of it, too, and to appreciate that. I have come to see it, at least most of the time, as one of the actual perks of marriage. But I have also had to watch this very carefully, to not let it overtake me.

For example: A while back, a catty friend told my husband that I had purchased an exorbitantly expensive cashmere sweater. This, my husband pompously told his friend, was impossible—his wife would never spend that kind of money on clothes. He came home and relayed the wild story he'd heard. "I bought it," I replied thoughtfully.

He went ballistic. How wasteful! How decadent! It was one of those click moments for me. I looked at him and I remembered what Mr. X. had made me understand about respecting my sovereignty, my desires—however trivial they might seem to someone else. If I didn't, I knew I would become resentful and cypherish. I would disappear. I said, "Well, I'm your wife and I did it—so now you'll have to choose. Me with the sweater, or no me."

The battle raged for days. Finally I told him that if he kept talking about the sweater I would wear it while I painted the kitchen. (HA!) But the truth was, I didn't even really like the sweater that much. On closer inspection, I realized it wasn't worth the price.

Long story short, I let him return the sweater. It made him happy, and secretly it made me happy, too, because I'd compromised: I'd let him "win," but with the knowledge that if I'd *really* wanted the sweater, I would have found a way to keep it. The decision had been mine. We had knit our way through the difficulties. I made him feel like a whacked-out South American dictator, while not sacrificing something I really wanted. Plus, I'd bought an expensive skirt to go with the sweater that I hadn't told him about. This, to me, is the art of marital negotiation.

The problem is that the marital negotiation, by its very nature, can suck the passion and mystery out of any relationship. As husband and wife, you work to become such a well-oiled team, running your small fiefdom, that you can wind up feeling more like siblings than lovers. That is sure to kill the interest for most people. Historically, no one ever expected the wife to be the lover, the inamorata. It was understood that marriage quells desire. Saint Paul, a first-century social critic, wanted to rid his lands of the dirty act of intercourse altogether. His percipient advice: "To avoid fornication, let every man have his own wife."

The Elizabethans weren't expected to give up wild passion or the comforts of marriage; they just weren't supposed to mix them up. According to some scholars, Shakespeare, who had his lovers and his loyal wife, Anne, wrote *Romeo and Juliet* as a cautionary tale: Look what happens when you actually try to marry the person you desire—death, destruction, and "a plague on both your houses!"

It is the corrosive closeness and the tendency to act wifey that seem to drain marriage of its eroticism for me. (Does any husband ever even use the word *erotic* when talking about his wife?) Back when women were making the New Rules, in the high days of feminism, there was never any real examination of the wife role—as long as you had a corporate job, too. Feminism doubled the woman's workload (in the name of respect) and then turned around and killed the femme fatale. She became seen, somehow, as the dumbed-down woman, a subspecies of our gender, so she got garroted and buried by women in business suits and scarf ties.

What was the problem with killing the seductress off? She's the one who kept sex alive in the marriage. Sincerity, clarity, straightforwardness, compromise—these things are antithetical to Eros. Carnality snorts at these modern ideas of marriage—and one way or another takes off in search of new quests. We respond sexually to the stranger, the unknown, the unfamiliar. The dirty urge has no interest in the known, the picked over, the fully examined. The femme fatale knows that it is not simply a question of acrobatics but a way of being, a way of conducting yourself, that fosters passion. I discovered her mystery and power with Mr. X.; I learned to be creative, to find and explore and cultivate a place for *myself*. There was no obvious spot for that person in my first marriage, because that ever-present, octopus-armed wife had hogged up all the space. In my second marriage, I knew that if I didn't want to wind up drunk in front of the television again, I had to work to cultivate that other side—and I did. And I do.

I once heard a man say that he knows his wife's fall dance, winter dance, spring dance. . . . That idea gives me the creeps. I do not ever allow my husband to think that he fully knows me, that he has that access. I am constantly on my guard to protect my private sphere, patrolling my borders in ways that might seem small but that are monumental to me. In our backyard there is a vegetable garden. He doesn't get any say about what is grown there, and this is important to me because the garden is something I have created, something I cultivate. And in the evenings when I go out, with a glass of wine, to pick vegetables, I often smoke, because this is truly forbidden. I break other little agreed-upon covenants and lie to my husband. He eventually finds out, gets frustrated, and knows that he'll never get to the bottom of me. Is it a game? I don't think so. I'll never get to the bottom of myself, either, but I am less concerned with pretending that I actually have. In other words, the self I met through Mr. X. and came to know over the years—the self that didn't have limits—is someone I have come to deeply respect.

The wife is about striving for some notion of perfection. The mistress is about games, invention, closeness. One is high and one is low. I was afraid of diving down there in my first marriage, which is part of what killed that marriage. Now I go there to keep my marriage alive.

My Marriage. My Affairs.

Hannah Pine

It is getting light outside, and my husband is not yet home. It is getting light outside, and I go to the hamper, pull out some of his dirty socks, and put them on. He does not like when I do this, wear his dirty socks, and because of this it is a habit I vow to break. But in his absence his socks are a comfort to me.

It is getting light outside and the dog follows me downstairs, looking worried. She does not like it when only one of us is home. Or is it me who does not like it? No, I think that I do. I like to be alone in the house. It reminds me of things, things that meant something to me in the past—an old boyfriend, sad Carpenters songs—and it makes me dreamy and depressed in a way I enjoy. How to explain, then, that my husband and I spend nearly every waking minute together that we can?

It is five in the morning and the fog is thick. I pull on a bathrobe and brew some coffee. I've been up since three. It is so quiet in the house that I can hear the neighbor's cat on the porch, crying for food. I turn up the heat—something I do when my husband is not home, and I feel particularly justified this time. He is staying over with N.

I go out to the porch, and sit bundled up. The cat and the dog eye each other warily, competing for my affection. I feel very calm. How lucky I am to have this morning alone!

But I am not pleased when my husband comes home a few hours later, at 9:00 A.M. No, not pleased at all. By then, I am tired of being alone, and annoyed with myself for wondering if he is happier with her than with me. (I know he is not, but the mind does wander.) Sometimes I am more successful than other times at hiding annoyance.

My duty is simple: to do no harm to my husband, whom I adore. And yes, to protect myself from harm, too. Does it really harm me that he has had an affair for four years, with a lawyer he met, a Catholic girl who lives with her parents and toils tirelessly at her job, representing all sorts of underprivileged people? (I call her a girl because she is seven years younger than I. I call her a girl to bother my husband.) I saw her once at a bar when we ran into her, before their affair. She wore rings on most of her fingers and used lots of lip balm. She seemed sweet. That night, she and my husband were wearing the same outfit, by coincidence: a T-shirt over waffled long underwear, and dungarees. I knew by the way my husband noted their matching outfits what he was thinking, and what would occur. This girl is very shy. She won't even call him at home, even though he has told her she can—though tact is, of course, encouraged. One only wants to know so much.

I am in love with my husband, so I could read right into his mind that night, before he even knew what would happen with her. I've read *Anna Karenina,* after all, so I know all about this sort of thing, reading his mind. And I know the difference between love as it exists in my marriage, and the sort of love-lust that can happen in an affair. More on that later. When I see what my husband is thinking, I try to be gentle.

I live by kindness, and by my brain. That is, I try to *think kindly* whenever I can. It is through kindness that I can feel peace replace fear. My great love with my husband has helped me learn this. Until I met him, I was a wreck, consumed with a fear of being alone.

For a while, when I was young, I had nightmares about a certain fairy tale, that story of the girl who literally spoke snakes and toads. When her sister, or perhaps just another little girl, would talk, out came diamonds, flowers, and pearls. The mean girl—you assumed she was mean because of the snakes and toads—sometimes disguised herself as the good girl. When the good girl is supposed to get married, the bad girl pretends she's the bride. Of course, she gets caught when she speaks. Nowhere in the story does it tell you why the snake-speaking girl is so bad. Nowhere does it say why she isn't the bride. This is all simply a given. One is pretty and kind, and the other is bad. One deserves to be loved, and the other does not.

As a girl, I would imagine myself in this world, and I'd wonder: Did I speak diamonds or snakes? And if the latter, then what? I worked myself into a frenzy at times. Did I have anything to offer that was unique, that was *lovely*? No, I surmised.

This condition lasted into my mid-twenties, and it was in it that I met my future—and present—husband. I was living alone. I was afraid of being with someone because I thought that eventually he might leave me. (In retrospect, I realize I liked living alone, though I was not confident enough to admit that at the time.)

Is it any wonder that, for a while, before these sanctioned affairs (if we must call them something, let's call them that), my husband cheated on me? I think not. What is surprising is that no snakes came out of my mouth after he did. Well, at first some tiny toads came out, and maybe some bugs. But soon, only flowers. Laugh all you want. I do, laugh, sometimes.

I don't mean to imply that it was my fault he "strayed." There was so little to stray from, because I was so worried he would. This is not to say that my insecurities caused our problems. It was *not* fair of him to have that first affair without telling me, even if I was insecure and became frantic at the tiniest hint that he wasn't thinking about me, but perhaps something else. It was unfair, it was mean, of him to lie. He admits this. But so do I, for my part, admit the cruelty my panic on this front comprised. I was so terrified of his wanting someone else that I am sure I guaranteed it. This is different from blaming myself for the thing.

There is always a third person in every marriage, someone said that. I agree. A third at least. If I let myself hate that person, real or imagined, what does that make me? Hateful, hateful, I say.

So now, I am no longer scared of the girls, the ones with diamonds or toads. The secret is, both of those girls could be me.

I choose diamonds.

. . .

When girls started dating at my elementary school, at the beginning of fifth grade in 1976, I wore purple cat's-eye glasses, a scoliosis brace, and a bowl haircut that even a girl with the most remarkable cheekbones (which I was not) ought not attempt. The dungarees that were in fashion announced one's size quite unceremoniously on a leather patch on the waist, and mine measured such that I would scrape at the numbers with a pencil until there was no trace left. This didn't help, of course, as everyone knew what it meant when, in place of your waist size, there was a scratched-out hole instead. In fifth grade, E. asked out M. M. wore a bra already, which the boys whispered about in code. "It's cloudy out," they'd hiss, pointing at her back. ("Cloudy" meant that one could not see through the shirt to the skin, because of the bra.) My next-door neighbor, T., who had also "developed" early (a horrifying phrase), dated all of the boys, except one, J., whose nickname was "Boogie." (Yes, he picked his nose.)

We all looked awful, all of us, even the prettiest girls; now, of course, I am guiltily glad when I see our class picture from then, and note lovely T., stomach protruding, in unflatteringly tight-fitting velour. But at the time, I thought it was only me, trapped in ugliness.

Often—and frighteningly, to me—girls at school replaced their friends with other girls. One friend, who had been a Love's Baby Soft model, was my best friend for two months in fifth grade. She had transferred to our school because she got kicked out of her other school for beating someone up. She was fantastic! She had long brown hair that fell in perfect waves down her pastel angora sweaters. She told me about how her father punished her for things by locking her, naked, in the basement. Once, my mother and I drove to her house and somehow got her out (I don't remember how, but I do remember throwing a towel over her shoulders, a towel that said I'm With Stupid! on it, inappropriately enough). But one day, I got to school and there was a note shoved into the slats on my locker. "Dear H., I am very sorry but I cannot be friends with you anymore. I am friends with L. now and she says that if I stay friends with you I will be a loser and no one will talk to me. I didn't know you were a loser because I was new. I'm so sorry and I will love you forever but please don't talk to me at school!" I am not kidding. Word for word. I still have it.

So, for the rest of fifth grade, I read *Anna Karenina.*

With my purple cat's-eye glasses and scoliosis, I'm sure I made a pretty picture weeping over a thick Russian novel. I was a bit oversensitive, I guess. But frankly, all I remember from *Anna Karenina* is that Anna and her lover, Vronsky—ah, what a masculine name! and even in fifth grade, I knew the affair to be illicit—were so entwined, so in love, that they could *read each other's minds.* Yes! I remember it well. They were psychic. I learned, from *Anna Karenina,* that true love means you know what a person is thinking just by looking at him. This struck me as remarkable. So imagine my horror when Tolstoy kills Anna for being unfaithful. The author's the one, after all, who throws her under that train. Why?

Ah, so many questions troubling my eleven-year-old head. While the other girls had bras and deodorant—one with the unfathomable brand name Tickle—and boys, I had Anna. In fact, I was in training to *be* her, right from that ripe little age.

It is really no surprise, then, that since I've been married, I've had affairs.

But I will not die under a train. My husband wouldn't have it.

And I'm happy, I think. Or rather, I am as happy as my nature allows me to be. I don't believe I'd be happier without these affairs. In fact, I think there's a good chance I would be less happy without them.

Why am I happy in marriage? I'm afraid I can't answer that question without sounding dumb. I adore my husband so much that sometimes I stay up at night to watch him sleep. While he works in his study, I often stand outside the closed door to listen to his silly little mechanical pencil scratching against paper, and breaking. He insists upon using these cheap plastic pencils that are supposed to "retract." Instead, they snap and they snap and they snap. I want to remember the sound if someday he's gone. But it is not just because I love my husband that my affairs won't destroy me or my marriage.

My husband knows about my affair with J., you see. It has lasted five years, we—my husband and I—figured out just tonight. It's intermittent, because J. is unstable. A genius at music, but troubled. I manage it by seeing him only sometimes, not too often. My husband also knew about my affair with A., which took place on a cross-country drive. Now that was romantic! We took Polaroids along the way. It was my first affair, and I was very, very shy. We'd gotten a motel room in the middle of Nebraska that had only one bed and a blue light on the wall. I paced around the room for a few hours before finally getting into the bed.

My husband also knew about my affair with P., though it wasn't really an affair so much as two dates, mostly taking place in a dirty band van, which was sordid enough that I acted ashamed. (Though I never told my husband that detail, I still felt sheepish. A van? I was thirty-five, for crying out loud.) But between us, it was sort of a thrill. I'm not proud, mind you. And I am not, I repeat, I am not ashamed of any of my affairs. I was ashamed when I almost had an affair with a mutual friend, M., who was really not worth it, and about whom I moped, unfairly, for days. My husband should not have to deal with my disappointments in lust. I mean, even our patience has limits.

. . .

I do like to pretend, in a sort of misinformed salute to my insecurities, which are many, mind you, that this was all my husband's idea, this business of having affairs. But it was my idea, actually. It was his, too, but I demand some credit.

To be honest, I don't know why I thought it up—perhaps Anna Karenina herself had taken up permanent residence in my vulnerable preteen brain. Those themes embroidered themselves indelibly in me early on, and sometimes, I admit—now and then, for an hour or two—I regret our capacity for this sort of relationship: say, if I'm feeling particularly low on a rainy day, and he's whistling around the house because he's been with his girl. Or if I'm a bit bored with J., and I think of my husband at home with the dog, reading a book. I long for him then in a way that seems immutable. I will have a flash of a thought: *What am I doing here with J.? Am I this foolish?* But it passes, and I no longer regret things; I come to think of the emotions I've had as something valuable, something from which to experience passion or learn. In any case, I don't ever regret it in a *serious* way. I don't feel that I am making sacrifices. I get so sad when I hear a friend complain that her boyfriend looked at another woman in a way that upset her, or that she caught him reading a dirty magazine—sad for the boyfriend, because it just seems *mean,* this sort of judgment on him. Not that I haven't had flashes of jealousy. No one is immune. But I've learned to think consciously about how my criticism of his natural pleasures might make my husband feel.

When I was a kid, around fifth grade, again, I was caught by my mother under my bed with a *Playboy* magazine. I'm sure I had no idea what I was looking at—I think I was looking at a cartoon that took place in an office, and feeling a little bit ill, but turned on—and when my mother found me, she said, "*What* are you doing?" and I felt so full of shame I could barely stand it. I was eleven then. My desire was offensive to her. She didn't mean to make me feel bad, or maybe she did, I don't know. I certainly don't blame her. She did the best she could. But because of that, I promised myself never to do the same, never to punish anyone for what they desire, as long as it doesn't hurt someone else. And I—like all of us (when we think about it the proper way, I believe)—know the difference between what can hurt me and what cannot, at least when it comes to this sort of thing.

. . .

Growing up in my family: our house was not full of peace, it was full of recriminations, accusations, envy, scorn. There was always a last piece of bacon (my brother would snatch it). Only one of us got to sit on my father's lap when he read us *Santa Mouse* (my youngest sister). Who got the best room in the house, with the fancy three-way mirror? My older sister. Jealousy ruled my and my sisters' lives. We eyed each other suspiciously all of the time. If my sister got brand-new white corduroy knickers—however unfortunate the fashion—I wanted them, too. When dieting came into style, I would not eat a French fry if my sister didn't swallow one, too. And if my mother so much as smiled at me instead of at one of them, there'd be tears, sobbing, the others were stricken. Why was this so? I have no answer to that. My parents are very loving. Perhaps because they are so loving, things were somehow overwhelming. But the point is: that atmosphere wasn't—it isn't—something I want to repeat now in my home.

. . .

One year—we'd been married about a year by then—my husband and I were living in a small town in a sparsely populated state, where frequently the weather was awful. Our neighbors often sat on the porch listening to cheerful songs about Jesus. I enjoyed this music. It was so cheerful it was forlorn. My husband did not enjoy the music and often drank whiskey to dull its sound. Finally, late at night, a hot wind would blow, the cicadas sang, and then their terrible music would fill up the air. My husband liked the cicadas. I did not. They made me feel insane.

So, one night, he was naked in the shower, and I was in the bathroom wearing a sweater and jeans. I remember that very well. Pink acrylic, the sweater had glitter and itched. He was in the shower and I was waiting for K. to come over, because we were going to have dinner. He worked with K. at the school where he taught, and I liked her. Often she wore a brown leather vest that was sleeveless. Her blond hair had beautiful streaks, and inside her green left eye, there was a fleck of black, an imperfection that was mesmerizing when you looked into it. She had been first in her class in graduate school and terrorized the men she worked with, just with her brain. So I wanted to be friends with her, and he, my husband, wanted me to be friends with her, too. He was standing in the shower, and I was putting on lipstick, and it was steaming hot in the bathroom but my body, it went suddenly cold. I just knew. How? I have no idea. I remember saying, "It's her, it's her, tell me it isn't her, is it her, it's her, it's not her is it . . ." He didn't have to answer. When K. came over and I opened the door, I could tell that she knew I knew.

That was the first time, and the only time we now think of as cheating. That was more than eight years ago.

That terrible night, I will not recount for you too closely here. I went out to dinner with K., in a daze, incapable of even saying I knew. Later, there was what seems now a sort of hilarious interlude in the local bar when my husband showed up, hoping "everything was fine." Soon there was much yelling, there were tears, and poor K. had a terrible anxiety attack, and I ended up comforting her in her car, and when I got home, there was more yelling, more tears. I even moved out for a while.

However, soon enough, I moved back home. I missed him, my love, the man I adored. And—I don't know why, maybe I just convinced myself or maybe time, like the sea, dulls all things—I became less distraught about it. Still, I was very surprised when, barely two weeks later, I heard the words "Go see her" come out of my mouth. "Go see her again," I said. "I don't care!" I was crying, but a strange smile was creeping onto my face. I wasn't angry. I was sad, in a way, but I was, had always been, aware of a sadness in myself. This situation had not created that sadness, but only exposed it to me. But the thing that surprised me was that this sadness was different from the kind I'd felt before. This was a peculiar sadness I can only call pleasant to me. It's hard to explain beyond that. I'm not masochistic. But it's the truth. I was sad in a *happy* way. Perhaps this is because I knew that I was playing a role in this sadness, making a decision that was right even if it caused me to suffer. Storybook heroines often banish their lovers, if only to revel in pining for them. The difference here was, I was also doing my husband a favor. Sending him off was not intended to hurt him or us. And so I accepted the sadness, I suppose. Earlier sadnesses had seemed unacceptable to me. This one did not.

Still, I thought nobody in her right mind would send her husband to see another woman. Some people might try to convince me that I just wanted to be different from everyone else. But to that I would counter that all my life, I have done nothing but try to fit in. Where did I get the idea that he should see her again? This wasn't a form of permitting him to see her, of granting permission—I would never want that power. It was simply that I thought he wanted to see her, and I thought I could handle it if he did. It wouldn't harm me. So I told him to go.

After my husband left in the rusty truck we'd bought together, something happened to me that I have never admitted even to him. I was *happy*. This is the truth. Perhaps this was simply because I felt I had given him a gift. That must have been part of it. Later, when I left the car's headlights on in the video store parking lot (I'd wandered around the store in a daze, feeling happy, still, feeling *I know something they don't know* as I met the eyes of others)—later, when I found out the battery had died and, because I could not call my husband—he was with *her,* where I'd sent him—later, I was not happy, of course. But moods change often, every day, for bigger and for smaller reasons, do they not? You must agree that my selection of a movie about a woman who becomes very, very ill in her fancy suburban house, from the smell of a new couch, from hairspray, from sex, and goes to live alone in a podlike structure out in nature, utterly weakened—was not a good one. I watched it anyway, three times in a row, refusing to look up from the screen in the morning when my husband came home.

. . .

Why is our marriage still pretty to me after that?

You could say we've "survived" an affair. But that makes our lives into a battle. And I choose to decline. I think, quite simply, we made a decision, just as you have made yours, whatever it may be. For myself, *I refuse to pathologize adult, consensual sex, especially when I'm not involved.* Not the most graceful sentence, but the content is sweet. Any time I try to write it out point-blank, it becomes clumsy like that.

I'll try again. There are many ways to choose to live erotically—or not. I simply believe that for culture to flourish, sex *must* not remain a morality tale. This renders nobody happy.

And I'm not talking about stupid, foolish pleasure—pleasure can have its consequences, to be sure. Though, yes, I've had sex for sex's sake, and liked it a lot. It's more complicated than that, of course.

. . .

That affair-gone-wrong, the very first one, was a long time ago—or at least it feels long, eight years or more.

The question of how we got from there to here is difficult for me to answer. I've asked myself often. I do remember many late-night conversations in which we tested the waters, negotiated possible scenes. Somehow, then, words were put into action. I wish I could pin it down in time.

Well, one November, five years ago, I was out hearing some music. My husband's affair with K. had ended when we moved somewhere else. He was seeing N.; it just sort of happened and I didn't protest. I thought I was different and would be just with him, not with other men, too.

But that changed the night J. drove me home from a show he played at a quiet, peaceful bar. I sat by myself until the very last set, watching him closely. He had such grace. He offered the ride. And sometime during the drive, he leaned over and kissed me. I didn't say no. I may even have kissed him back. Okay, I did. I kissed back. It felt—well, how does it feel to kiss and be kissed by a man you just watched play music for two hours, a man you've never kissed before? Nice. It feels lovely. I thought, *This is what I have given my husband, and what he has given me.* J. dropped me off soon after—after we drove to a playground near my house, and sat on the hood of his car, watching the wind in the trees, and held hands. When I came in, my husband said, "Who drove you home?" "J.," I answered. It was like that.

The idea of betrayal threatened our love, starting with K., and we made a decision going from there. A progression of serious thought led us here.

And we continue to think. Sometimes I ask him, "Would you still see other women if I said I didn't want you to?" He says, "No." "Really?" I ask. "Really," he says. And I believe him. Recently I was surprised when he added, "Actually, I think you're the one who'd be more likely to cheat." This had never occurred to me. But it's true: I'm the romantic, secretive one. I'm the one who will stay out until four in the morning with J., having a funeral for a dead bird we find on his lawn, and listening to records. I'm the one who feels tinges of guilt, coming home in the dawn. My husband is more likely to be completely pragmatic. To say, "I like her. But I keep my feelings for her in a certain place."

. . .

Perhaps this is one reason our lives aren't wild; at least, they don't feel that way to me. I have had three affairs, and he has had one, since K. He would argue with that, because he would count a few of the women he spent only one night with, or a couple of my friends who made out with him—can you believe them? I can, actually. He is intelligent, beautiful, kind. My best friends know about our agreement, so why not, is what I say to that. Anyway, people have lived crazier lives than we do, and in fact, mine is less crazy than most that I see. My household is peaceful and productive. We fill it with pretty amber lights. I cook dinner nearly every night. Soon, I might try to get pregnant. Neither of us can imagine life without the other one in it. These affairs, they just don't matter that much—which isn't to degrade them at all. But in light of the rest? Well, affairs matter in a certain place, a place that is decent, cherished, and fine. It resembles love, even, what I feel for those men. But my husband, he matters all the time. I'm in love with him.

. . .

It is light outside, and my husband is upstairs, asleep. When he came through the door this morning, I tried to say simply "Good morning." He said "I love you" as he went up the stairs. I think today, I will let him rest. He is probably very tired. And so am I. I spent some sleepless hours, waiting for him to come home. But then, there are some things worth losing sleep over. And, as I said, I like those early morning hours. Even the chilliest, loneliest ones.

Mommy Maddest

One of the reasons it's hard to express satisfaction with your life when you have children is that everywhere, every day there is anger . . . the quick summer storm kind of anger, the slow burn of anger, the underground anger that sometimes affects what you do or say without your even knowing that it was there. There are the terrible twos when a child asserting independence refuses to wear mittens on a freezing cold day and for a moment your frustration turns you into a wild thing. There's the other kind of anger that comes when you need sleep and the child wakes or you need to soak in the bath and the child wants you to see his block tower. . . . Anger is everywhere in the rough-and-tumble of child rearing as you find out what you can't tolerate, what kind of a demon witch you really are, what causes you to flare, to stifle fury or to stuff it back down the throat, to let it out all of a sudden. . . . None of this is simple. Domestic squalor is dark and serious. It leaves behind guilt or sadness. Anger bestows on you a portrait of your soul. It is often followed by guilt. The portrait is more detailed if you have children.

—Anne Roiphe, *Fruitful: A Real Mother in the Modern World*

My Mother's Ring

Caught Between Two Families

Helen Schulman

Y MOTHER WAS starving the day she got married. Before the wedding, she says, she was locked away by herself in a little room so that my father wouldn't see her—bad luck and all that. He was out on the floor, eating and drinking, greeting their guests. After the ceremony, no one thought to save her a plate of food; there was so much hobnobbing to do, so many people to talk to. So when it was all over and they were finally on their own, my parents got into their car and went out for pizza. They were wearing their wedding rings, of course—identical rings, silver and black and wide, with blocky silver letters on them that spell out in Hebrew "I am my beloved's, and my beloved is mine." At the restaurant my mother went into the ladies' room to wash her hands. She took off the ring and left it on the sink. The night she got married my mother lost her wedding ring in some pizza parlor bathroom. You don't have to be a Freudian psychiatrist to get the significance, but that is exactly what my father was, a Freudian psychiatrist.

That's the first story I want to tell you about those rings. The second starts here: Three years ago—forty-two years after my parents' wedding night—I was scheduled, along with my husband and kids, to leave for California the next morning to visit my mother-in-law for Christmas. Here was my life: thirty-eight years old, married, mother of two children, ages three and one; teaching graduate-level fiction writing in New York, where I lived with my family and where my parents also lived, across town. So that night, before I left town, I went to visit my parents. My mother and I were in their living room when we heard my father politely call her name from the bedroom. "Gloria," he said. We somehow both knew something was wrong. We ran in and found him on the floor, shaken but not hurt. It took both of us to lift him back onto the bed. It was the first time I carried the man who had carried me so many times.

So I found it very hard to leave my parents and my city that next day. But my husband and my kids were counting on spending Christmas with his family, so we went. Once I was across the country I proceeded to call my parents morning and night. It seemed that with every phone call, my father was getting worse: his memory was diminishing, his sense of balance was off, there was an undiagnosed stiffness in his limbs. The doctors were thinking Parkinson's. Each time my mother answered I felt as if I had sent her a life preserver. The day we were coming home, I called them from California before we left and then again when we arrived in New York that night. I asked to speak to my father, but my mother said he was too tired. He was lying next to her in the bed, but he just liked to hear her talking to me.

About five hours later the phone rang once more. "Daddy fell again," said my mother. But this was a different kind of fall. "He's having brain surgery right now." He'd needed to go to the bathroom, she told me. He hadn't wanted to wake her. At the hospital, the emergency room doctor—a Jewish girl, said my mother—had asked him who was president and what his own name was and he'd said to my mother, "I'm sorry, Glor," because he couldn't answer the questions. Then he went into a coma.

It was the middle of the night. "I'll be there in fifteen minutes," I said. But I took a shower. Without that shower, I don't think I could have faced it. We had been traveling all day; once we'd gotten the kids home and unpacked and gone through the mail and gone out to buy milk and combed through the phone messages and I had spoken with my parents, I'd just collapsed into bed. By the time my mother called, I could smell myself. After I got out of the shower, I told my husband what had happened, and what needed to be done with the children in the morning. I knew they would be very upset to wake up and not find me home. They'd never woken up to not find me home before. But I went to the hospital to be with my parents.

. . .

My daughter loves my father; he had been an active, doting grandfather until his health began to deteriorate. Now that he had fallen and there had been such terrible damage to his brain, the situation was devastating. If he survived, none of us knew what kind of shape he would be in—would he continue to resemble Karen Ann Quinlan? Would he ever walk and talk again? Would he ever be able to play with my children in his same thoughtful and loving manner? How was I to discuss the situation with a three-year-old child? I needed help.

After my father fell, I made an appointment with the social worker at my daughter's nursery school; the twelve-thousand-dollar tuition has its benefits. So I sat on the social worker's couch in my daughter's school and explained as much as I could about my father and my daughter, and as I was explaining I began to cry. "Look," said this woman, "if you are lucky enough to live this long and have children of your own and feel as attached to a parent as you are to yours, then you are a fortunate person." But at that moment, I didn't feel fortunate. I felt angry and scared and devastated and overwhelmed and utterly torn. I listened to her words, but I couldn't hear them properly, couldn't take them in. Right then, lucky was not how I would have characterized myself.

. . .

Months later, when my father had made a recovery of a fluctuating, roller-coastery nature, I took my children to a playground and met my parents there for a picnic. My father was in a wheelchair but, being my father, wanted to try to walk. My mother was playing with my daughter on the jungle gym. I was guiding my father back to his wheelchair when I looked up and saw my son hanging precipitously off a climbing apparatus. Where was King Solomon when I needed him? If I let go of my father, who wavered like a feather in the air, he would have no choice but to fall. If I didn't run to my son, he would surely topple and hit the playground's cement hardtop.

What would you have done?

My son fell to the ground, scraping both his palms.

I held on to my father.

. . .

Sometimes, when he was still in the hospital, I would spend the entire morning by my father's side. My mother came every day, but the mornings seemed especially hard for her. She couldn't sleep at night, and then there were a million phone calls—friends and colleagues, relatives, private nurses to employ, the nightmare labyrinth of health insurance companies to navigate, her own fear. I thought she appreciated my early arrival. I would call her and tell her what to expect when she finally came in, disheveled and shaky, lipstickless, still determined to protect her husband. So the morning was my time.

When he was awake, I had to tell him over and over again what had happened to him. Remember that movie *Groundhog Day*? Each time I told him the story—you fell, you had two brain surgeries, you had a seizure, you are in the hospital—the story was fresh for him. Each time I told him the story he was devastated all over again. But for me, the story took on a rote sameness. I told him that story ten times a day. Sometimes I varied the details to entertain myself. Usually, after I told him the story he would pass out. He was passed out this particular morning and I was waiting for a doctor to come and evaluate him for the hospital's rehabilitation unit. If they did not accept him, we would be forced to move him to whatever nursing home in the five boroughs became available next. My father could not sit up, he could not eat, some days he did not achieve consciousness. He was hardly a candidate for rehab, but in a nursing home he would die. I needed to find this doctor and convince him to find a bed for my father in rehab. Finally, the nurse told me the doctor would come in twenty minutes. I decided to run out and get a cup of coffee.

On the way back, I saw an old woman hyperventilating in the lobby of the hospital. She looked about to faint. It was my mother. Very distraught. What should I do, help her and miss my chance with the doctor?

I guided her over to a marble bench. I laid her down. I said, "Don't you fall, too," and gave her my cup of coffee. Then I left her there, alone on the cold marble, and I returned to my father.

There are no stories from this time about me and my husband.

. . .

What happens to a person when she suddenly finds herself more powerful than the most powerful people in her life? My parents, who after all gave me life, shepherded me through a childhood that surprisingly seemed to extend itself way into adulthood, gave me love and advice, lent me money, cared for me when I was sick, baby-sat my kids so my husband and I could go to the movies . . . my parents were suddenly both weak, vulnerable, small. As a middle child in a family of strong personalities, I had often felt overwhelmed, too sensitive, too dependent. Once, when I'd published my first book and I was looking for even more ego stroking, I'd asked my father what he'd thought I would be when I grew up. He said, "You were like a little flower. I thought someone would take care of you." But now I was taking charge, now I was taking care of everyone. It was a stunning role for me. My father had required six pints of blood during his surgery. One afternoon, as a break from sitting by his side, I decided to return the favor and went to the hospital blood lab. As I watched my blood flow out of my body and into that little plastic sack, I thought, *Now you need me, you even need my blood for your survival,* and the very thought was more dizzying than the blood loss. It made me feel very strong. And like everything else that was so conflicting and complicated during that time, it also made me feel very, very lost.

. . .

The bitch in the house? I was the bitch in the hospital. My mother talked to the nurses, the social workers, the doctors, told them about how my father had worked in that very hospital for forty years, about how, when he was a resident on call, she'd sneak into one of the residents' rooms at night and sleep with him, how twice a week they would have dinner together in the cafeteria. She tried to engage them, to warm them up to us. Not me. I was cold and animal. Each time the nurse brought my father medication I asked what it was and why they were giving it to him. I begged the physical therapist to come and see him, even though he couldn't walk or talk or sit up or even lift his arm, because if someone didn't keep him moving his pneumonia would worsen and kill him. I yelled at the little speech therapist with the curly hair who wouldn't give him any liquids because she was afraid he'd aspirate them, but who wouldn't give him an aspiration test because she was too busy. I shouted at the intake worker that my father gave forty years of his life to this hospital and goddamnit they better find a bed for him in rehab. I begged, reasoned, yelled. I never gave up. I exercised his limbs while he was unconscious, and when he was conscious I begged him to take a sip of thickened juice and prattled on for hours about my kids, who were back home without me. I poured every drop of myself into the big black hole that took up so shockingly little of his hospital bed. And when, after ten hours of that, I slogged back home to my family, my mother would call and say, "Daddy woke up and wondered why you haven't come to see him today."

. . .

I had two children and I had two parents. Oh, and I was supposed to be working. I had a job. That semester, I was supposed to be writing a movie, about a schizophrenic who pushed an innocent young woman to her death. So at night, after I'd bathed and fed the children and put them to bed, after I did the laundry and the bills, after I'd ignored the phone messages from my friends and made dinner for my husband—elaborate gourmetish things like risottos and fish in parchment, just to remind him that he had a wife—I read trial transcripts and autopsy reports and everything I could about schizophrenia, until I passed out, dirty clothes still on my body, reference books in hand.

. . .

My mother-in-law came to New York to visit, and my husband and I went out to dinner with her and a couple of her girlfriends. One of them asked me about the kids, and then she asked me about my work, and then she asked me about my parents. "You know what you are?" she said, after I'd answered all her questions. "You're part of the sandwich generation."

What did she mean by that? She meant if we hadn't had children so late in life, if we'd had children at the normal age—say, twenty-five, twenty-eight—our parents could have helped us when the kids were little, and only staggered their way downhill toward helplessness after the children were grown. I was thirty-five, my husband thirty-eight, when our first child was born; I had my career, I'd already published four books, I kicked in my part of the family income. I hadn't planned to wait so long to have kids, but that was beside the point now. Now I was a victim of my own arrogance and biology, taking care of both of my families, the first one and this one, at the same time. And didn't I resent that? asked the friend. After all, I'd waited so long, this was my time to enjoy my children. I thought, *Resentment is the wrong word.* But what was the right one? I didn't know where to be, who to go to, who needed me more. One evening, when I came home from the hospital, I started to sob in the kitchen. "Why are you crying, Mommy?" my daughter asked. "Because your grandpa is so sick," I said. My daughter took a napkin from the table, which was set with a dinner I had not made for her, and used it to wipe my eyes. Then she said, "Drink a little bit of water." So I obeyed her and drank from her sippy cup. Then she said, "Now don't talk about it anymore."

"Those are my genes," my rather reserved Waspy husband said proudly. I was almost startled by his voice. I hadn't even noticed him there in the room, hadn't noticed him for so long.

That year, the only time I felt free of either set of my familial obligations was the few times I got to a yoga class and the teacher said, "You have to practice the art of nonattachment." And so I did. I practiced the art of nonattachment with my head on the ground and my feet in the air, and I floated off the planet in my mind, untethered by the very people who make me feel most tethered to the earth.

. . .

My father came home from rehab after six weeks, brain-damaged but doing better. He could eat, he could walk a little, he could talk, although he often couldn't find the right words to express what he wanted to say, and he had a great deal of trouble following or sustaining a conversation. As the weeks and months passed, this situation changed and did not change. Sometimes my father could walk, sometimes he couldn't. Sometimes he could carry on a conversation, sometimes not. Sometimes he possessed all the wisdom and humanity of his being, and other times I looked in his eyes and it felt like he wasn't there. On those days he looked terrified to me. Several months of this seesawing later, my mother was diagnosed with breast cancer.

It was decided that I would accompany her to the hospital for her mastectomy while my brother, my partner in all things terrible and hard, stayed at home with my father. The morning of the surgery, as I was rushing out of the apartment, my two-year-old son got his fingers stuck in a closet door. For a few long horrible seconds, my husband and I didn't know how to get them out; if we moved the door in either direction it would pinch harder. You never heard such screams. Finally, I just closed my eyes and said to my husband, "Just do it." Whatever my husband did—I don't know, I had my eyes closed—the kid's fingers came out of the door. They were red and flat and my son cried his heart out in my arms. But I had to get to the hospital, the same hospital my father had been discharged from just months before, the hospital where my mother was now being operated on. I had to leave my kid to go help my mother. I made the choice. I disengaged my son's arms from around my neck, handed him over to my husband, and walked out the door.

. . .

Here's the end of the second story about my parents' wedding rings. Shortly after my mother lost hers, on her wedding night, she had another very similar one made, which she was still wearing forty-two years later, the day of her mastectomy. At the hospital, as she waited to go into surgery, she wore a blue hospital gown and that ring. Next to her, on her bedside table, there was a phone. My mother asked me to call home to check in on my father. "How come your mother never calls?" said my father when I did. She had been away from home about an hour and a half. "We're waiting to go into surgery, Daddy," I said. "We're waiting here, too," said my father, and he sounded angry. Of course he was angry. She was his entire world.

I said good-bye and hung up. It was almost time. I said, "Ma, you should give me your watch and your earrings, and your wedding ring. I'll hold them until the surgery is over." She handed over the watch and the earrings, but not the ring. "It doesn't come off," she said. She'd been wearing it for so long her knuckle had swollen and locked that ring into place. Then the surgeon came in, and I went out so the doctor could mark my mother's chest, and then the surgeon called me back in and the surgical nurse said, "It's time, but first you better take off that wedding ring." "It doesn't come off," I announced, but my mother interrupted, "Yes, it does," and she slipped it off and held it out to me. My mother. I don't think she had ever lied to me before. "I guess I didn't want to take it off," she confessed. I said, "I'll take good care of it, Ma." And I put it on my finger.

I wore it out to the waiting room. I sat in the waiting room, wearing her ring.

It was the first time in months that I was alone. No parents, no children, no screenplay, no grocery shopping, no housecleaning, no bill paying, no husband to completely ignore only to wonder, later, if he would get fed up and leave me. No screaming or yelling at anyone. Instead, I read a book. It was the first book I had read in as long as I could remember that wasn't written by a friend or a student, that wasn't assigned for reviewing, that wasn't about schizophrenia, that nobody had asked me to blurb. I curled up on a couch in the waiting room and I read that book for most of the next nine hours. I did not pay attention to all the families that were waiting so anxiously around me, I did not look up when I heard their sobbing, or when I smelled their ad hoc picnics or when the couples involved began to fight. Where was my family? My families? I was by myself. These people were all there together; they had each other. That was their misfortune.

I was alone. And I don't mind telling you, it was like a little slice of heaven. Waiting for my mother to come out of surgery was like a mini-vacation for me. I read my book and I drank my coffee and for the first time that miserable year, I felt like myself.

. . .

I sat there for the next nine hours wearing my mother's ring. And then, when I visited her in recovery and yelled at the nurses that no, I would not leave even though I'd been there half an hour already and the legal limit was five minutes, not until she was given more pain medication, not until she was given Compazine, I still wore that ring. I wore it in recovery because her arms were swaddled to her body and she looked like one big nauseated, suffering head. Eventually I put it on my middle finger and then I put my own wedding ring on top of it so it wouldn't fall off, because in the days that followed, my mother's hand was too swollen to wear the thing. Day after day it rattled around my finger. In truth, I didn't have the substance or the heft to fill the space.

Finally, when my mother had stopped puking her guts up, when she was able to sit up and hold up her head, my brother and I brought my father to the hospital to see her. My father couldn't lift himself out of the wheelchair and stand, and my mother couldn't bend forward in her hospital bed to meet him because of the pain and all those tubes and wires hooked up to all those machines, but still by some miracle of determination my parents managed to kiss each other.

That's the way they were, my parents. "Kiss me quick in the elevator," my mother would say, when we all still lived together on Eighty-sixth Street and were going downstairs.

"Give me a kiss, Glor," my father would say, when they'd been fighting for weeks and it was enough already.

Kiss, kiss, kiss. I'll tell you, sometimes when I was single and lonely all that kissing drove me crazy.

Eventually, when my mother came home from the hospital, I gave the ring back to her, and thank God it fit her hand again, because frankly I couldn't stand wearing it anymore.

It wasn't mine. I wasn't worthy of it. For weeks, for months, I had barely seen my husband.

So I went home to my family. To the bills and the laundry, to the cooking, to my two little children, to my desk and its ever-growing pile of work, to my husband. And I started over again, with the newfound knowledge I'd gleaned during those weeks and months, months of being the mother-in-the-middle, the daughter-in-the-middle, the non-wife. The knowledge of what that nursery school shrink had tried to tell me long ago, but I couldn't grasp at the time. That I was lucky.

Attila the Honey I'm Home

Kristin van Ogtrop

It's a typical night:

I arrive home from work, after first stopping to pick up my two boys from my friend Gabrielle's house, where my nanny has left them on a play date. It's seven thirty. No one has had a bath. Foolishly, I have promised that we will make milk shakes. The boys have eaten dinner. I haven't. My husband is at a basketball game and won't be home until ten.

Owen, who is six, tosses a bouquet of flowers—a gift from Gabrielle's garden—onto the grass as we get out of the car. Three-year-old Hugo sees the moon. I mention that the sun is out, too; he runs from one end of the front walk to the other, trying to find it, getting closer to the street with each lap.

Owen says he wants the milk shake *now*.

I unlock the front door and step in. George the cat meows and rubs against my legs, begging to be fed.

I walk back outside to pick up the flowers, the wet towel (swimming lessons), and my own two bags from work (contents: three unread newspapers, two magazines, a birthday party invitation for Owen, a present for the party, and a folder of work that, ever the optimist, I'm hoping to do tonight).

Back into the house with flowers, towel, bags. As I put my keys in the bowl next to the front door (small attempt at order), I knock over a framed picture beside it. The glass in the frame shatters.

Hugo calls, insistent, for me to come back outside.

Owen hovers behind me, barefoot. He wants to know why, when you combine chocolate and vanilla, does the ice cream turn brown instead of white?

I maneuver Owen around the broken glass and ask him to get the Dustbuster as I begin to pick up the shards. He disappears into the kitchen for what seems like ten minutes. I glance out for Hugo, whose voice is fainter but *definitely* still audible. George stands on his hind legs, clawing holes in the screen.

Owen reappears with the Dustbuster, revving the motor. He wants to know exactly how long until we make the milk shake, and are we sure we even have chocolate ice cream?

I am talking in my Mr. Rogers voice as my desperation rises. Any minute now my head is going to blast off my body, burst through the screen door, and buzz around my little town, eventually losing steam before landing with a thud somewhere near the train station, where it will be run over by one of my smiling neighbors being picked up by what I imagine are calm spouses who will drive them calmly home to houses calm and collected where the children are already bathed and ready for bed.

As for me, it's time to start yelling.

. . .

The next day:

I get up at 5:30 to leave the house at 6:00, to be driven to the TV studio for hair and makeup at 6:45, to go on the air, live, at 7:40. I'm the executive editor of an enormously popular women's magazine and am appearing as an "expert" on a local morning show to discuss "what your wallet says about you." I have a hairstylist I've never met and he makes the back of my head look ridiculous, like a ski jump. At 7:25 the segment producer hands me the anchor's script; it contains five questions that weren't part of yesterday's pre-interview. I make up answers that sound informed-clever-peppy enough for morning TV with two minutes to spare. Total airtime: ninety seconds.

By the time I get to the office at 8:30 I have six voice mail messages (boss, nanny, human resources manager, unhappy writer, underling editor wanting guidance, my mother), twenty-seven e-mails, and, on my chair, a 4,000-word article I need to edit by the end of the day. I run to the cafeteria to get something to eat, then call boss and nanny and answer most of the e-mails before my 9:30 meeting.

At 10:45 two fact-checkers come into my office to describe the problems of a recent story, which kept them at work until 4:00 A.M. the night before. Are fact-checkers or editor to blame? Editor, I decide, and call her in. She is flustered and defensive, and starts to cry. My tissue box is empty, so I hand her a napkin. We talk (well, I talk; she nods) about the fact that she's made similar mistakes in the past, and perhaps this isn't the job for her. After she leaves I call the human resources manager to discuss the problematic editor, a looming legal problem, and staff salaries.

I have lunch at my desk and a second cup of coffee while I edit the piece, until two editors visit to complain about coworkers. A third tells me she is overloaded. A fourth confesses her marital problems and starts to cry; now I'm out of napkins, too. I give her the number of a counseling service and suggest she use it. Someone calls to ask about the presentation I'm giving tomorrow; I haven't even begun to think about it, which probably should worry me but somehow doesn't.

I finish the edit and drop it in my out box. Before leaving the office at 5:30 I pick up all the paper that blankets my desk and divide it into four discrete piles for the morning. I very well might forget to look through the piles and something will get overlooked, but when I return to work, the neat stacks will make me feel organized and calm. And at work, I usually am.

Here are a few things people have said about me at the office:

- "You're unflappable."
- "Are you ever in a bad mood?"
- "You command respect as soon as you walk into a room."
- "Your straightforward, no-nonsense style gets things done."
- "You're good at finessing situations so people don't boil over."

Here are things people—OK, the members of my family—have said about me at home:

- "Mommy is always grumpy."
- "Why are you so tense?"
- "You just need to relax."
- "You don't need to yell!"
- "You're too mean to live in this house and I want you to go back to work for the rest of your life!"

That last one is my favorite. It's also the saddest, because it captures such a painful truth: too often I'm a better mother at work than I am at home. Of course, at work, no one shouts at me for five minutes straight in what parents universally refer to as an "outside voice." No one charges into my office, hands outstretched, to smear peanut butter all over my skirt or Vaseline all over my favorite needlepoint rug. At work, when someone is demanding something of me, I can say, "I'll call you back" or "Let's talk about that in the next meeting." When people don't listen to me, they do so after they've left my office, not right in front of me. Yet even if shouting and random acts of destruction were to become the norm at work, I probably would not respond with the angry tantrums that punctuate so many nights at home. We have our own form of chaos in the office, after all. I work with creative people—temperamental, flaky, "difficult"—but my job is to be the eye of the storm.

So why this angel-in-the-office, horror-at-home division? Shouldn't the skills that serve me so well at work help me at the end of the day? My friend Chrissie, heroic stay-at-home mother of four, has one explanation: My behavior simply reproduces, in the adult world, the perfect-at-school/demon-at-home phenomenon that is acted out daily among children throughout America. I am on my best behavior at work, just as Owen is on his best behavior at school, but at home we have to ask him seven times to put on his shoes and by the seventh time it's no longer a request but a shouted, boot-camp command. And I am on my worst behavior at home because that's where I can "unwind" after spending eight (or ten, or fourteen) hours at the office keeping my cool.

Arlie Russell Hochschild has other ideas about this apparently widespread condition. In her 1997 book *Time Bind: When Work Becomes Home and Home Becomes Work,* she writes, "In this new model of family and work life, a tired parent flees a world of unresolved quarrels and unwashed laundry for the reliable orderliness, harmony, and managed cheer of work." At the office, I do manage, in all senses of the word. I am paid to be bossy—a trait that, for better and worse, has always been a predominant part of my personality. But at home, that bossiness yields unpleasant dividends, both from two boys who are now officially Grade A backtalkers and from a husband who frequently lets me know he's not someone I need to supervise. Still, the impulse isn't likely to go away, as long as I remain the only one in our household who knows where the library books/soccer cleats/car keys have gone—and what to do with them. At home I am wife, mother, baby-sitting and housekeeping manager, cook, social secretary, gardener, tutor, chauffeur, interior decorator, general contractor, and laundress. That many roles is exhausting, especially at those times when my mind is still in work mode. The other night I said to Hugo, "Do you want to put on your pj's in Owen's office?" It's a messy juggling act, and when a ball drops, I'm never laughing.

Last Friday I picked up the cheery note that Owen's kindergarten teacher, Ms. Stenstrom, sends at the end of every week. "We had an exciting morning!" it began. "We finished our touch unit by guessing what was in all the bags—thanks for sending in SUCH mysterious objects!" I had forgotten that Owen was supposed to have taken something interesting to touch in a brown paper bag to school that day. Standing alone in the kitchen, I started to cry. I read the note again, feeling miserable for Owen, miserable for me, miserable for lovely, infinitely patient Ms. Stenstrom. Then I climbed the stairs, cornered Dean, and cried some more. Is that appropriate? To cry for an hour and then have a long, tedious, completely unproductive discussion with an equally sleep-deprived husband about All The Things We're Doing Wrong? How did I turn into this?

. . .

Start with my mother, end with my father. In 1976, when I was twelve, fully two-thirds of all American households that consisted of married couples with children had one parent staying home full-time, according to the U.S. Census Bureau. My mother was one of those parents. With her tuna cashew casserole recipe, I won the 4-H Ready Foods Contest at the Delaware State Fair when I was in fourth grade. From my mother I learned that when you assemble a place setting, the knife should be one thumb-knuckle distance from the edge of the table; when you arrange flowers in a vase, the largest blooms should be at the bottom; when you hem a skirt, you should turn the ends of the fabric under twice. From my mother I also learned that grades are important, that feelings are neither right nor wrong, and that I am capable of just about anything I make up my mind to do.

College, graduate school, first jobs (art gallery, film production company); they all happened without much planning. Along the way I met Dean, and for a few years nothing else mattered. Then, when I was twenty-seven, I landed at *Vogue*—and suddenly found myself living on a planet where I spoke the native tongue. Dean left graduate school and got a magazine job, too. Of course, while he and I were fetching coffee and confirming the spelling of proper names (standard duties for editor wanna-bes, for a salary dangerously close to minimum wage), our closest friends were finishing law school and business school and accepting $100,000 jobs and getting pregnant and buying houses. I despaired: we would never have children! never buy a house! never pay off my student loan!

But I got promoted. I got pregnant. By the time Owen was a year old, the charms of our romantic brownstone floor-through in Brooklyn were obliterated by overflowing closets and a litter box in the living room. For the sake of matrimonial harmony Dean allowed himself to be talked into the suburbs (hello! nearly the happiest day in my life!). Our once-minuscule salaries got bigger, our once-mansionlike house eventually felt smaller, but we're still here; our choice has stuck.

I left *Vogue* and had job after job, and as I moved from one magazine to another, this thought formed on the border of my consciousness. It got less peripheral, gradually bigger, until it was large and clear as day: in spite of years of training, I had not become my mother. I was my father, with ovaries. I have his square shoulders and his ease with strangers; I also have his extraordinarily short fuse. Like my father, I am polite to people in the workplace because I am trying to charm them, to win them over—and to be fair, to do the right thing. At work I give people the benefit of the doubt. At home there is no such thing. At home I—like my father—blame first, ask questions later. My mother is the soul of patience. My mother is nothing like this.

I can still arrange flowers and set a table, but I can't remember how my mother disciplined without raising her voice. Where my kids are concerned, I am volatile but deeply sentimental, like my father. I keep locks of their hair, a drawer full of their drawings. And when they're asleep, I kneel beside their beds in atonement for my sins, press my nose to their sweaty blond heads, and ask forgiveness for my take-no-prisoners parenting style.

I work because I have to financially, and because I love to. Like my dad, I get enormous personal satisfaction from career success. But the smoothness with which my career flows makes life at home even harder to manage. Like me, my father is missing the microchip that processes chaos. When his three daughters were small, he would come home from work (by six, in time for family dinner) and pour himself a drink before he'd even taken off his tie. The drink was not a reward for a hard day's work, but a buttress for what he'd face over the next four hours. On a recent visit to our house, while attempting to work an ice maker that had been broken for four months, he announced, "If I lived in this house, I'd have to drink all day long." Ice makers, you see, don't stay broken for four months in his house. My father has a wife.

· · ·

Ah, a wife. Sometimes when describing the work my nanny does to women of another generation who find my life perplexing, I say,

"Basically, she's a wife," and wonder if it's horribly sexist or insulting to use that description. Lauren does wash the kids' clothes, make their dinner, help with homework, cuddle after naps. She does not, however, write notes to the teacher or plan vacations or figure out where we're going to put the hamster Owen desperately wants. And Dean, God bless him, is terrible at those things. I used to think it was lack of training; now I think it's that Y chromosome. Dean is spectacular at spelling Kyrgyzstan and remembering who won the 1976 World Series. Ask him the first name of Hugo's nursery school teacher and he's stumped. Ask him to remember to pick up cat food and it goes in one ear and out the other; on really frustrating days he'll deny ever being told at all (note to self: don't say anything important if the sports section is within ten feet). So there are duties—and they seem to number in the thousands—that fall in the vast gray area that is not-husband-not-nanny, and therefore they are mine.

I come home on an average Tuesday to find the Scholastic book order form submerged in a pile of drawings and Pokémon cards and disemboweled pens on the kitchen counter. I look at the pictures of Clifford paperbacks, boxed sets, games. How many Clifford books do we already have, anyway? Did I order a Clifford cassette the last time, or was I just considering it? Did Dean's sister give Owen a Clifford CD-ROM for Christmas? The questions (unanswerable without a substantial investment of house searching or phone calling) start to jam my circuits, and I think I might burst into tears. I just can't make one more decision. I have a sudden, overwhelming desire to be George Banks, the clueless and routinized father in *Mary Poppins,* when he bursts into the house at six on the dot singing, "I feel a surge of deep satisfaction!" Slippers, sherry, pipe at 6:01. Then: "It's 6:03, and the heirs to my dominion/are scrubbed and tubbed, and adequately fed/And so I'll pat them on the head, and send them off to bed/How lordly is the life I lead!" George at least has a song's length of ignorant bliss before he learns that the children have gone missing. . . .

Unfortunately, the fantasy doesn't quite sustain me as the bathwater sloshes all over the floor and the choice of *Bread and Jam for Frances* over *If You Give a Moose a Muffin* results in fraternal civil war. That's when the exhaustion wins. I call to Dean, who has just arrived home from work, "I can't deal with this anymore!" and he steps in before I really start to yell. I wash my face and brush my teeth and fall into bed the minute I can make a break for it, the millisecond Hugo is finished with his nightly forty-five minutes of getting in and out, in and out of bed. I crawl under the covers like a woman who has walked forty miles through a snowstorm, and remember all over again that—pathetic or not—this really is my favorite moment of the day.

. . .

And so there's the guilt. This is one area in which my father and I differ. He has never Wrestled with His Identity as a Parent. He has never, as far as I know, overcompensated for anything. He didn't ever play duck-duck-goose after work, as I did two nights ago, even though it was dark and the grass was wet and I would rather—who are we kidding?—have been inside with a glass of wine. The guilt seems centered on the things I'm missing in my children's lives. I know I miss much, because I feel it: there is a purity to their everyday world that makes my heart ache. When I walk into one of their schools, I feel as if I'm walking into a church; the halls are filled with noble souls who are trying to save the world. I am not of that world in the way that nonworking mothers are—I'm more a frequent visitor—and I suspect that my guilt and sadness about that are part of what makes me so cranky at home.

But my guilt is diminishing as I evolve, and I consider the process of shedding it a significant act of liberation. The older my kids get, the more I'm beginning to realize that they're happy and smart and loving, despite the fact that Mom works. I am trying to eliminate the stubborn fear that children of working mothers grow up to be unhappy adults. I'm making progress, although I'm occasionally derailed by news items like the one I recently saw in the *Wall Street Journal* that described the math scores of children who don't have two parents at home from 6:00 to 9:00 P.M. (Let's just say the chances of Owen and Hugo ever reaching AP calculus are slim.)

There's guilt where my marriage is concerned, too, but it's a Mobius strip: guilt and resentment, and more guilt because of the resentment. We are just like many two-career, multiple-child couples I know. I could write a script for one of our arguments and pass it out to half of my suburban neighbors (the 51 percent in my town with working moms); simply change the names and everyone could act out the same neat little domestic drama. Whereas Dean and I used to argue about money and where to live, we now bicker constantly about one thing: who is doing more. Before we had children we were broke but had fun doing effortless activities that didn't cost a dime, like sleeping in. Now we have money but no time together (and, obviously, no sleeping in). We are still partners, but often partners in martyrdom, burning ourselves at the stake on a bonfire of diapers that need to be changed, mittens that need to be found, plumbers who need to be called. We often have a semifight at three in the afternoon to see who is least required at the office and can take the 5:58 train to relieve the nanny. During the week we are rarely, if ever, both home awake with the kids at the same time. Although Dean points out that this is true of most working parents we know, it troubles me that, schedule-wise, we might as well be divorced with joint custody. Because we spend many weekend nights with friends and their children, we eat dinner together as a foursome only about once a week, not five or six times as was the norm in our own childhoods. Is this the worst thing in the world? Is this damaging to my children in the long run? As with everything, it depends on who you ask.

It's these questions without answers that make me insane. Most work questions somehow have ready answers, and when I doubt my abilities as an editor, the moments are fleeting. I doubt my skills as a mother every day. I measure myself against a Platonic motherhood ideal and I'm always coming up short. You could argue that the doubt itself makes me try harder, means I continue to strive. But the doubt is also what makes me irrational, moody, even angry when faced with the chaos that accompanies such fundamental childhood joys as jumping on Mommy and Daddy's newly made bed.

. . .

Was my mother ever this angry? It's hard to believe, and scares me when I contemplate it. When I was little, reading a book on the hammock or playing foursquare in the driveway, was my mom actually looking forward to the day when I would go away to college so she could have the house to herself? Didn't she love me more than that?

This, I fear, is how it will be: I will love my children, but my love for them will always be imperfect, damaged by my rigid personality and the demands of my work. I will never be able to share the surprise they feel when they find a cicada in the grass, because stopping to marvel at the cicada means I will miss my morning train. I will never fully love, without qualifiers, the loud, messy place that is the home of two energetic boys. The years will pass, Owen and Hugo will grow, and I will continue to dream about the time I can walk in the front door and feel relaxed.

I will long for a time when I will never yell at my kids just because I am late. Long to be a mother who simply doesn't care that there's Vaseline on my needlepoint rug. To be on my best behavior at home, just as I am at work; to treat my family with the same kindness and respect that I at least pretend to give everyone in my office.

Because before I know it, my boys will be grown. The house will be spotless, and so will I: nice, calm, both at work and at home. Four little feet jumping on the bed will be a distant memory. And things like cicadas will have lost their magic, and my children will be gone for good.

The Myth of Co-Parenting

How It Was Supposed to Be. How It Was.

Hope Edelman

THROUGHOUT MUCH OF 1999 and 2000, my husband spent quite a lot of time at work. By "quite a lot" I mean the kind of time Fermilab scientists spent trying to split the atom, which is to say, every waking moment. The unofficial count one week came in at ninety-two hours, which didn't include cell phone calls answered on grocery checkout lines or middle-of-the-night brainstorms that had to be e-mailed before dawn. Often I would wake at 3:00 A.M. and find him editing a business plan down in the living room, drinking herbal tea in front of his laptop's ethereal glow. If he had been a lawyer tallying billable hours, he would have made some firm stinking rich.

He was launching an Internet company back then, and these were the kind of hours most people in his industry were putting in. Phrases like "window of opportunity" and "ensuring our long-term security" were bandied about our house a lot, usually during the kind of exasperating late-night conversations that began with "The red-eye to New York? *Again?*" and included "I mean, it's not like you're trying to find a cure for cancer," somewhere within. I was working nearly full-time myself, though it soon became clear this would have to end. Our daughter was a year and a half old, and the phrase "functionally orphaned" was also getting thrown around our house a lot, usually by me.

So as my husband's work hours exponentially increased, I started cutting back on mine. First a drop from thirty-five per week to twenty-five, and then a dwindle down to about eighteen. At first I didn't really mind. With the exception of six weeks postpartum, this was the first time since high school that I had a good excuse not to work like a maniac, and I was grateful for the break. Still, there was something more than vaguely unsettling about feeling that my choice hadn't been much of an actual choice. When one parent works ninety-two hours a week, the other one, by necessity, has to start picking up the slack. Otherwise, some fairly important things—like keeping the refrigerator stocked, or filing income taxes, or finding a reliable baby-sitter, not to mention giving a child some semblance of security and consistency around this place, for God's sake—won't get done. A lot of slack was starting to pile up around our house. And because I was the only parent spending any real time there, the primary de-slacker was me.

How did I feel about this? I don't mind saying. I was extremely pissed off.

. . .

Like virtually every woman friend I have, I entered marriage with the belief that co-parenting was an attainable goal. In truth, it was more of a vague assumption, a kind of imagined parity I had superimposed on the idea of marriage without ever really thinking it through. *If I'm going to contribute half of the income, then he'll contribute half of the housework and child care.* Like that. If you'd asked me to elaborate, I would have said something impassioned and emphatic, using terms like "shared responsibility" and "equal division of labor." The watered-down version of feminism I identified with espoused those catchphrases, and in lieu of a more sophisticated blueprint for domestic life, I co-opted the talk as my own. But really, I didn't know what I was talking about beyond the fact that I didn't want to be the dominant parent in the house.

When I was growing up in suburban New York, my mother seemed to do everything. *Everything.* Carpooling, haircuts, vet appointments, ice cream cakes, dinners in the Crock-Pot, book-report dioramas—the whole roll call for a housewife of the 1960s and 1970s. My father, from my child's point of view, did three things. He came home from work in time for dinner. He sat at the kitchen table once a month and paid the bills. And, on weekend trips, he drove the car. Certainly he did much more than that, including earn all of our family's income, but my mother's omnipresence in our household meant that anyone else felt, well, incidental in comparison. The morning after she died, of breast cancer at forty-two, my younger siblings and I sat at the kitchen table with our father as dawn filtered through the yellow window shades. I looked at him sitting there, in a polo shirt and baseball cap, suddenly so small beneath his collapsed shoulders. I was barely seventeen. He was fifty-one. *Huh,* I thought. *Who are* you?

There were no chore charts taped to the refrigerator, no family powwows, no enthusiastic TV nannies suddenly materializing outside our front door. My father taught himself to use a microwave and I started driving my siblings for their haircuts and that, as they say, was that.

My cousin Lorraine, a devout Baha'i, once told me it doesn't matter how many orgasms a potential husband gives you; what really matters is the kind of father he'll be. At first I thought she said this because Baha'is disavow premarital sex, but the more men I dated, the more I realized Lorraine was right. Loyalty and devotion are undoubtedly better traits to have in a spouse than those fleeting moments of passion, though I can't deny the importance of the latter. When I met John, it was like winning the boyfriend jackpot. He was beautiful and sexy, and devoted and smart, *so* smart, and he had the kindest green eyes. The first time I saw those eyes, when I was negotiating an office sublease from him in New York, he smiled right at me and it happened, just the way you dream about when you're twelve: I knew this was someone I would love. *And* he wanted children, which immediately separated him from a cool three-quarters of the men I'd dated before. I was thirty-two when we started dating, and just becoming acutely aware that I didn't have unlimited time to wait.

What happened next happened fast. Within two years, John and I were parents and homeowners in a canyon outside Los Angeles. By then he was deep into the process of starting his own company, which left us with barely an hour to spend together at the end of each day. And even though I so badly wanted him to succeed, to get the acclaim a smart, hardworking, honest person deserves—and even though I was grateful that his hard, honest work earned enough to support us both—well, let me put it bluntly. Back there when I was single and imagining the perfect partnership? This wasn't what I had in mind.

When John became so scarce around our house, I had to compensate by being utterly present in every way: as a kisser of boo-boos; a dispenser of discipline; an employer of baby-sitters; an assembler of child furniture; a scary-monster slayer, mortgage refinancer, reseeder of dying backyards. And that's before I even opened my office door for the day. Balancing act? I was the whole damn circus, all three rings.

It began to make me spitting mad, the way the daily duties of parenting and home ownership started to rest entirely on me. It wasn't even the additional work I minded as much as the total responsibility for every decision made. The frustration I felt after researching and visiting six preschools during my so-called work hours, trying to do a thorough job for both of us, and then having John offhandedly say, "Just pick the one you like best." Or the irritation I felt when, after three weeks of weighing the options, I finally made the choice, and then he raised his eyebrows at the cost. *I didn't sign up for this!* I began shouting at my sister over the phone.

How does it happen, I wondered both then and now, that even today, in this post–second wave, post-superwoman, dual-income society we're supposed to live in, the mother nearly always becomes the primary parent, even when she, too, works full-time—the one who meets most or all of the children's and the household's minute-by-minute needs? We start out with such grand intentions for sharing the job, yet ultimately how many fathers handle the dental appointments, shop for school clothes, or shuttle pets to and from the vet? Nine times out of ten, it's still the mother who plans and emcees the birthday parties, the mother who cuts the meeting short when the school nurse calls. Women have known about this Second Shift for years, the way the workday so often starts up again for women when they walk through the door at the end of the *other* workday—a time mandated perhaps by the baby-sitter's deadline, but also by their own guilt, sense of responsibility, tendency to prioritize their husband's job first, or a combination of all three. Still, I—like many other enlightened, equality-oriented women having babies in this era—had naïvely thought that a pro-feminist partner, plus my own sheer willpower, would prevent this from happening to me. I hadn't bargained for how deeply the gender roles of "nurturer" and "provider" are ingrained in us all, or—no matter how much I love being a mother to my daughter—how much I would grow to resent them.

When it became clear that my husband and I were not achieving the kind of co-parenting I'd so badly wanted us to achieve, I felt duped and infuriated and frustrated and, beneath it all, terribly, impossibly sad. Sad for myself, and sad for my daughter, who—just like me as a child—had so little one-on-one time with her father. No matter how sincerely John and I tried to buck convention, no matter how often I was the one who sat down at the kitchen table to pay the bills, there we were: he absorbed in his own world of work, me consumed by mine at home. My parents all over again.

. . .

The intensity of John's workplace was, originally, supposed to last for six months, then for another six months, then for only about three months more. But there was always some obstacle on the horizon: first-round funding, second-round funding, hirings, firings, had to train a sales force, had to meet a new goal. And meetings, all those meetings. Seven in the morning, nine at night. How were all those other dot-com wives managing?

There was no time together for anything other than the most pragmatic exchanges. When he walked through the door at 10:00 P.M., I'd lunge at him with paint chips to approve, or insurance forms to sign, or leaks to examine before I called the plumber first thing in the morning. Fourteen hours of conversation compressed into twenty highly utilitarian minutes before we fell, exhausted, into bed. A healthy domestic situation, it was not.

I was angry with the kind of anger that had nothing to do with rationality. A lot of the time, I was mad at Gloria Steinem for having raised women's expectations when I was just a toddler—but at least she lived by her principles, marrying late and never trying to raise kids; so then I got mad at Betty Friedan for having started it all with *The Feminine Mystique,* and when that wasn't satisfying enough, I got mad at all the womyn in my feminist criticism class in graduate school, the ones who'd sat there and so smugly claimed it was impossible for a strong-willed woman to ever have an equal partnership with a man. Because it was starting to look as if they'd been right.

But mostly I was mad at John, because he'd never actually sat down with me to say, "This is what starting a dot-com company will involve," or even, "I'd like to do this—what do you think?"—the way I imagine I would have with him before taking on such a demanding project (which, of course, we'd then have realized together was not feasible unless he quit his job or cut back dramatically, which—of course—was out of the question). Legitimate or not, I felt that at least partly because he was "the husband" and his earning power currently eclipsed mine, his career took precedence, and I had to pick up the household slack, to the detriment of my own waning career—or in addition to it. Before our marriage, I had never expected that. I don't remember the conversation where I asked him to support me financially in exchange for me doing everything else. In fact, I'd never wanted that and still decidedly didn't. I was not only happy to put in my portion of the income (though it would inevitably be less than usual during any year I birthed and breast-fed an infant), I expected to and *wanted* to contribute as much as I could: Part of who I was—what defined me and constituted a main source of my happiness and vitality—was my longtime writing and teaching career. I didn't want to give it up, but I also didn't want hired professionals running my household and raising my child. It felt like an impossible catch-22.

. . .

Face-to-face, John and I didn't give ultimatums. At first, we didn't even argue much out loud. Instead we engaged in a kind of low-level quibbling where the stakes were comfortably low. Little digs that didn't mean much in isolation but eventually started to add up. Like bickering about whose fault it was we never took vacations. (He said mine, I said his.) And whether we should buy our daughter a swing set. (I said yes, he said not now.) And about who forgot to roll the trash cans to the bottom of the driveway, again. (Usually him.)

I'd been through therapy. I knew the spiel. How you were supposed to say, "When you're gone all the time, it makes me feel angry and resentful and lonely," instead of, "How much longer do you realistically think I'm going to put up with this crap?" I tried that first approach, and there was something to it, I admit. John listened respectfully. He asked what he could do to improve. Then it was his turn. He told me how he'd begun to feel like a punching bag in our home. How my moods ruled our household, how sometimes he felt like wilting when he heard that sharp edge in my voice. Then he said he was sorry and I said I was sorry, and he said he'd try to be home more and I said I'd try to lighten up. And this would work, for a while. Until the night John would say he'd be home at eight to put Maya to bed but would forget to call about the last-minute staff meeting that started at six, and when he'd walk through the door at ten I'd be too pissed off to even say hello. Instead, I'd snap, "How much longer do you realistically think I'm going to put up with this crap?" And the night would devolve from there.

Neither of us was "wrong." Neither was completely right. The culpability was shared. Both of us were stuck together on that crazy carousel, where the more time John spent away from home, the more pissed off I got, and the more pissed off I got, the less he wanted to be around.

. . .

One day I said fuck it, and I took John's credit card and bought a swing set. Not one of those fancy redwood kinds that look like a piece of the Alamo, but a sturdy wood one nonetheless with a tree house at the top of the slide, and I paid for delivery and assembly, too. On the way home I stopped at one of those places that sell the fancy redwood kind and ordered a playground-quality bucket swing for another seventy bucks.

Fuck it.

There were other purchases I'd made like this, without John's involvement—the silk bedroom curtains, the Kate Spade wallet I didn't really need—each one thrilling me with a momentary, devilish glee. But the swing set: the swing set was my gutsiest act of rebellion thus far. Still, when it was fully installed on our side lawn, the cloth roof of the tree house gently flapping in the breeze, I felt oddly unfulfilled. Because, after all, what had I really achieved? My daughter had a swing set, but I was still standing on the grass by myself, furiously poking at gopher holes with my foot, thinking about whether I'd have time on Thursday to reseed the lawn alone. When what I really wanted was for my husband to say, "Honey, let me help you with that reseeding, and then we'll all three go out for dinner together." I just wanted him to come home, to share with me—and Maya—all the joys and frustrations and responsibilities of domestic life.

On bad days, when the baby-sitter canceled or another short-notice business trip had just been announced, he would plead with me to hire a full-time nanny—we'd cut corners elsewhere, we'd go into savings, whatever it took, he said. I didn't want to hear it. "I don't need a nanny, I need a husband!" I shouted. Didn't he understand? My plan hadn't been to hire someone to raise our child. My plan had been to do it together: two responsible parents with two fulfilling jobs, in an egalitarian marriage with a well-adjusted kid who was equally bonded to us both.

. . .

In writing class I tell my students there are just two basic human motivators: desire and fear. Every decision we make, every action we take, springs from this divided well. Some characters are ruled by desire. Others are ruled by fear. So what was my story during the year and a half that John spent so much time at work? He claimed that I was fear-driven, that I was threatened by the loss of control, which may in fact have been true. When I try to dissect my behavior then, reaching beneath all the months of anger and complaints, I do find fear: the fear that I'd never find a way to balance work and family life without constantly compromising one, the other, or both. But mostly what I find is desire. For my daughter to have a close relationship with her father, for my husband to have more time to spend with me, for me to find a way to have some control over my time, even with a husband and a child factored into the mix. And then there was the big one: for my husband to fulfill the promise I felt he made to me on our wedding day, which was to be my partner at home and in life. Somewhere along the way, we'd stopped feeling like a team, and I wanted that fellowship back.

I wish, if only to inject a flashy turning point into this story right about now, that I could say some climactic event occurred from which we emerged dazed yet transformed, or that one of us delivered an ultimatum the other couldn't ignore and our commitment to each other was then renewed. But in reality, the way we resolved all this was gradual, and—in retrospect—surprisingly simple. John got the company stabilized and, as he'd promised, finally started working fewer hours. And I, knowing he would be home that much more, slowly started adding hours to my workday. With the additional income, we hired a live-in nanny, who took over much of the housework as well. And then, a few months after Francis arrived, Maya started preschool two mornings a week. Those became blessed writing hours for me, time when I was fully released of the guilt of paying others to watch my child. Between 9:00 A.M. and 12:30 P.M. Maya was exactly where she was supposed to be and, within that time frame, so was I.

With Francis came an additional benefit: a baby-sitter on Friday nights. For the first time since Maya's birth, John and I had a set night each week to devote to each other, and as we split combination sushi plates and did side-by-side chatarangas in a 6:00 P.M. yoga class, we began to slowly build upon the foundation we'd laid with our marriage—and, thankfully, even in the darkest months, we'd always trusted hadn't disappeared. Yes, there were still some Friday nights when I watched TV alone because John was flying back from New York, and other Fridays when I had to sit late in front of the computer to meet a deadline. And there were some weekend days when John still had to take meetings, though they became fewer and fewer over time.

. . .

It has taken real effort for me to release the dream of completely equal co-parenting, or at least to accept that we may not be the family to make it real. We're still quite a distance from that goal, and even further when you factor in the amount of household support we now have. Does John do 50 percent of the remaining child care? No. But neither do I contribute 50 percent of the income, as I once did. Ours is still an imbalanced relationship in some ways, but imbalance I've learned to live with—especially after the extreme inequity we once had.

What really matters now—more than everything being absolutely equal, more than either my husband or me "striking it rich"—is that John is home before Maya's bedtime almost every night now to join the pileup on her bed, and that we took our first real family vacation last December. This is the essence of what I longed for during those bleak, angry months of my daughter's first two years. It was a desire almost embarrassing in its simplicity, yet one so strong that, in one of the greatest paradoxes of my marriage, it might have torn my husband and me apart: the desire to love and be loved, with reciprocity and conviction, with fairness and respect; the desire to capture that elusive animal we all grow up believing marriage is, and never stop wanting it to be.

Daddy Dearest

What Happens When He Does *More* Than His Half?

Laurie Abraham

"The friends, dolly, *two dollies . . . trot old jo, trot old jo, best horse country ohhh. . . .*" The chattering travels from her crib down the short hall to our bed. The light is still gray, too early to tell whether the day holds clouds or sun, though maybe I could get a read on the weather if my husband didn't insist on pulling the bedroom curtains closed every night. Ankles throbbing, wrists—"bone tired" is such an apt cliché. Rolling onto my stomach, I pull the pillow over my head and breathe musty sheets—I wish I could get this smell out; I want my sheets to smell like a fabric softener from my childhood, the one our neighbors used but my mother didn't think was necessary—but wait. Is my husband stirring? Has he heard? Of course he's heard. He never doesn't hear. Tim is the fox of our house, ears always pricked, eyes always darting, nose twitching for baby sounds, baby movements, baby scents. I have to act quickly if I'm going to beat him into her room: "Good morning, Edie! Hello, my darling girl. How was your sleep?" But maybe this morning he's exhausted, too; maybe he's going to stay in our musty cave for a while. No, no, he's turning over, he's going. I have to get moving. Now. We roll to our respective sides and jump up.

"I want to go first," I say as we jostle against each other in the narrow hall.

"Let's go together," he says.

"OK."

I don't always agree to this mutual good morning, and he doesn't either: "I didn't see her yesterday," he'll say. "OK, go ahead," I'll answer, after weighing his claim. And sometimes he lets me go first, too, after doing the same.

Today is a Sunday; the stakes are higher for me on weekdays, since I work full-time. Tim does, too, and we come closer to splitting the care of our twenty-month-old daughter fifty-fifty than any other parents I know: I spend the mornings with her, from about 7:00 to 9:30, when our baby-sitter comes, and he takes the late afternoons, until I return home at 7:00 and take over for the next hour and a half. Except that my time is increasingly overlapping with Tim's. He's leaving for work later and later, so he's around to "chase, chase Daddy, chase" most of the morning. When I come home in the evenings, he doesn't disappear. Not that I really want him to: It's good for us to be together as a family.

Today we're going on an outing, we three. I'm nervous, because I made the plan. Tim usually decides where we're going. "Do you have anything you want to do this weekend?" he'll ask early on a Friday. "Uh, I haven't really thought—" "Because I have three options," he'll say. What's making me particularly skittery today is that I haven't figured out when we're leaving, and Tim, I know, is busy factoring in various departure times and their impact on Edie's nap. I'm factoring, too; I mean, I'm her mother; I want Edie to get a good nap, too, but not with Tim's fervency. "I don't have to go," he had offered, partly, I know, so he could get Edie down at 1:00 P.M. on the nose, and partly because he isn't especially enamored of my plan. We're going to visit some river towns outside the city, with lovely grassy banks, parks. Yes, a couple hours' drive. But Edie likes the car; she can ride a good hour without displaying a twinge of restlessness. The idea is to hook up with my best friend, Lisa, who's considering a move. "You hardly ever see her," I tell Tim, rejecting his bid to stay home. Lisa and I didn't settle on a time to meet, which is what we do—we leave things open until the last minute.

In fact, it will be a while before Lisa even gets out of bed, so I'm going to get bagels for our breakfast. It's a sunny, warm fall day, it turns out, and though every potential moment (every moment, that is, when Edie is awake and I'm not at work) lost with my girl can feel like a blow, I'm pleased to be alone—yet, as always, slightly disconcerted at my relief at getting away. Tim never seems to need a break. I've heard him use a sharp tone with Edie exactly once—and the memory of it still gives me joy. ("Did you hear what I said?" he barked at her near the end of a long drive during which Edie had grown increasingly demanding. "Stop asking for Barney!") For one shining hour, I wasn't the parent who lost her cool. The rest of the way home, I expertly and lovingly soothed a truly miserable Edie, and when Tim pulled up to the door, I outdid myself. "I'll put Edie to bed; just go to a movie," I offered, glowing with magnanimity. *This is why Tim clings to his calm,* I thought. *You feel so right, so righteous, so . . . beyond reproach.*

Today, I'm happy to be alight on the quiet morning street, walking to the bakery where the man will silently but not begrudgingly put the bagels in a brown paper bag, will quietly grunt out the price. In Edie's Saturday music class, the teacher says, "Tim and Laurie are my most loyal parents." Or maybe he just thinks we're weird. We're the only parents who both accompany our child. I imagine the other fathers at home contentedly munching bacon and reading the paper.

"Cowboys, watch the cowboys," Edie is screeching when I return. She is wearing only a purple cotton T-shirt, a diaper, and scuffed white baby shoes. "Read that, read that," she says, pushing *Winnie the Pooh and the Pebble Hunt* into my hands. Her eyes are large and beseeching, darkly beautiful. People notice her eyes: the steadiness, almost stubbornness, of her gaze; the way she pleads with them or opens them exaggeratedly wide, tilting up her chin, mimicking adults. Her eyes crinkle and squeeze shut when she's hugging the tiny plastic boy she's named Ricardo; they flutter as she puts her mouth on yours.

I set down my bag of bagels and gather Edie on my lap. "Are you going to have any clean blankets for her?" Tim asks before I can read a word. When you're truly sharing parenting, no arena is too small in which to assert your will. And it's an intricate matter, our positions on the cleanliless of baby blankets, one of which (there are five of them) Edie must at all times have available for sucking. I insist that these scraps of flannel be soaked in stain remover before they're washed so that they're not permanently blotched yellow and brown. This process takes about eight hours, which means there are times when the blanket Edie's clinging to is relatively dirty but I don't have a replacement ready. (I do the laundry because I'm particular about it, obviously, and feel that it would be unfair to ask Tim to adopt my methods.) Tim cares more about the cleanliness of the blanket Edie is holding at any one time—germs scare him—and so would wash them constantly. "But how can she get sick from her own saliva?" I ask. "Who cares about permanent stains?" he replies.

As we charge and countercharge, I feel myself putting my arm around Edie's waist, blocking out Tim. *She's mine,* I think. Does he notice? I drop my arm. *Ridiculous, Laurie, you're being ridiculous.* Tim and Edie are talking about the cowboys again (how did that happen?), who've yodeled their way into my girl's heart via a video. Should I be jealous, aggravated at Tim for pulling her in his direction? Edie and I were reading, after all. Or she was thumbing through the few heavy cardboard pages. That's how she reads. "Horsey ride," she commands. She doesn't want to wait until after breakfast, as we'd urged. She's on the floor now, almost jumping up and down in her eagerness to get to that mechanical horse outside the deli. "OK, OK," Tim says. "We'll go on the horsey first." That's a departure from our usual informal system: We'd already told her it was time for breakfast, and we try to stick with the plan, rather than immediately acquiescing to her desires. But, really, who cares which comes first? I don't want every interaction in her life to follow the same template: task, reward, task, reward.

"You can fix her breakfast while we're gone," Tim tells me. "Sure, I'll dump the cereal in the bowl," I mutter. He orchestrates our every move. "Daddy will take you now," he says, addressing her. "Or Daddy and Mommy," he quickly adds, thinking that though I've said I want some time to write this morning, my snapping at him about the cereal might mean I want to come with them. No, no, no, I don't. I have to get going on this essay, only the second piece of any length I've taken on since Edie was born. I would never say I enjoy writing like I enjoy my job as an editor—it's fun to kibbitz with writers, brainstorm ideas for future pieces, be the boss. But in its elusiveness, its difficulty, its opportunity for discovery, writing is infinitely more absorbing. When it's working, it's a physical thing, a glorious loss of self-consciousness that I can only compare to two other experiences in my life: having orgasms and playing high school basketball.

In the Colette biography I'm reading, the author, Judith Thurman, at one point drops her omniscient narrator voice to say how difficult, if not impossible, it is to write and mother at the same time. Thurman is clearly talking about herself here—she has one daughter, who was born as she started researching the Colette book and had celebrated her tenth birthday by the time she finished. Thurman's aside, coming as it does in the midst of a section about Colette's shocking abandonment of her own daughter—she shipped the girl off to the country to be cared for by a German nanny and never looked back—is chilling. Chilling, because Thurman doesn't relegate Colette to the category of "other"; she doesn't treat her acts as singularly evil, beyond recognition to living, breathing mothers—or at least living, breathing writer-mothers. So how can I, of all people, do both well?

Edie howls, absolutely howls, when Tim tells her I'm not coming. I want to come, I do. Should I? But I must try to carve out some time to write. Tim picks her up. "It's Daddy time, Daddy time," he says over her protests. Guilt, a tugging toward her, an urge to stanch the tears. Yes, but also greedy delight that she wants me. Not that in general she doesn't slightly favor me; she does. I don't know what I'd do if the situation were reversed. I don't know what I will do, because surely it will happen when she's Oedipal, if not long before, because she is no less bonded to him than to me. An old friend told me that her passive relinquishing of the primary caretaker role to her husband (she hadn't even been sure she wanted children, but her husband knew he did; by the time she was twenty-five they had two, and well, he just stepped in) almost destroyed her. Too many cultural imperatives ignored; each time her little boy or girl ran to their daddy for comfort, asked him to give the bath, it chipped away at her self-worth. What kind of woman was she? It's one thing to believe that children aren't necessary for a woman to lead a happy and fruitful life, as I adamantly do; it's another for a woman to have children and to refuse, or fail to be granted, the prerogatives of motherhood.

"Your position is secure," my shrink tells me in strangely appropriate martial language. Unlike my friend, I never let my husband take over everything, though he would, and sometimes it can take monumental energy to resist him, to keep "sharing" the power. *The power?* Before Edie was born, I was just worried he wouldn't share the work. I thought I wanted a child, unlike my friend, but I never had baby lust. I was thrumming with ambivalence, worried about, alternately, cheating my child and cheating my work, myself. During my pregnancy I practically made Tim sign a contract to split the parenting exactly in half. I'd heard about too many husbands who'd promised to distribute the burden equally, but then somehow didn't. From reading I'd done, I knew that studies of "co-parenting," as it's called, suggested I had about as much chance as any woman of getting my due: Tim and I earned about the same amount of money; he was going to take paternity leave for a few months after I went back to work (the key to this apparently being that men who are exclusively responsible for their babies for a time are more likely to become true parenting partners); and his office was closer to home than mine, meaning that even once we had a baby-sitter, he'd be the one to schlep her to doctor's appointments, come home if there was a problem, and so forth. But I didn't expect to love Edie as passionately as I do. And now I wonder: Is hierachy *necessary* for peace at home, as well as at work? Are we destined to compete—in my mind, if not in Tim's—for the next eighteen years? "Three is a very hard number; someone's always on the outside," my therapist says. "Have another child." He's joking but he's not.

They're back from the horsey, and we are both being careful, trying to adore Edie as a team. As I spoon cereal into her mouth—and we snatch bites of our bagels—he brings up Micalah, a baby in singing class. My daughter loves musical names, the curious, delicious sound of new words in general, which is a gift to me. Here, Tim, here's a gift for you, my husband, not her father: I tell him a story about my sports-addled mother, and we laugh about her together. My mother's boundless passion for football and basketball is pretty funny, but following the predictable in-law dynamic, I normally don't encourage Tim to poke fun, even gently, at my mother. Three is a hard number. "Ready, ready," Edie is saying. It's a little after ten, and Lisa hasn't called. "I'm ready, too, but we're going on Lisa-time," Tim says. "Fuck you," I say quietly. Edie is saying she's "ready" to go outside, as Tim knows, not that she's itching to go on our trip.

We decide to take Edie to the park. Tim will go first while I shower; then we'll meet and switch. This is a rare opportunity to wash and dry my hair straight, how I like it, I remind myself as they leave. I don't have to race to get done, like I do on those mornings when Edie is standing staring dumbstruck at me on the threshold of the bathroom, blanket hanging from her mouth. "Hi, Edie," I say over the roar of the dryer—buying time, straining to engage her, give me a few more minutes and my hair will be done. I only wash my hair twice a week these days, but now I deeply understand those short, perky mama-dos. I still hate them, though. So instead, I stand nearly naked—I strip off my robe, I get so sweaty—yanking at my hair with the brush.

This morning, I dry and dry and dry. I'm drying so long, I'm baking my scalp, my brain. No moisture left anywhere. Then how come I feel like crying? I lean toward the mirror and note the tiny lines around my eyes.

Minutes later, approaching the park, I see Edie toddling around the blacktop in her pink-and-white-checked sun hat. There is no one in my life whom I've ever been so grateful to escape and so grateful to see—moment to moment, day in, day out. When I push through the heavy iron gate, Edie breaks into a smile. "Mommy!" She grabs my hand. "Did Lisa call?" Tim asks. I shake my head no, and he leaves it at that. "Walk with Mommy. Walk with Mommy," Edie says. Tim follows about twenty paces behind as she pulls me about. "Do you want to swing?" I ask. I lift her into the swing, give her a push. Tim comes up beside us. "Remember the Band-Aid on the swing that time?" he asks her.

She doesn't respond, and I'm glad. Does Tim do this on purpose, try to carve out a space for them that doesn't include me? "I see your husband in the park all the time with Edie," says Abby, stopping me on the street. Hmm . . . She'd been in my new-mothers group, with her baby daughter, and I'm sure she remembers how agitated I got when my fellow mothers admitted they didn't feel they could ask their husbands for more help. The final straw had come when a fortyish woman related how she'd acquiesced to her husband's demand that she not return to work. She liked her job, he hated his, but she was going to quit, she told us, because her husband believed babies should be with their mothers. I looked around the group to see if anyone else felt like screaming, "This is the new millennium, for Christ's sakes! What are you doing?" All I saw was mildness, we're-all-in-this-together capitulation. Unable to hide my frustration, I sputtered something about how, while I understood that traditional roles were sometimes what we actually wanted, if we didn't, we *could* resist. To my amazement, nobody seconded me, and before I knew it we'd resumed talking about the mechanics of breast-feeding and the proper consistency of baby shit. "We are for the most part more lonely when we go abroad among men than when we stay in our chambers," Thoreau said.

"Bye-bye, Edie," Tim says, waving to her in the swing. It's the changing of the guard. Edie doesn't return his wave, and when he turns and walks off, I can see the dejection in his sagging shoulders. But, Tim, you should know her eyes followed you until you were out of sight.

Back and forth, back and forth Edie swings, and time blurs. We move to the ground, where Edie arranges her hat, a leaf, and her blanket, all very deliberate. "That's better," she announces, before starting all over again, seeking some Platonic order. One of my favorite parts of being Edie's mother is watching her get lost in her play. And I'm good at not intruding, not requiring her to see me, include me. I've become a devotee of the renowned British child analyst D. W. Winnicott, who wrote about how babies develop "false selves" when they must regularly "react" to (or manage) their mothers' moods. "[T]here is not sufficient ego-strength for there to be a reaction without a loss of identity," he wrote. Indeed, in my house, I find myself falling back when Tim moves forward—which he does so much more forcefully and regularly than I—both because I can't match his intensity and because I don't want to overwhelm Edie. I worry about interfering with the developmental project of knowing her own desires, as Winnicott would have it. Of her finding her authentic self.

We return home in the stroller at a little after eleven. Lisa has called, Tim informs me as I walk in. "What should we do?" I immediately ask. "When should we leave?"

Why am I asking him? I think as soon as the question is out of my mouth. *Why can't I figure this out on my own? I can take into account Edie's nap and lunch schedule—I'm a grown-up.* Tim is unusually impassive: This trip was my deal, and he's leaving it in my hands. Except there is watching in his cool demeanor. This man watches me make bottles (he worries that too much cow's milk will leave her congested, too much soy will hinder her digestion); he scrubs sippy cups I've already cleaned; in the beginning, in those eight long months (yes, eight) when Edie was nearly inconsolable due to gastric upset, colic—essentially a tautology for "cries all the time"—or just general unhappiness at being thrust into this world, he advised me on how to hold her, how to quiet her. He's sure that I (or perhaps our baby-sitter) has done something "wrong" vis-à-vis the application of Desitin whenever she gets a rash. He tries to stop judging, but I feel his eyes.

I flop into an armchair in the living room, stewing in indecision, knowing I should simply declare when we're leaving and move into action, but the more I tell myself to take command, the more paralyzed I become. Let's see, we could wait to give her lunch and then leave around 12:30, which would be good because she'd probably fall asleep quickly in the car and get a decent nap. But she won't be hungry now, because she ate breakfast late, so maybe we should just leave now and have lunch when we meet Lisa—a picnic together would be nice—but what if she stays awake till the end of the trip and only gets half a nap? Well, she could sleep in her stroller . . . but she may not fall asleep again, and then she'll probably be fussy, easily inflamed. And I'll be blamed, subtly, silently, and even if I'm not, I'll still feel guilty. Maybe I should just call Lisa back and tell her we can't go. That would eliminate the potential for uncomfortable moments, keep the calm—the boring, deadly calm. No way. I *want* to go on this trip! *Do* I want to go on this trip? "When should we leave?" I wail. "Neither is perfect," Tim responds. "I'm not looking for perfect," I spit.

But I am looking for perfect, just like him. I'm like a kidnapping victim who's absorbed the values of her captors. Speaking of kidnapping, a friend of mine, the only woman I know whose relationship with her husband and child is comparable to mine, tells me she finds herself "kidnapping" her daughter to get some time with her; a half hour or so before her spouse is scheduled to arrive home from his (low-pressure) job, she spirits the girl away to a craft store. "Where have you been?" he demands when they get back. "Oh, nowhere exciting," she says casually.

This same friend also read her husband's diary, which is reprehensible, undoubtedly, but more reprehensible was what he'd written: that he was a "better" parent than she. It takes my breath away. The truth is, I don't really think Tim believes that, even deep down. Oh, sometimes he thinks he's better, but not in any all-encompassing kind of way. In fact, he acknowledges that he's overbearing; he's not proud of it. If only I could be more generous. If only I could remember that Tim's efforts to regulate Edie's existence aren't a challenge to me but a measure of his own struggles, the porousness of the boundaries in his family and the resulting narcissistic insult he suffers when he can't keep peace among those he loves. To this day, he avoids telling his mother bad news for fear she'll be consumed by his pain. As he "controlled" her—as he imagined he could prevent her suffering—he labors to control the most unpredictable and frustrating of beings, a baby, a toddler. Edie.

And what about me? Why do I so insistently see Tim as an adversary? I obviously believe that the explanation is in part beyond our little family—there simply aren't models for sharing the work and the power and the love of parenting. But I also bring my own messy platter of experience to the table. And pondering that, I'm not sure I should be worrying about intruding on my daughter, in the Winnicottian sense. Maybe letting Edie be is Tim's work as a parent, while mine is to devour my girl. Because I probably can't do it, not in the menacing sense of that word. My mother, who lives in the Midwest, once said to me sadly but not accusingly, "I was so good at teaching you girls to be independent, to go your own way, and now look what I've got, one daughter in New York and one in L.A."

Like mother, like daughter. It comes naturally to me to give my daughter room, to back off, and there is a fine line between giving a child enough room and too much. Because what is too much but abandonment? The truth is—and I don't think I'm deceiving myself here—I haven't come anywhere close to emotionally abandoning Edie. (Neither, for that matter, is Tim in danger of consuming her.) But in the complicated way fear and longing express themselves, I wonder if my competitive feelings toward Tim aren't heightened by the fact that, first, I doubt I'll ever feel entitled to love her with the same heedlessness that he does and that, second, in my assiduousness about giving her space, I'll hold her so lightly that she'll abandon me. Like mother, like daughter.

All this drama goes on in my head, usually beyond articulation, even to myself. It's good that Tim said that word, "perfect," I realize now, because it reminds me there is no such thing. And it pisses me off that he expects perfection, which is galvanizing. Anger is a reflex for me—too much of one, I know, but there it is. And so, we'll leave now to meet Lisa. We'll risk it. And that's what it feels like, that I'm taking a risk, daring to cheat the nap gods, who may show their wrath in Edie's prickliness, Tim's censoriousness, my own guilty heart. "Let's go," I say. I scoop Edie up and kiss her, on the mouth.

Crossing the Line in the Sand

How Mad Can Mother Get?

Elissa Schappell

N THE PHONE I tell my mother about the essay I am working on.

"You're writing about anger?" my mother says with surprise.

"Well—yes," I say. "About, you know, my anger, and how can you teach your kids to express anger constructively, when you yourself never learned how to."

"What do you mean?" she says. "You weren't an angry child."

There's this pause. Sickening as it is, my mother and I rarely argue or fight—and even then it's a war of kid gloves, not boxing gloves, all politeness and barely raised voices. (If you supposedly love someone, you don't hurt their feelings.) When I was a child, my mother would, when put out with me, yank me not so gently by the arm, or—far worse—torture me with a lengthy discussion of my crime, and our feelings. She didn't yell, and never hit. I don't remember ever being afraid of my mother.

Nor can I remember my mother and father having a real fight, ever. In terms of my sister and me, my father got mad the way fathers, historically, are permitted to: He'd yell some, shake his fist, and on very rare occasions spank. Once I got slapped across the face for insulting my mother, but only once. I can count on one hand the occasions on which my father's anger seemed excessive, or frightened me.

For the most part, my family didn't do anger in the raging, rampaging, veins-bursting-in-the-neck way. My family stopped anger in its tracks. We drowned it in cocktails, or ate it with chocolate frosting, or left the room and let it starve.

. . .

"I could get pretty mad," I tell my mother on the phone, feeling my chest start to tighten in defense of my girl-self's anger.

"About what?" my mother asks.

She has a point. Even now, I can't truly pinpoint the source of my childhood anger. Clearly, I was put together with different parts than my parents. I was high-strung and overly sensitive—especially about being taken seriously, which is hard when you're under five feet tall and your nickname is Pip.

"I don't remember you being *that* angry," my mother says, but what I hear is, *Oh, come now. You're exaggerating.*

"Well, I was angry," I say. "I was angry a lot."

I want to hurt her a little.

"I threw a high-heeled shoe at Rob's head in a French restaurant," I say.

". . . When?" she says, finally.

"It was early in our marriage. I was in my twenties. Lots of stuff happened, actually. Some of it much worse than that."

"Really?" she says, but I can tell she does not want or need to hear one more thing. "I'm sorry to hear that, honey. You seem just fine to me."

"It's good I found a great shrink," I say, thinking, *Blessed is more like it.* Over many years, Dr. B., my therapist, has helped me understand that I'm entitled to my anger and to express it, but not to slap a man across the face or rip off all his shirt buttons simply because he annoyed me.

"I agree," my mother says, the relief palpable in her voice. "Dr. B. sounds wonderful."

"She is."

And that's that. We are in agreement on something, so we can stop. Nothing has been lost. The key is to keep the peace.

. . .

What I don't tell my mother, then, is that the reason I went back to my therapist in my early thirties, after stopping for a time, wasn't depression, but a fear of losing control of my anger. I was humiliated by my behavior; it shamed me and made me feel guilty (for now, as in childhood, what did I really have to be angry about?). I was concerned because my husband, Rob, and I were thinking about having a child, despite the fact that I'd always considered babies shrieking menaces—glorified larvae—and children irrational, needy, unpredictable, and narcissistic (much like myself, I suppose). And if and when we did have this child, I didn't want to be a bad mother. I wanted to be *my* mother—safe, protective, rational, calm—but (and here's the catch) without giving up *all* my anger, for if it sometimes scared and shamed me, it also fueled me: my drive, my ambition, my work. It was a fundamental part of who I was, and I didn't want to bury it completely—only to tame it. I had horrible fantasies of shaking my children until their teeth fell out, yanking their limbs out of their sockets, burning them with cigarettes, or smacking them around. I was terrified of what my anger might make me capable of.

. . .

Now, seven years later, I am mother to two very cool, very wonderful children: Isadora, six, and Miles, three. So far, neither has felt the need to flee from me, that I know of. There has been, so far, no fodder for an afterschool TV special.

Still, every day I feel as if I have to draw a line in the sand, a line I have to promise myself not to cross. Depending on the day's psychic weather—my mood's tide—the line can fade or move slightly, only to re-form again and again. For example: Some days it seems all I do is yell at my kids, then apologize for yelling at them, then feel guilty for being such a lousy mother, then start to feel resentful about being made to feel like a bad mother. I mean, how crappy of a mother am I really? It isn't like they exist on a diet of Happy Meals and Ho-Hos. I don't knock them around in public or humiliate them by screaming, *If you don't stop crying, I am going to really give you something to cry about!* I read them books and play pretend, I make sure they have mittens or some such facsimile in the winter, and I insist we eat dinner together as a family. I tell them they are loved so often they sometimes roll their eyes.

And yet, as I wash my face some mornings, I already feel overwhelmed; not even dressed, I am already pulling myself back from that line. I have a novel under contract, long overdue; I need to add eight more books to a monthly book review column I write, revise an essay for a collection I've been asked to contribute to, and, oh yeah, dress the kids appropriately while allowing for their individuality (read: fairy wings and lion suits) and try to keep Miles from undressing and tying another balloon string around his penis before we can get out the door. I must make breakfast, pack lunches, collect homework, hunt for library books eventually discovered in the fireplace, walk kids to school without resorting to dragging on collars, avoid eye contact with the terminally chirpy Class Mother who will press me to bake peanut-butter-free cupcakes or chaperone the upcoming field trip to a turkey farm.

Most days, Rob is there to help me with all this. Other days—like today—he has his own deadline. So today, after dropping off Isadora, I will carry Miles to preschool—if necessary, upside down. Then I will coordinate his pickup and play date with Nicole, our precious and most adored baby-sitter, without whom my life would skid into a ditch and explode. Next I will ride my bike to my studio, flipping off the car that cuts me off, nearly dropping my messenger bag which contains my laptop, and work frantically (Novel or essay? Flip a coin.) for a few hours. Just as I get into a groove (Hey, I finally seem to be writing in English—as though it were my first language!), I will notice the time, briefly panic, and race out to pick up Isadora and take her to tumbling class, where, watching her learn forward rolls on the balance beam, it will occur to me that I never added those books to my column. Debating what to do if I lose my job—shepherd? evangelist preacher?—I will drag my by now worn-down daughter into the store for juice boxes and pasta bunnies, giving in to her request for ice cream studded with what appear to be army men. Greeting us at home is Miles, who has apparently markered Japanese swearwords all over his naked body. Indefatigable Nicole will look ready to quit. I will give her a bottle of wine and make her swear to come back tomorrow.

The light on my answering machine flashes, ten messages. Can't I just push the erase button? Rob is working downstairs, checking online for anthrax updates and putting out any fires flaring at *Tin House,* the literary magazine he's co-founder and editor of. As I watch the kids run out to dig for beetles in the dirt with what appear to be fish forks from the family silver service, my head pounds. I am never going to finish this novel. The publisher is going to ask for the money back, and I will have to say, *Ha-ha, I have spent it all on tinfoil shoes and applesauce!* The only solution is to put "free kitten" signs around my children's necks and plop them in a box on the curb.

I will take deep breaths, remember that I'm in control, that I'm *allowed* to be mad but I can also *choose not to* get angry. So minutes later, when the kids come inside and find me on the phone (not returning calls but actually stealing a moment to talk to a real friend) and begin to pull on my sweater and whine, I will recall, somewhat sheepishly, anger-management strategies pulled out of magazines and parenting books, and I will count, make myself smile, whisper that I'll be right with them. I will hold myself in check, and eventually they will run off and leave me to finish my call. This night, I will be able to push my anger back into its cage with the stick of hard-earned, well-managed patience.

But a couple of nights later—I am steaming artichokes and laying out chicken nugget stars and guitars—it creeps back out. Miles has pinched Isadora's Triscuit and, with charming malevolence, slowly licked it top to bottom.

Isadora screams.

"Miles, stop licking your sister's food!" I scold. *Keep calm,* I think.

Isadora grabs the cracker and smashes it into his face.

"It's my cracker!" Miles yells, grabbing back what's left of it.

I slam down the cookie tray, the chicken nuggets leaping as if alive. I cannot bear it when they hurt each other. "Stop it!" I say, grabbing Isadora by the shoulder, and, to Miles, "No taking Izzy's food—"

"But, Mommy—"

"Do you understand? Jesus!" I'm yelling now.

These days, not only does it seem as though I am constantly shrieking in frustration, I am boggled by the banality of what I am yelling about. *Don't hug the cat that way! No, you can't have beef jerky for breakfast! Did I hear a thank-you?! Barbie's head doesn't go on Ken's body! Get up! Sit down! Are you trying to kill me?! Do you want my head to explode?! And who do you suppose is going to clean it all up! Huh? Don't look at me, pal!*

But when they refuse to hear me, when they refuse to turn off the TV in favor of a painting project or building with Legos, the effort to keep from screaming "Barney is Satan!!" is sometimes beyond me. I ought to wear one of those bracelets that say WWMBD on them. *What would Mrs. Brady do?*

The first thing, of course, would be to sell a kidney so I could afford my very own live-in Alice, who would not only run our house like a fancy hotel, but also lovingly dress and deliver Isadora and Miles to school on time, freeing us from rumors that we're carney folks living out of tents by the East River. At school she would greet the Class Mother and happily agree to fashion a three-foot statue of the school mascot out of ladyfingers, then accompany the entire first grade to an outing at the local prison. After school, she'd provide a tasty snack not concocted in a lab and help them with homework; then they'd all construct a baking soda volcano.

Thus, when Mr. Brady came home, I would not be tired and stressed, having worked, bathed, perhaps had coffee with a friend, and maybe even changed the leather pants (a mother's best friend, as they wipe clean) I've been wearing for three days . . . so I'd be able to see him not as the bastard who got me into this mess, but as my lover whom I am thrilled to have home again. I would be capable of sparks, of lively flirty adult conversation, and—over a sumptuous turkey-frank-free dinner—I might even run my stockinged foot up the back of his calf, causing him to wonder if I am truly his wife or, in fact, the robot love slave he asked Santa for.

. . .

Despite the noisy cracker-licking debacle, Rob, unshaven and bleary-eyed, comes up from his basement office, where he has spent the day reading page proofs. So much for the Brady fantasy.

Though he looks tired and cranky, I know he's not likely to lose his head, except as a somewhat understandable (at least to me) response to an unbearable situation. *Daddy broke the kitchen window with a flying fork/threw the chicken carcass off the table and into the dishwasher because, Isadora, you again swore you'd never read when you plainly can, upset your milk, and declared the wild rice yucky; and, Miles, you jumped out of your chair for the thirteenth time, raspberried your mother, and, finally, stuck the filthy spoon you'd artistically spackled with modeling clay into your juice.*

With me, in contrast, so often what sets off my anger is pure stress and fatigue. Likewise, sometimes I am just too damned tired or lazy to discipline my children calmly and effectively (unless, of course, they are being unlawful or are in danger of, say, *losing an eye*). But my exhaustion is coupled with my guilt that I am one of the lucky ones. I shouldn't complain. I have money (usually), a partner (always), and child care (generally when I want it). Unlike so many husbands, mine is a true partner; I can always tag him to take over when I am about to grab the folding chair. My kids are happy, safe, and healthy, and I get to do the work I want, more or less. How many people can say that? I am rich beyond words.

And yet, where once seeing a mother dragging a kid down the street like a wildebeest would have made me shake my head in horror, I now sigh in sympathy—for the *mother,* not the child. I can relate to the pure adrenaline—and fireman's carry—it sometimes takes just to get your kids from point A to point B.

. . .

Have I said yet that I've never hit my children? I have not. What I have done: grabbed their wrists and yanked their arms. Dressed them roughly and pushed them out the door. Let the brush catch and pull their hair when they squirmed. On occasion, let them fall when I could have caught them. Thrown things—near them, but not—never—at them. I have swatted Miles's bottom (somehow, I don't really consider this hitting), hard enough so that he turned to me, hurt and surprised.

I can live with this. I can even live with the fact that someday I might spank them, if they deserve it and I am under control. The key is control. Which is why I find it harder to live with the experience I had not so long ago, one that has—I think—changed the way my children look at me, if not the way I look at myself.

On this night, my husband was out seeing a band. The kids and I had dinner at a friend's, so we segued into our bedtime routine later than usual. They were coming down from spending time in a house with different rules: people eat chocolate bars; people jump from the sofa to the chairs playing hot lava and alligators; no one says *please* or *thank you*.

Reentry was hell.

It was all I could do to get them into their pajamas without a whip and a shoehorn. Mouths had to be pried open to brush teeth. They battled bare-fannied to see who could slide onto the john first. A bloom of wet toilet paper spread out on the floor like a squashed corsage.

Finally, they toddle off toward their room. "Get into bed," I call out to them from the bathroom, where I'm on hands and knees cleaning up the mess. "Go to sleep, and have pleasant dreams." *Goddamnit,* I add, sotto voce.

As I finish rinsing the sink, I realize it's actually quiet. But when I enter their room, they scream with laughter and scurry up to the top bunk. Playing Pirate Ship.

"Guys," I say. *They're just wound up,* I think, *having a little fun.* "Come on, scallywags."

Up in the crow's nest, Isadora accidentally elbows her glass of water off the top bunk, showering the bean bag chair, magazines, paint sets, puzzle pieces.

"Dammit!" I yell.

Isadora bites her lip.

I count to three again, trying to chew my anger into swallowable bits. "I know it was an accident," I manage. Even as I praise myself for being so generous, it isn't lost on me that permitting a child to have an open container in bed is not a stellar practice. And whose fault was it that their floor was such a colossal mess?

Still.

Isadora looks peeved, then upset. She hates doing anything wrong; it embarrasses her, which in turn makes her bratty. Of course, I relate to this, but I still can't stand it.

She stares at me, and for a moment I am afraid she's going to start bawling or pitch a fit. When Isadora was small I was determined to teach her it's okay for girls to get mad—that it's normal, human, and not gender-specific. Together, with the assistance of a few well-chosen "How to care for and maintain your child" manuals, Isadora and I learned the language of anger. And while it seems goofy and makes me feel self-conscious to hear myself parroting, *Use your words to tell me why you are angry. It's fine to be angry, it's good to express your anger, anger is poison, don't swallow it* . . . well, embarrassing or not, this actually works for us. Admittedly, she is better at it than I.

"I am allowed to be angry about the water spilling without being angry at you," I say now.

She is visibly relieved.

"Jesus!" I can't help adding.

I go get a towel and mop up the water. "Now, in your bunks, pirates," I say. "Please don't make me tell you again, mateys."

I glance at my watch: 9:30. Already 9:30. And I still have work I want to do tonight. No, *ought* to do—because clearly the message from my control tower is, *Darling, relax! Recline! You've got magazines on the sofa, Halloween candy in the freezer, Independent Film Channel on TV!*

Wringing out the towel in the bathroom sink, I look at myself in the mirror. *Count to ten, ha-ha. I ought to make 'em walk the plank. Yo-ho-ho, I want a bottle of rum.* Anger makes me look old. My young handsome husband is out listening to music, talking with our friends, childless friends, so the conversation is perhaps topical! Philosophical! Any opical! Not that he doesn't deserve it, but still, here I am in the domestic wasteland turning more and more shrewish by the moment.

Isadora and Miles are giggling over a book in the top bunk now when I return. It is as though I don't even exist. I'm in no mood to count to ten. I am inching closer to the line. "What did I tell you?" I say, loud but not quite a yell yet. "Get in bed, *now*!"

Miles grins. He picks up the book they're reading and, like a midget supervillain in a Bond movie, turns and hurls it at my face, clocking me, with great accuracy, right on the brow bone.

Flashbulb of agony. Brought to my knees, I scream like the freaking Cyclops.

Then, for a moment, I just stand there, holding my eye. Miles is staring down at me, smiling. Amused. Waiting to see what I will do next. He doesn't know that the line of acceptable/unacceptable behavior—*my* line—has just been kicked into invisibility.

"My God, you hit me in the face!" I scream. *"What the hell is wrong with you?"*

My blood, spiked with stress, rage, and guilt, surges in my veins, and I feel almost dizzy. In a fury, I jump up on the ladder and make to grab Miles around the throat. He and Isadora both skitter backward, bolting to the wall to get out of my reach. Now they know: I can see it in their faces. I am going to take Miles down, or better, take both of them down, and I can't wait. I want to hurt him. An otherworldly bellow of hell and doom swells in my gut, and a terrible sound rises up out of me, as though this ugliness has been boiling in my bowels for years. I roar at them.

In slow motion, I watch my children's faces draw into masks of fear and shock. Miles yelps. Isadora presses her face into the crook of her arm. "I'm scared!" she cries, her voice breaking.

"Good!" I scream, meaning it. "I'm *glad* you're scared! You *should* be scared!"

But I am scared, too—scared of hurting my children, of not being able to protect them from myself. Scared of how much I both love them and hate them in this moment.

Miles grabs hold of Isadora, and she throws her arms around him and pulls him close, sheltering him with her body. He shakes and sobs. "Mommy," Isadora whimpers, her face wet with tears. "Please stop. Please. You're scaring us."

Mommy, please stop!

My daughter's pleading is like taking a knife to an elevator cable, snap! And my rage goes into free fall, leaving this great emptiness, this hollow ring of silence, and all I want, all I *need,* is to morph into a daisy or a doormouse. I want to be impotent and innocent. I want the whole thing never to have happened.

My children tremble and cling to each other on the lifeboat of the upper bunk. *Thank God they have each other.* I step down from the ladder. I can't believe how I am shaking, as if I'm coming down from some thrilling and terrifying high. "Miles," I say. "Isadora." My voice is hoarse and foreign.

They watch me closely. Are my eyes wild, pupils dilated? Is my hair electric?

"You hurt Mommy," I say. "That really really hurt." I can feel the bump rising on the ridge of my brow; my whole eye socket aches. At least there is evidence. I hope it hurts for a while.

"We're sorry, Mommy . . ." Isadora says. Miles says, "Sorry, Mommy." They look at me as if I am a stranger they must be polite to. Neither of them moves, not even to wipe their noses, now running from their crying.

"It's late," I say, finally. "Let's get into bed."

There is a second's hesitation as they turn their backs on me, as though they no longer trust me. And why shouldn't they be suspicious? Miles shinnies down the ladder, keeping an eye on me; Isadora pulls up her knees and slides between her sheets. What are they thinking? I kiss her good night. Her face is hot.

"I am sorry we made you so mad," Isadora says again.

I swallow hard. I feel unworthy of her apology.

In his bunk, Miles lies on top of his blankets, in the baby pose of tummy down, fanny in the air. He lets me cover him with his quilt and hug him, then he rolls on his back and his T-shirt rides up so I can see his smooth white stomach, his navel a delicate whorl where once we connected.

"I love you," I say at the door. Neither of them says a word.

I want to cry. They are so small. How goddamn small are they? It doesn't seem fair that anyone so small should have a mother like me.

It's not like I hit them, I tell myself. *I stopped myself in time, didn't I? Isadora is fine. And Miles has to know there are consequences to his actions, and better me to teach him than somebody else, a sadistic gym teacher, or, God forbid, a cop.*

Upstairs, I pour myself a glass of red wine and sit on the sofa, still shaking. *But still, I lost it. It wasn't what I did, or didn't do, it was what I could have done. And the truth is, it felt so good to scream, so very good. Even now, after all the books, all the therapy.*

After a few minutes, I get up and go downstairs to check on them. They are both fast asleep, fingers of moonlight touching their faces. They are perfect.

And suddenly I have this urge to get into bed with them. I want to curl up around them; I want their arms slung across my face, their windmilling limbs pedaling dream bicycles across my ribs and shins. I want them to beat me up. I want to whisper in their ears, *Mommy loves you. Mommy will never hurt you.* I want to wake them up *now,* letting not another minute pass, so they can see in my face that I mean it when I say, *You are safe. You can trust me. I could never not love you.* I want this for their sakes, but also for mine.

But to wake them or climb into their beds would be intrusive and unfair. I do not deserve, nor do I have, the right to demand their forgiveness.

So instead, I crack the door, letting the hallway light illuminate the corners of their room. I stand outside the door for a minute, then walk away.

And I draw a new line in the sand.

Maternal Bitch

Susan Squire

IN THE HOUSE of my first marriage, my inner Bitch was comatose. She was Tinker Bell without Peter, languishing away in a forgotten drawer, losing wattage by the hour—while I congratulated myself for suppressing her so well. I'd been planning this strategy since I was a suburban teenager with two younger siblings and two parents who didn't get along. Through careful observation of the family dynamic, I'd decided rather sweepingly that if every husband is an infant-in-waiting, every wife is a Bitch-in-waiting. The waiting ceased when they became parents. Motherhood, whatever else it did, sooner or later made the woman feel put upon, which released her bitch, who deprived the man of the lavish attention he secretly needed, which turned him into . . .

This line of reasoning led to an inevitable conclusion: If you avoid motherhood, you avoid activating the Bitch. That was my simple plan. At fourteen, I announced to my father, "I never want to have children." He seemed disturbed by this and reacted defensively, blurting, "That means you're unable to love." It sounded to me like a death sentence, but for the next two decades, my attitude didn't change a whit. I truly did not want children; that is, I did not want to be a Bitch.

The plan worked perfectly—until, in the house of my second marriage, I subverted it, willingly, consciously, recklessly. For the love of Husband B, I broke my vow to avoid maternity. And as I'd suspected long before, it was motherhood, not marriage, that sprung the Bitch.

But first a few words about Husband A. I met him at work. I was twenty-three, just out of college. He was thirty-two, divorced, with custody of two young sons. My aversion to motherhood suited him just fine. On our first date, this being L.A. circa 1974, we dropped acid and went to a transvestite bar. A year or so later we married, a decision that, in retrospect, was made rather casually. Three weeks after our low-key wedding, A scheduled his vasectomy. We went together to the pre-op appointment with the urologist. It had been A's idea, of course—I knew enough about the neuroses of men where their penises were concerned not to propose surgical alteration myself—but to say I was supportive would be an understatement.

The urologist, however, was openly skeptical of my resolve. He seemed more focused on discussing my psyche than on the imminent procedure. I had many childbearing years ahead of me, he said. Did I not foresee even the possibility of changing my mind? I said no. He pressed harder but got nowhere. The vasectomy went smoothly. A had no regrets, and neither did I.

. . .

So the Bitch was comatose in the house of my first marriage, despite my stepsons. I cared about them, they cared about me, we got along—in fact, twenty-five years later, we're still in touch—but I operated at a fond remove from them, like a mildly curious big sister home from college for the summer. Only thirteen years separated me from the older boy (almost as many as separated me from their father), and it was their father who dealt with their daily needs. I'd fill in as A's surrogate when he was out of town, making dinner or checking the kids' homework, but otherwise the time I spent with them was at my convenience. I approached the marriage with a similar attitude of benign indifference. More than once, I wondered if my father had been right after all: Had I chosen to enter this particular family because I was incapable of love and sensed that A and the boys wouldn't demand it? Only much later, after the Bitch made her presence known, would I understand that I had settled into this life not because I couldn't love but because I was afraid to.

. . .

My marriage to A took place during the 1970s and early 1980s, when "open marriage," cocaine, and ludes had replaced "free love" and psychedelics in our social circle. A and I dabbled in these fashions as we'd dabbled in their predecessors. Why not? I had an enviable job, a presentable husband, an appealing house in a canyon high above Beverly Hills, and easy access to the recreational drugs of the moment. But despite my pursuit of pleasure, I wasn't finding much. Again, I was the observer, only it wasn't my parents I was watching now, but a restless young woman pretending to have fun and occasionally remembering to pretend to be someone's wife. I was aware of my chronic detachment but not perturbed by it. I seemed to lack nothing worth having. Specifically, I lacked the Bitch, along with the ticking biological clock that would have sprung her.

Thus, I felt quite safe. After all, I was over thirty now, and she was nowhere to be seen. Meanwhile, I kept myself very, very busy. I indulged in intense flirtations that never exceeded the limits set by Bill and Monica, accumulated major credit card debt feeding my clothes habit, swam laps obsessively at the health club, and, most distracting of all, worked like a maniac. With virtually no domestic responsibilities except those I selected, like cooking for friends (it was A who cleaned the house meticulously, kept us in groceries and lightbulbs, dealt with the kids' schools—and never complained), I could handle my full-time job plus whatever other work I felt like accepting. The marriage took up so little of my energy that sometimes it felt like I wasn't married at all. Inadvertently, A colluded in this masquerade. His expectations of life, conjugal and otherwise, were minimal. His first marriage had been volatile; peace seemed to be what he most wanted from his second. Peace I could give him, if nothing else.

My passion was for my work: that's what felt real to me. Perhaps the workaholic had filled the void meant for the Bitch, though I suspect that the Bitch only concealed herself in workaholic's clothing to slip past my alarm system. Meanwhile, the marriage—remember the marriage?—was entirely too calm, too polite. Too nonmarriage to work. It was a well-run business partnership that happened to include unmemorable sex. The emotional disconnect between A and me was profound. I was very, very well behaved in that first house. Husband B, lucky guy, wouldn't have recognized me.

. . .

A and I split up after a decade. The divorce was as civilized as the marriage had been. We shared the $500 cost of an assembly-line "do-it-yourself" legal process, sold our house in California, split the proceeds to pay off joint debts, split the few pennies left over from that. There was no need to split our friends. We were far too reasonable to force anyone to take sides, and besides, I moved to New York, which nullified the potential for social awkwardness.

My eggs had aged ten years, but still I heard no clock ticking, let alone an alarm ringing. My friends, one by one, heard what I didn't. The married ones got pregnant or consulted fertility specialists; the others went to great lengths to find a partner, or at least some decent seed. My younger sister and her husband conceived a second child soon after my divorce went through. Toward none of these women did I feel a shred of envy. Something more complicated than mere disinterest was going on in me; I was well aware of that. I knew where I was coming from: the house of my childhood, which included its Bitch-in-residence. Mom.

. . .

In that house, the Bitch was pretty much a morning person. My sister and I called her "Mrs. Monday," after the meanie who ran the orphanage in our favorite book about two parentless sisters. Our Mrs. Monday would appear in the kitchen at breakfast, still in her bathrobe, moody as hell. Although we were careful not to spill our cereal or otherwise provoke her, somehow she was provoked anyway. Most days, she was snarling by the time we left for school.

At night, she was different—and worse. Instead of being mean Mrs. Monday, she became a morose and friendless little orphan, albeit one sipping a Canadian Club on the rocks. I suppose she felt abandoned because my workaholic father was rarely home, though I wasn't entirely sure she felt any better when he was around. Anyway, the booze, far from perking her up, sunk her. She became needy beyond my endurance, begging me (as the eldest) not to go to my room or out with a friend because she didn't want to be left alone. Usually I complied; she seemed so lost, so hopeless.

I couldn't even get angry, which would have been preferable to what I actually felt: pity, guilt, and claustrophobia. It's far easier for a kid to fight a snarling parent than a crying one. For one thing, you can snarl back. You can storm out the door with your sister, muttering about Mrs. Monday, but you can't—I couldn't—wage war against this defenseless little girl. She seemed pathetic, and nobody wants a pathetic parent, because where does that leave you? Unprotected at best. And guilty. I struggled with that terrible, irrational child's guilt that insists, "It's all my fault that Mommy's sad."

I was the first to sense that the psychic torture Mom inflicted—on us and on herself—might have little, if anything, to do with us personally. It was mostly about marriage to my father and her domestic role. (She is now, in her seventies, an accomplished and published writer, an adored grandmother, one of my best friends, and living proof that divorce can be a good thing.) This was back in the 1950s and 1960s when, on TV at least, women like my mother were considered the lucky ones, floating through a permanent suburban idyll subsidized by their husbands, who, poor things, slogged through long, high-pressure days at the office, then came home half-dead and sank into their armchairs, expecting to be revived by chirpy wives in pearls and full makeup who plied them with dry martinis, delicious casseroles, and carefully orchestrated playtimes with freshly bathed, well-behaved offspring.

My sister and I, however, knew better. My father was the chirpy one. He wasn't stuck at home with the kids and the station wagon, wondering why he bothered to get a B.A. in English literature from Smith College in order to do nothing much. (I don't know if my mother wondered about this, but I certainly did.) My father was out in the world, having fun and feeling good about himself, or so I surmised—because when he did make an appearance at home, he was never sad or mean or depressed. It was the dad's life I wanted, but being female, the closest I could get to it was to avoid being a mom.

I was still convinced of this in 1976, when I married for the first time. By then the happy homemaker myth (with an early assist from Betty Friedan's *The Feminine Mystique* in 1963) had been exposed as fraudulent. Now it was considered anathema to be stuck at home. Women were supposed to be out in the world with men, earning money. I was all for the career thing—the dad thing. I wasn't against marriage, either. Just motherhood.

. . .

But then, with one marriage and one divorce behind me, I fell in love. Within the first fifteen minutes of meeting the man who would become Husband B, I felt it: a wordless soul-deep entanglement that gripped me and would not let go. There was no hope of detachment. "Will you have babies with me?" he asked, early on. I was stunned to hear myself respond, "Of course." *Of course?* But I wasn't thinking about the Bitch just then; I wasn't thinking at all. I was feeling. Inescapable, irrational, unbounded love. He could have said, "Will you have scorpions with me?" and I would have reacted no differently.

So, at thirty-seven, I got pregnant. Then I got scared. My primary emotions for the next nine months fluctuated between terror and deep ambivalence. When I went into labor at a dinner party, I whispered to a friend as we rushed out for the hospital, "Make it stop." By "it" I didn't mean labor (though I would have gladly skipped that, too) but what it would bring: a baby. The thing that was going to make me mean in the morning, sad at night, and miserable all the time.

For the moment, I felt only panic. The best moment postdelivery wasn't when they handed me the wrapped-up bundle I'd just ejected—I was relieved when the nurse took it away again—but just before they wheeled me to my room, when the two Percocets I'd been given kicked in. So much for "maternal instinct."

. . .

I came home from the hospital two days later in a state of alternating hysteria and catatonia. I knew about the postpartum depression thing and the exhaustion thing, but *this*? Killer waves of incompetence crashing through my body and making me too frantic to even understand what was happening to me? Where was my observer-self when I really needed her? I'd been sucked into an emotional maelstrom I'd created. As a firm believer in worst-possible-scenario thinking so as to feel grateful for anything that fell short of it, I had pictured the initial entry into newborn hell as Dead Woman Walking, on Seconal or something, like Neely in *Valley of the Dolls.* That turned out to be excessively optimistic. The reality was teeth-grinding, like coming down from weeks of being force-fed crystal meth and nothing else with my eyelids pried open with toothpicks the entire time. This tiny, scary baby . . . I didn't know what the fuck I was doing. Husband B, meanwhile, was as clueless as I was, and just as bad at covering it up. This had been a source of hilarity in the ancient prepartum past. (Put the two of us in a hardware store trying to buy the right lightbulb or nail, or at home trying to use them, and we're a Lucy and Ethel routine.) Now it was motive for murder. So much for gut alliances and soul-deep entanglements. Look where unbounded love had gotten me.

I could see now that having a baby is, pardon the understatement, a crisis—at least until it settles down into being just your life. And the last thing I needed during this crisis was my psychic twin. The diapering alone was a challenge neither of us could hope to meet. This live, squalling object was nothing like the plastic doll we practiced on in Lamaze class. I needed B to soothe me, if not show me the way. Was I, as the Mother—God help me—supposed to soothe *him*? Was I supposed to be thrilled that he was trying to master the Pampers Challenge, even though, like me, he was failing? I was not thrilled. I was freaked out. Weren't women supposed to know how to be mothers automatically? But I'd already noticed that I was missing that instinct.

B had, by now, fully regressed to his own level of helplessness, whimpering and fiddling in frustration. The number of mangled yet unsoiled diapers in the shiny new pail was up to four. When B gamely reached for number five, I knew I was about to snap. Not me, actually; it was the Bitch, rattling her cage. At that moment, B got the diaper on. The Bitch was, for now, silenced.

Naturally, I had planned to breast-feed. *Naturally?* I don't think so. I could not get it (I mean *her*—you know, the baby) to suck. In fact, I couldn't get either of my suddenly humongous nipples anywhere near that teensy mouth. I'd had trouble in the hospital, but the nurse had said my milk probably hadn't "come in" yet, keep practicing, babies don't need to eat in the beginning anyway, blah-blah-blah. Now "the beginning" was over. The baby was four days old.

I was sick with worry about this tiny little creature, whose life depended entirely on me. The elusive "maternal instinct" had finally kicked in. I felt engulfed by excruciating waves of love. I was desperate to save her. I had the means on my body, two enormous boobs flopping around, but I couldn't figure out how to use them. I was on the couch, pillows sliding from under my elbows despite my efforts to hold them in place, trying to guide tiny wailing newborn to giant nipple, sobbing. Where was my tumbler of Canadian Club on the rocks?

B took in the scene. I watched him through a curtain of tears, saw his face turn panicky. His eyes flitted back and forth, trying to gauge what exactly was happening. "What's wrong?" he said finally, idiotically. I choked out the tragic news: She was starving to death, and I would die with her because I couldn't stand to live without her. He stared, looking less panicked now and more confused. I was losing it. I had lost it already.

. . .

And then I had it, my first moment of clarity since that labor-inducing dinner party centuries ago, and it wasn't pretty: I'd become my mother at her most forlorn. I was inconsolable yet desperate for consolation, crying and clinging to my firstborn. I flashed on the story my mother had told me about my second day of life. We were in the hospital, surrounded by beaming family members. I was the firstborn of the new generation. The phone rang. My mother, all too rarely the object of so much love and attention, was too busy soaking it in to answer, so my father did. The call was about Uncle Jack, the family patriarch. He'd dropped dead of a heart attack. Everyone, including my father, left immediately. My mother was alone—"abandoned" was the word she used.

But she had me. And for the next twenty-four hours, she said, she wouldn't be parted from me. More than once I heard the story: "I cried and cried. My tears fell on your little head. Thank God you were there. I needed you so much."

Oy. Now, with my own baby, I could not let history repeat itself. I stopped crying. Just like that. In the meantime, B apparently had been having an epiphany of his own. "Why don't I go to the market," he said, "and get some formula?" He seemed quite pleased with himself, enough to add patronizingly, "She doesn't *have* to starve, you know."

"Is that what you call being helpful?" I snarled. "I can't feed her formula!" The Bitch was back to help me fight the good fight. In the most withering tone I could summon, I filled B in on the currently conventional wisdom: Good mothers breast-feed. Bad, lazy ones don't. I threw in some medical factoids for good measure—how breast-feeding protects the baby's immune system, helps the mother heal, and so on.

B waited until I was done. "But isn't some food better than no food?" he said.

Could he be any more annoying? Okay, he was rational, and I was not (that was the annoying part). But guess what? I was no longer hysterical. It occurred to me then that annoyance and helplessness are antithetical. Annoyance, I decided, was preferable and would prevail—and it already was, as I was now yelling at B instead of . . . how did Mom put it? . . . letting my tears fall on the baby's little head. B could take it. He was a big boy. Besides, the Bitch wasn't so bad, not at all. She was, to my shock, good company. She was sassy, feisty, not depressed, and (so far) harmless; B seemed unfazed by her as he headed out to the store.

Fifteen minutes later he returned, clutching a grocery bag and looking smug. From the bag he produced four cans of premixed, liquid formula—precisely the kind no one recommends. "Thanks," I said, "but I—we—don't need it." In B's brief absence, Emily had clamped her mouth on my nipple and was gulping away. Had snapping at B boosted my confidence in some Thelma-and-Louise fuck-it way? Had I snapped off my own despair? Or had it happened by chance, just because I'd moved from the couch to a chair in B's absence and stumbled on a position that worked? Whatever the reason, something was flowing from my body to the baby's.

B watched with fascination and tenderness. And I watched B with love. Which, according to Erich Segal, means never having to say you're sorry, a misguided sentiment that has always irked me. So I said I was sorry. "For what?" B asked. I couldn't help smiling. Maybe I hadn't been as nasty as I'd thought. Or maybe, just maybe, he preferred the Bitch to the sob sister I'd been before she lent me her muscles. Had he known the faux wife I'd been in Marriage A, he'd have traded her for the Bitch, too. Maybe B sensed (being a guy's guy, he would never articulate it) that the anger and frustration that sometimes accompanies deep emotional engagement is a price worth paying. You can't connect without friction. And now there was this baby. More friction. More connection.

Thus the Bitch made her debut. There would be many more appearances, sometimes daily. She roared at B to keep me from doing something worse, like roaring at a little kid not yet equipped to understand that moms, even good ones, sometimes lose it a little so as not to lose it all. B wasn't always as friendly to the Bitch as he'd been that first time, but he got used to her pretty quickly. Generally, once she'd finished her business of protecting me, she vanished, and no one suffered permanent damage. And she's still around, keeping me vital and strong, enabling me—and my daughter—to weather those inevitable working-mom stretches of feeling put upon from "having it all" (as in, *doing* it all). I have my little outbursts, I get cranky and irritable, but I tell her why: bad day at work, maybe, or a fight with a friend. If it's her, if she's been careless or indifferent or uncooperative, or I'm sick of picking up her room, I'll tell her that, too. It doesn't kill her to hear it. Sometimes it pisses her off, and that, I hope, is the worst of it. I know for sure that she doesn't feel sorry for me or find me sad. It's okay if my kid is exposed—courtesy of the Bitch—to my bad moments; in fact, I count on the Bitch to keep me honest and my family informed of my whereabouts.

It's okay, that is, as long as I make it clear to them (and I think I have) that a bad day does not make a bad, or a sad, life. I've learned that while motherhood guarantees quite a few of the former, it does not guarantee the latter; quite the opposite. On that assumption I was way off. And who taught me that?

Thank you, Bitch.

The Origin, Procreation, and Hopes of an Angry Feminist

Natalie Angier

THIS MORNING MY four-year-old daughter, Katherine, donned the mantle of Freud and drew a telling picture of me. She started with the usual details: the wild foam of hair; the hands and feet with each twiglike finger and toe carefully indicated; the belly button; the two boobs with their bull's-eye nipples. But then she added a couple of new elements. She drew big tears dripping from my eyes, and a thought balloon above my head, with another figure inside it, lying prone.

I asked her to explain.

"You're crying because you're so upset about the news," she said. And I was indeed visibly and raucously distressed by what I had been reading in the newspaper—specifically, that our newly anointed tsar, I mean president, planned to reinstate the old Reagan gag rule, forbidding any international family planning organization that receives American aid from so much as lip-synching the word *abortion*.

And the figure in the thought balloon?

"That's President George Bush," said Katherine. "You're wishing that he was dead."

After laughing with surprise, not to mention maternal pride in an offspring's cleverness, I hugged her close and insisted that I didn't want George W. Bush to die; I merely wished that he weren't president. "Your mother is a crank, isn't she?" I said. "Always mad and complaining, right?"

She shrugged against my hug; so what else is new? I hugged her tighter and cooed, "But you're going to be a good little revolutionary, aren't you? A fighter for the cause?" At which point she pushed me away impatiently. She's never been a huggy-kissy kind of child, and besides, she wanted to keep drawing, not yakkety-yakking.

It's true, I'm a crank, by avocation and provocation. I luxuriate in indignation; it feels so, well, righteous. Every morning at the breakfast table I read, or rather jackhammer, the newspaper, stopping often to share fragments of my disgust, incredulity, rage, and despair with that captive audience otherwise known as my family. In recognition of my filibustering skills, my husband a couple of years ago bought me a genuine antique wooden soapbox, which is far too beautiful to stand and preach on, but serves quite nicely as an annex to my daughter's dollhouse. I complain about many, many issues, from the fragile state of our Mother Gaia to the laughable state of our mother-?*& %*;#! government, but the issue that has obsessed me the longest and sets me ranting the loudest is feminism. I am an unrepentant advocate of women's rights, one of those creatures that the Rush Limbaughites deride as a feminazi. From the moment I was aware of being female, I realized that girls and women inexplicably were considered imperfect goods, inferior to boys and men in virtually every way that counted. As a young bookworm in the 1960s, I noticed that the books I read, in school and out, featured far more tales of boys than they did of girls. I saw that men got to do all the fun things in life, like fly to the moon and utter awkwardly exalted, and notably female-free, lines about small "man" steps and giant "mankind" steps; while the closest women got to outer space was in commercials for Comet. I noticed that boys were asked what they wanted to be when they grew up, while girls were told what they could be. Nurse, teacher, or stewardess: any questions?

Well, this sucks, I thought to myself. *Why couldn't I have been born a boy?* I remember getting into an argument with my friend Cheryl in the second or third grade. "I wish I were a boy," I said. "Don't you?"

"No," she replied. "I like being a girl."

"You like being a girl?" I said, my surliness happily snapping to attention. "How can you like being a girl?"

"I don't know," she said, shaking her decidedly girlish blond curls. "I just do."

I refused to back down. "Well, what part do you like? Wearing dresses that fly up when you're in the playground so your underwear shows? Or being told to act like a 'lady'? Or not being allowed to do stuff because you're a girl?"

"I enjoy being a girl," she said firmly, and I'm pretty sure she didn't learn the line from Rodgers and Hammerstein. "I'm sorry, Natalie, I don't feel the way you do, and I don't want to quarrel about it anymore." (As the daughter of a minister, Cheryl was unfailingly polite, and she really used words like "quarrel.")

Deciding that my best friend was lying, blind, stupid, or some chimera of the three, I retreated to another part of Cheryl's room and waited in sullen anomie for my mother to come fetch me home.

. . .

In the late 1960s, my mother discovered the fledgling Women's Liberation Movement, which in one sense wasn't fledgling at all—feminism has been around in one form or another for many centuries, if not millennia—but which in another felt revolutionary, as spanking new as the airfoil of a Pan Am jet. My mother joined a group called OWL, for "Older Women's Liberation"—older meaning thirty and up—and started attending consciousness-raising sessions. The spirit of her awakening suffused our household, inciting ever more acrimony between her and my father but finding an eager and fully primed pupil in my grouchy, righteously indignant self. I became a feminist long before I had a bra to burn, which is just as well, since, despite the cliché, rabble-rousing feminists never burned their bras but merely, in one demonstration against the Miss America pageant, removed them and dumped them in a public trash can. I read all the feminist classics, including *The Feminine Mystique, The Female Eunuch, The Dialectics of Sex,* and bits and pieces of that gargantuan bible of the business, *The Second Sex.* I argued with my street-smart Bronx friends, who ridiculed the women's movement as the province of "man-haters," "dykes," and "dogs."

And I hated history. Oh, how I hated history. I hated the pantheon of great artists, scientists, and political leaders for being almost exclusively male. I hated the things that our certified geniuses have said about women over the ages, such as Aristotle's contention that "the male is by nature superior, and the female inferior; and the one rules, and the other is ruled" (Any questions?), or Charles Darwin flakking for his team with the assertion that "the chief distinction in the intellectual powers of the two sexes is shown by man's attaining to a higher eminence, in whatever he takes up, than can woman—whether requiring deep thought, reason, or imagination, or merely the use of the senses and hands." Where were the women? I wondered. Why didn't they fight back? Why did they put up with being put down for so long?

Sometimes it seemed that feminism was the only thing that mattered in my life. And to be honest, it wasn't making my life very happy. I felt disenfranchised, marginalized, and perpetually disappointed. When I was a teenager, and by then having moved from the Bronx to a small town in Michigan, my mother and I decided to start a consciousness-raising group of our own, and we invited a ragtag collection of friends and neighbors to join us. But after a few weeks, I began to feel that our meetings were off-track. We weren't talking about important things, notably the Oppression of Women, or how pissed off we were by that oppression. We were, or rather the other women were, gabbing. They were talking about their daily lives, their kids, their husbands, their in-laws. And they weren't even angry about anything! What was the point? This was supposed to be a CR meeting, not a bridge club!

So I began to complain. I began to rant. I scolded the others for not passing the feminist purity test, for neglecting the political in favor of the personal, and for wasting their time on trivia. I didn't want to discuss the minutiae of when and under what amusing circumstances Barbara had nursed her baby the other day. I wanted to know why Barbara assumed complete responsibility for child care and let her husband off the hook every time! And then a funny thing happened. After a few weeks of being put down, the women wouldn't put up with it anymore. They kicked me out of the group. I was a founding member, but they asked my mother to ask me to leave, and she did, and I did. In truth, I don't blame them. I didn't even blame them back then. I knew I was a pocket of broken glass.

Through the years, paradoxically, I've lost many a female friend over the issue of feminism, or rather my rendering of it. My girlfriends simply have not cared enough about feminism to suit me; most of them wouldn't even have called themselves feminists. They didn't see it as a betrayal of the cause, for example, to allow a man to take them out for dinner and then pay the whole bill, rather than splitting the tab. They didn't like calling men and asking them out on a date, as I insisted on doing regardless of how irritated the men might be by my "pushiness." Worst of all, my girlfriends were just a bit too noncommittal about the whole friendship business. I wanted profound friendships, glorious friendships, friendships that fattened the spirit and sharpened the mind. I wanted a friendship as close and as revolutionary as that between my heroines, Susan B. Anthony and Elizabeth Cady Stanton. I pined for that sort of gynocentricity, but I never found it. That failure has been one of the great disappointments of my life, a sorry paradox: I am a soapbox-certified feminist who believes abstractly in the principle of female-female bonding as a source of enormous strength, and I have virtually no close female friends. I have plenty of casual girlfriends, even a handful of good friends, but no great friends, no best friends, no Elizabeth Cady, no Susan B., mine forever.

The one woman I've been able to count on over the years, whose feminism and commitment to the revolution have never flagged, is my mother. I can say anything to my mother, bitch and thunder and claptrap against all the world's misogynies and idiocies, and my mother won't recoil from me, or roll her eyes or belittle my complaints. Most of the time, she agrees with what I'm saying, and when she doesn't we at least can fight loudly about the issue. She doesn't sigh, "Oh, Natalie, I just don't feel the way you do," or "Natalie, I don't want to quarrel about it anymore." She's a warrior, as I am, although she's always been a lot peppier in spirit, less gloomy about the future. She's a warrior, all right, and my best girlfriend when it comes down to it. And lately I've been seized with the worry of, What in hell am I going to do when she dies? Who will I kvetch to? Sure, I have my husband, but his breakfast-time burden is heavy enough, I know, and besides, he's not a woman, so there's a limit to how much he can sympathize with my feminist natterings. What am I going to do? Who am I going to turn to?

Which brings me to the subject I began with: my daughter, Katherine. My poor brilliant beautiful daughter. My daughter, I fear, is doomed. My daughter, I pray, will take up the feminist torch, and whip its flame higher and brighter than I ever could. I don't want my daughter to be like me—no, not at all. I don't want her to be angry about the world and its injustices. I don't want her to carry a checklist wherever she goes and be embittered by the male-female ratios she finds. I don't want her to go to a jazz club or a rock concert and not be able to enjoy the music because, goddess-damn it, all the musicians are male. I don't want her to spend her time writing letters to magazine editors or conference organizers complaining about the lack of female voices and female speakers. I don't want her to feel alienated and dispirited by the majestic sweep of human history, its achievements in philosophy, science, technology, painting, architecture, and literature, solely because name after immortalized name is masculine. I want her to be able to appreciate, absorb, and metabolize our species' best thinking, and use those thoughts as a glorious slingshot, the way a well-aimed spacecraft exploits the gravitational energy of a planet to impel it forward on its cosmic trek. I want her to feel as much a player in the game that began long before her as she is a master of the destiny that awaits her. Hell, I'm a mother. I'm allowed to be grandiose about these things.

At the same time, I don't want my daughter to take her liberty for granted, or view feminism as a bit of mildewed history, of no more relevance to her life than a horse-drawn barouche or a manual typewriter. I relish the line in a letter that Elizabeth Cady Stanton wrote to Lucretia Mott about the birth of her fifth child—a girl at last! "I am at length the happy mother of a daughter," she said. "Rejoice with me all Womankind, for lo! a champion of thy cause is born." Sure enough, Harriot Stanton became a defender of the cause and a fighter for suffragism and women's rights. Did Harriot have a choice? Does Katherine?

As many have pointed out over the years, the surest and most insidious enemy of freedom is not dictatorship, but complacency. If you don't keep struggling to move forward, you don't stay put—you slide backward. For any number of reasons, from the sociocultural to the evolutionary and biological, women and men are locked in a push-me-pull-you struggle for control over the keys to the future, which, for a sexually reproducing mammal, amounts to an ongoing struggle over the female body, female sexuality, and female behavior. This doesn't mean that women and men can't get along gorgeously or cooperate lovingly toward a desired end—healthy kids, regular pleasure, a joint 401(k), the occasional sapphire-ring-in-the-morning-bagel surprise.

It does mean, however, that we women must pay attention, and never get lax or laissez-faire. It means that we must be cognizant of the lessons of history, primary among them the tendency of men to seek, consciously or otherwise, to restrict women's itinerary and keep the miraculous forward-facing womb safe in sweet seclusion. I know all this intellectually, and I feel it right down to my totipotent stem cells. I want Katherine to know it and feel it, too, but I want her consciousness to stay aloft without her having to expend so much emotional fuel, not to mention hortatorical hot air, to keep it there. Yes, I'm selfish, and as I said earlier, I worry about what will happen when I don't have my mother to kvetch to, and I have fantasized about turning my daughter into my surrogate mother, who herself has been my surrogate best friend.

I predict that my daughter will resist the imposition, and rightly so. She's not here to entertain me, or shore me up, or even listen to my cereal-hour sermonettes. I want her to be a warrior, a champion of the cause. I'd feel as proud as a mighty blue she-whale—the largest animal ever to grace this planet—should my daughter choose to call herself a feminist. Yet I want her to be a feminist without the litmus paper, the indignation, and the barbed wire. A feminist with close friends who aren't kin. A feminist without portfolio, if you will, and a citizen of the world.

Look at Me Now

Look at me!
Look at me!
Look at me NOW!
It is fun to have fun
But you have to know how.

—Dr. Seuss, *The Cat in the Hat*

Married at 46

The Agony and the Ecstasy

Nancy Wartik

WHEN I WAS a little girl, it was never as clear to me as I think it is to some little girls that I'd fall in love and marry when I grew up. Yes, I loved dressing my Barbie in her white wedding gown and walking her down the aisle with George Harrison, just as girls today probably marry their body-pierced Barbies to a member of 'N Sync. But there was also a childhood poem I liked and suspected might apply to me. It started out, "If no one ever marries me— And I don't see why they should, For nurse says I'm not pretty, And I'm seldom very good. . . ." I don't know why I didn't take for granted something so much in the natural order of my particular world. I'd like to think I was just a precocious little feminist, but that's probably crediting myself with an awareness I didn't yet have.

Whatever the reasons for my childhood presentiments, they were on the mark. I did have a boyfriend for a year in high school, but that was apparently a fluke because after that, throughout college, there were long droughts punctuated only by vain crushes or abortive stabs at love. I hung on to my virginity for so long it got embarrassing. Finally, on a break from school and living in California, I went to Mexico with a friend in the same awkward situation and we picked up the first men we met in a bar and got the problem taken care of. I had a tendency in those days to divide men into two categories. There were those who were dubious candidates for love, by virtue of being emotionally or geographically distant, or tragic tortured souls; these were invariably men with whom I became obsessed. Then there were nice, nearby men who really did like me, which meant something was horribly wrong with them and caused me to treat them with a mixture of ambivalence and scorn.

I traveled through most of my twenties on my own, and then through much of my thirties. During those years, I managed to untangle some of my unhappiest relationship patterns, through thousands of dollars donated to therapists and with knowledge bred of painful experience. By my forties I'd had affairs lasting long enough for the parties involved to memorize my phone number, learn my cats' names, and meet my friends. I'd had boyfriends I cared about, if never with a certainty that made real commitment possible. I'd been "in lust." But I'd never been in love, never even officially lived with anyone. Sometimes I took this in stride, other times I wondered if I was a bizarre sport of nature. What were other people doing right that I was doing wrong? Not that my life was empty: I lived in a perfectly nice Brooklyn apartment equipped, urban-single-woman-style, with two adored cats, in a building where I knew and liked my neighbors. I had a schedule so busy it was hard to accommodate and a career as a writer and later a college journalism teacher that, if not without frustrations, moved basically in an upward trajectory. I had a loving family and good friends: men friends, married friends, and most of all a beloved circle of women friends with whom I traveled, kvetched, fought, got facials, rented summer houses, smoked the occasional joint, and talked incessantly. My fortieth birthday party, thrown by five of these friends and crowded with people from many parts of my life, was a wonderful thing that made me feel lucky and loved. But the dark side of turning forty was a feeling that if I was still unmated by this point, it would always be thus.

The older I got, the more I questioned whether I could be truly happy outside a relationship with a man. The feelings themselves made me feel guilty, and I fought them. After all, I'd long been an avowed feminist. I was a former staffer at *Ms.* magazine, propagator of such aphorisms as "A woman without a man is like a fish without a bicycle." Theoretically, it seemed to me that I should be able to live as contentedly on my own as with someone else; I didn't want to rely on another person for my happiness. But I felt lonely at a deep, unappeasable level, so lonely sometimes that I wasn't sure how I'd get through the rest of my life if this was how it was going to be. I was forty-three years old and I was tired of showing up for our big family Thanksgivings year after year, watching cousins bring along boyfriends or girlfriends, and then husbands or wives, and finally, growing broods of children, while time plodded by and I remained defiantly alone. I was tired of having only my cats to cuddle. I wanted to be somebody else's most important person. I wanted to understand what people meant when they talked about being in love. I didn't really care whether or not a fish needed a bicycle.

. . .

If I could have ordered a man out of a catalogue, I don't suppose Dennis is the first one I'd have picked. I'd always tended to go for men who were younger than I, by a little or a lot, but Dennis was in his early fifties—by far the oldest man I'd ever been involved with. He was, by his own admission, a shy person, quiet in social situations, whereas I, to compensate for various social neuroses of my own, was generally drawn to outgoing, gregarious men. He'd been divorced for almost twenty years and, though he'd been entangled with a string of women since then, had never remarried, which made me suspicious. If he was so normal and desirable, why was he available? He also had a selective memory and didn't always recall things I told him about myself. Poor memory has always been a trait that drives me crazy. Some of the most terrible, door-slamming fights we ever had happened when I took affront because he'd forgotten some vital piece of personal information: my high school boyfriend's name, or the list of my top five favorite short stories.

We met on a winter night in 1998, at a photography opening where we each had a tenuous connection to one of the photographers. I was on deadline, and I was exhausted and somewhat dazed from writing a magazine story about Viagra for which I'd been interviewing men in graphic detail ("So it was even bigger and harder than when you were sixteen?"). The story wasn't done and I shouldn't have left home at all. I'd like to say a psychic intuition forced me out the door, but it was mostly the usual vague sense that I should get myself "out there," that onerous chore expected of all single people who want to change their status. At the opening, I bumped into an acquaintance who was talking to Dennis, and he introduced us.

Again, it would be romantic to say an indefinable something drew me to Dennis immediately. He was introduced, however, as an editor at a well-known newspaper, so my first thoughts involved networking more than romance. I did notice he had an intense blue-eyed gaze and seemed nervous making small talk—staring down into his plastic cup as if he wished more wine would magically appear in it—which I found rather endearing. The fact that he didn't have a ring on the third finger of his left hand also interested me. Given his job, I figured I could probably check off "smart," "living above poverty level," and possibly even "not a potential psychopath" on the "significant other" checklist. As we talked, I kept expecting some woman to come swooping over to claim him. None did, and at the end of the evening, we exchanged e-mail addresses, as is the modern way. Being a wizened veteran of single life in New York, however, I didn't allow myself to get too optimistic. The idea that you could meet a man; have him call you; realize you liked each other; and discover he wasn't seriously in need of psychiatric help was a lovely one, but then, all the fairy tales I'd devoured as a little girl were lovely, too.

Yet from our first date—when I don't know if I was more moved by a sad story Dennis told me about his dog, Kuji, or the fact that he splurged and took me to Brooklyn in a cab before going all the way back to Manhattan's Upper West Side—there was an easy progression, a sense of growing potential, that I'd simply never experienced before. I'd had one date in the year before I met Dennis, and I'd alarmed him by trying to discuss what meaning our lives really had, in this world of pain and death. "She's a little morbid, isn't she?" he inquired of the friend who set us up. Dennis didn't mind morbid talk—or philosophical talk, or silly talk, or any kind of talk I wanted to have. We understood each other, we got each other's jokes. He liked my cats. I waited for him to announce he wasn't ready for commitment, or to stumble on evidence he had another girlfriend stashed somewhere, whom he'd forgotten to mention. It didn't happen. He continued to seem interested. He told me what he was feeling without dissembling. His refusal to hide his emotions delighted and astounded me. I often thought back to the first night we met, reveling in my luck. What if I hadn't blown off my deadline? What if the acquaintance who introduced us hadn't been there that night? I took nothing for granted because I knew, as only someone who's spent years "out there" can, just how serendipitously, precariously lucky I'd been.

But at the same time I was falling in love, I was busy battling it each step of the way. When I met Dennis, he was writing a biography of Albert Einstein, with a twin focus on Einstein's passions for science and women. He likes to tell the story of how one of the first things I asked him was, "So was Einstein an asshole like most other men?" Today, it doesn't seem to have quite the cynical wit I attributed to it at the time (though I should add that Einstein *did* behave atrociously to many women in his life). But it was my not-so-subtle way of warning Dennis that I knew the average man couldn't be trusted, that a potential suitor would have to break through layers of defenses to earn the incredible prize of a relationship with me.

My fears about opening up to another human being, forty-three years in the making, were as hardy and plentiful as a hydra-headed monster. I'd spent so long refusing to compromise in a relationship, it was hard to accept that some compromises might actually be healthy ones—and even harder to know which ones they were. I agonized over whether the things that worried me about Dennis were fatal flaws, or things I could learn to live with. I agonized alone. I agonized with friends. I agonized with my mother, who had the strength of character not to revert to Jewish mom-speak ("What, at your age, you can afford to be picky?"). And, unfortunately for Dennis, I agonized with him. ("How? How? How can I stay in this relationship when you can't remember if I like anchovies?")

Then I agonized over *being* in all this agony. When you met "the one," wasn't everything supposed to feel perfect? Since I'd never been in love, I only knew what it *didn't* feel like, not what it did. I can remember being acutely frustrated, at times, that there was no way to run a scientific test to see if this was love and Dennis was the right person; having to rely on myself for answers seemed so imprecise. Popular culture talked ad nauseam about love, love, love, but gave us virtually no useful information at all about it. It didn't seem fair.

In lieu of a scientific test, I minutely scrutinized every little incident for clues that might reveal if we had a future together. One night we walked by a woman begging for money, with a sick dog at her feet. I didn't think Dennis was as touched by their plight as I was, and when we got home I put him through an intense Q&A about whether he cared, truly cared, about the condition of other beings on the planet. And if so, why wasn't he off in Rwanda or Bosnia, doing something about it? Another night, after drinking copiously with a friend who'd discovered her boyfriend had been routinely cheating on her, I came home and called Dennis at 2:00 A.M., woke him from a sound sleep, and demanded to know if he was capable of this sort of thing. He told me he wouldn't ever lie to me. "Except that if you were lying, you wouldn't admit it, would you?" I cleverly asked. Finally, sensibly, he told me there was nothing more he could say; I'd have to make my own choice about whether or not to believe him.

I scrutinized myself, too. Was I really in love, or did I just think this was my last chance not to end up living like Eleanor Rigby? Dennis was an accomplished person, with a prestigious job and a higher tax bracket than mine. Would I feel the same about him if he was working as a dishwasher? Was I deceiving myself and "settling" for someone who could make my life more comfortable? If you loved someone, did you love them only for who they were, or were you allowed to count in their accomplishments and the lifestyle you'd have with them? Once again, what were the rules?

It's not that I think I shouldn't have asked myself any questions: about Dennis, about love, about relationships. But I asked the same questions over and over, then didn't always listen to the answers. Months went by and despite my myriad concerns, we grew ever closer and our lives grew more intertwined. A year and a day after we met, Dennis drove to

Brooklyn, picked up me and the two cats, and we all moved into his apartment. To my surprise, moving in with someone wasn't the ordeal I'd expected. In forty-plus years, I'd become ingrained in slightly eccentric habits and wasn't sure if they'd mesh with another person's. I saw no point in cooking if there was takeout to be had. I ate at my desk or the living room coffee table, after clearing off enough space for a plate and for the cats to sit there and keep me company. I hated doing dishes and let them soak in the sink for weeks or even months (yes, it's true) on end. I stayed up until all hours fiddling around on my computer, then slept as late as I could. I rarely answered the phone, on the theory that if God didn't want people to screen calls She/He wouldn't have invented answering machines.

None of those things ended up mattering much. Dennis got up early and I slept late, sparing us quarrels over who got the bathroom first in the morning. He wasn't compelled to make a ritual of dinnertime and didn't mind cats on the table; we both liked takeout; and he came with a dishwasher—in itself, almost an incentive to fall in love. True, he thought it was perfectly normal to pick up a ringing phone; in fact, he insisted on it, and when it was inevitably for me, he would refuse to lie and say I wasn't there. But for the most part, we lived well together. I liked having this new roommate, a person to snuggle with on the sofa and talk to, after a day spent home alone working.

Yet still, my doubts about the relationship didn't melt away. We'd spend an evening with friends during which Dennis stayed quiet rather than tossing out brilliant social commentary, and I'd launch into a mental soliloquy about whether I could possibly stay with someone who, on a high school scale, was more like a member of the chess club than the lead singer in the school rock band. Then I'd pick a fight and there we'd be, back at square one, as if all our bonding had never happened. A good friend took to calling these spells of mine "the chill winds of doubt." I never knew for sure when the winds would roar through, though often they followed in the wake of a new step we'd taken toward commitment: on our first real vacation, or right after I moved in. When they came full force, they rocked me to my roots. It felt as if all I could do was hunker down and hope they'd pass soon, feeling sullen and miserable (and generously sharing the wealth with Dennis).

I'd been stuck in this spot in past relationships, but never in one with so much possibility. My "chill winds of doubt" friend, who knew me well, told me whenever I needed to hear it that she firmly believed Dennis was right for me. My mother reminded me that even as a child, I'd always preferred the toy across the room to the one in my hand, which actually made me feel better. It suggested that my ambivalence was my own, solvable problem, not a result of inherent flaws in the relationship. Many times, I clung to the words of these people I loved to help me through my worst moments, trusting their judgment in ways I didn't always trust my own.

It goes without saying that if Dennis wasn't a generous, loving person, my spells of misery and doubt would have ended things between us. But while I was hunkered down, he hung in there with me, often justifiably infuriated, but never threatening to leave. He had a way of cutting through an argument by telling me something I needed to hear just then, something that innately felt true. He thought many of the fights I picked were an excuse for bailing out instead of staying the course. He also let me know that at his age, he wouldn't be undergoing any radical personality transformations: what I saw was what I got. But he let me discuss my worries and fears, no matter how petty or how often we'd been over the same territory, and once I'd finally aired whatever was bothering me—a task always easier said than done—our relationship would resume its erratic, zigzagging, but ultimately forward progress.

Two years minus one day after we'd met, I was slouched on our sofa in my sweat clothes. I'd just done something that felt heavy with finality. When I'd first moved in with Dennis, I'd held on to my Brooklyn apartment as a safety measure, but several days ago, I'd sold it, along with all my furniture. Now if Dennis and I had an argument, I couldn't even go slamming back home. Naturally, instead of feeling warm and romantic, I felt anxious and trapped. I was dirty and tired, because I was still unpacking boxes. It was at this moment that Dennis chose to hand me another box—this one small and wrapped—whose contents were fairly obvious. Despite my ebbing and flowing doubts, I'd let it be known for months now that one of these days I wanted to walk down an aisle in a white dress, just like my old Barbie doll. The strength of my desire to marry had surprised me; I'd always thought of myself as someone who wouldn't feel a need to bother with legal conventions. Another myth shattered: the drive to marry felt deep and not open to rational self-interrogation.

It would be lovely to report that as I opened the box and looked at my truly lovely diamond ring, tears clouded my eyes and all my doubts vanished forever. Of course, it didn't happen that way at all. I said yes, but I felt prosaically dry-eyed, and at the same time as if I'd been plunged into a mild stupor. We were living through the aftermath of the 2000 elections and, at least as my memory paints it, twenty minutes after getting engaged, we were discussing the Supreme Court's role in the Florida recount. Our engagement, for me, began a weeks-long siege of doubts as vicious as any I'd felt in the two years we'd been together. Each tiny flaw of Dennis's suddenly seemed magnified to a cardinal sin. Sometimes, with every fiber of my being, I wanted to undo our new commitment and flee. The feelings swarmed around me like Furies at the most inconvenient times, like at the start of a trip we took to Europe several weeks after getting engaged, when all should have been roses and romance between us.

A month or so after that, Dennis went to San Francisco on business and I came along to see an old friend there. Soon after I arrived, Dennis and I got into a horrible fight about something trivial, long since forgotten. It was Sunday and Dennis went off to a series of meetings; my friend picked me up because we planned to spend a few hours at an Asian bath in the city. I flung myself into her car and let spill a flood of anger and angst: Perhaps I was making a terrible mistake to go ahead with this marriage. Dennis wasn't enough like my idea of the kind of man I should be with. He was just too different than I was, except for all the unfortunate ways in which he was too similar. He didn't truly listen to me or understand me. I couldn't live anymore torn up with this wrenching back-and-forthing over the relationship.

My friend listened as I ranted. She'd been married for ten years or so. The marriage had seen some dramatic ups and downs but it had stayed solidly together and I respected her opinion; she'd always done love better than I had. She didn't seem shocked at my outburst, or as if she thought my lacerating doubts were especially unusual. I can't remember if she came up with the image that lingered from the conversation, or if I superimposed it on her words. But as we talked, I suddenly saw that I'd climbed up the steps to a high dive, where I now stood, looking down at the pool far below. I could jump in or I could give up, turn around, and climb back down (past all the other people ranged on the steps, waiting their turn). In the past, I'd always chosen to turn around and climb back down. Come to think of it, I'd never really *gotten* very far up the steps before. Could I forgive my own lack of courage this time if I never even tried to jump? Could I live the rest of my life wondering what might have been? I was forty-five and I had a choice to make. I needed to decide if I could viscerally accept the idea that Dennis didn't need to change; *I* did. If I stayed in the relationship, I would have to let go of the belief that true love never requires making even slight compromises. If I was willing to do that, I needed to stop second-guessing myself, marshal my courage, plunge in, and let the water splash where it might.

And so, reader, I married him. It was in June, on a grassy lawn, in a country woods. I wore a long white dress and Dennis and I walked down the aisle together, because I needed him beside me, holding my hand. It felt very right to stand in front of the interfaith minister who was performing the ceremony, to look each other in the eyes and say our vows. Almost all of the people we cared most about surrounded us. My parents were happy as only parents whose daughter has delayed marriage until her mid-forties can be. Mosquitoes nipped at our flesh, and at dinnertime, the skies opened up and thunder rumbled. Children ran around catching raindrops in their mouths, we all danced wildly to music with a calypso beat, and the evening flashed by in a multicolored blur. People reminded us over and over that rain at a wedding means good luck.

. . .

Looking back over what I've written, I see it's not quite the story I set out to write. I'd meant to talk about what it's like to marry at a later age, in a society that just a few years back kindly informed women they were likelier to die in a terrorist attack than marry for the first time over age forty (a comparison that seems even less amusing now than it did then). In that context, I'd meant to mockingly compare marrying at forty-six to achieving the single woman's Holy Grail and to explain how I've learned that this Holy Grail is an illusion of sorts, that love and marriage are as much a struggle as single life, just in a different way.

I was going to write about how painful it is—and it *is* painful—to see close friendships alter because you have less time to invest in them and because your role in the dynamic has subtly changed. About how difficult it is—and it *is* difficult—to give up an independent lifestyle you've cultivated for decades. About how hard it is—and it *is* hard—to become a "wife" when you've never even liked the sound of the word, with its connotations of an aproned female dishing up dinner for a hardworking male. All of these things involved a confusing adjustment period that's still not totally over for me. Only recently have I begun to use the phrase "my husband" without it sounding laughably awkward to my own ears. In an early version of this essay, I wrote, "In some ways, getting married helped me understand better than I ever did when I was single just how valid a choice staying on your own can be."

I didn't write that story, because I came to realize it's not the story that feels true to me—it's only the story that I *wanted* to feel true. Part of me still wants to believe I could be as happy single as coupled. I hate the stigma that even today hovers over women who, for whatever reason, don't tie their lives to a man's; I wish I'd been stronger in resisting it. I keenly remember what it felt like to cringe from each successive family gathering, wondering if relatives were asking themselves, "What's wrong with her? Why can't she find a man?" To drag myself out on another date because I felt I "should," then feel defensive when my date asked, "Have you ever been married?"—as if the answer would help him judge whether I was desirable. I know what it feels like to be simultaneously scornful and envious of smug, naïve couples who paired up early and haven't the remotest sense of what "out there" is like. I never want to vanish so far into coupledom that I forget . . . well . . . forget just how valid—but how difficult—a choice staying on your own *can* be. I've always come down on the side of those who prefer to fight through loneliness and other ghosts of solitude rather than compromise too much in love. Had I not met Dennis, I think there's an excellent chance that's the fight I'd still be waging.

I did meet Dennis, though. And so it turned out that my own difficult fight lay in the opposite direction, against all the self-created ghosts that kept me from embracing what I'd claimed to want as long as it existed only in the realm of fantasy: love, relationship, commitment. I'm happier now than I've ever been in my life; I recognize it, and people see it in me. That's not to say I think a lifetime of blissful certainty now stretches before me. Probably sooner rather than later, I expect the chill winds of doubt—my own personal nemesis—will blow again, though when they do, I hope I'll be better at recognizing what's at the root of the dissatisfaction and airing it in a way that helps it dissipate quickly. But if falling in love and marrying did call for revising some of my expectations, what I've gained isn't an illusion at all. It's a blessing, and one that I'm deeply grateful for—as grateful as a chronically ambivalent malcontent can be.

The Fat Lady Sings

Natalie Kusz

NOT MUCH IS delightful—I'm the first to admit it—about being fat: the joints ache and the lungs wheeze in mere anticipation of a staircase; any temperature above zero calls for extreme nudity and intravenous ice water; clothes shopping preparations include a motivational speaker and prescription narcotics; and the act of picking up, say, a dropped quarter is something to be accomplished only with the toes, lest bending the prominent midriff results in toppling, concussion, and death.

Moreover, a fat person is a pariah, subject to the kinds of vitriol once reserved for eighteenth-century witches. My sister, who is a supersized chick like myself, has had food hurled at her from passing cars (with accompanying size-related slurs) in two of these United States *when she was out for healthy strolls;* both she and I, idling our cars at traffic lights, have had drivers alongside us shout helpfully, "Get out and walk, fatass!" (and then what, they'll throw cheeseburgers?); and grocery cashiers have repeatedly—I kid you not—held up our purchases and speculated, "I guess you didn't notice the low-calorie version," or something similar. These are not infrequent incidents; some sort of confrontation, subtle or overt, occurs every time I leave my house, unless I am accompanied by a thin person (whose presence seems to discourage unseemliness, I assume because Smalls don't like other Smalls to see them behaving badly).

So, no, there is not much of an upside to being fat.

Can someone explain, then, why the General Populace believes that if enough people alert the fat lady (oh, so sympathetically) to the downside of her heftiness, she will suddenly come to her senses, see the error of her ways, and make haste to phone Jenny Craig? On how many occasions must I, sitting in a friend's living room—believing myself protected, for once, from assault—have that friend lean toward me, lay a narrow hand on my arm, and murmur, "I hope this doesn't hurt your feelings, but I love you and I'm concerned about your weight."

Imagine, if you will, what a fat lady feels at this moment. The fact that she is in this living room at all, that she calls this person Friend, means this person has aced specific tests, has indicated over time that he or she is "safe," disinclined to criticize, less presumptuous and more benevolent than the world at large; for the fat lady, like all circus freaks, has much to fear among regular folk, and is cautious about relaxing among them. And, once she has relaxed, imagine how it feels to find out she was wrong, that all along she was misreading the signs, that her body was, in fact, being evaluated and judged and, yes, weighed. Like the woman with an unfaithful lover, she must review every past visit, every reckless and liberated moment, wondering which of them was true and which false.

Let me be perfectly clear: the friend's supportive admonition may be *meant* less caustically, but it does not *feel* less caustic than the aforementioned "Get out and walk, fatass" incident. True, the friend, like the family doctor, talking not about my ugliness but rather about how unhealthy it is to be me, how likely I am to die young. Even so: How preferable to be shunned than exhorted; for upon hearing "Fatass!" I can flee the scene, anticipate never again meeting the heckler this side of Hades, while a friend's kindly advice is the start, not the end, of tortures—a thousand future opportunities to co-inhabit a room, pretending to overlook my benefactor's earnest and affectionate disapproval, clenching my abs and tucking in my chins, imagining myself petite, and palatable, and elsewhere.

The unfathomable question, I repeat, is *why*. Not so much why friends, Romans, and countrymen draw me aside to whisper admonishments—I believe some of them truly are well-meaning—but why do they suppose this will be effectual? Is it likely that in thirty-eight years of living I have never once noticed my own corpulence? Or that I have somehow missed those alarmist hourly news reports on obesity (Americans Are Fatter Than Ever!), weight-loss studies, and the mortal (and, some believe, moral) risks of overweight? Perhaps the thought is that I am having so much fun living the fat life (what with all those swanky clothes, adoring fans, and male model escorts) that I've neglected subtle details such as creaky knees and a pendulous, unfashionable belly. Last possibility: that for a Small to weigh in (so to speak) on a fat person's self-style is compulsory, a form of intervention similar to that imposed on alcoholics, drug addicts, gamblers—on anyone, in short, without the strength of will to make good choices on his or her own.

The term *willpower* always does, in fact, work its way into fat-related discourse, from media advertising ("Boost your willpower with ScrawnyQuik!") to exercise videos ("Just a little willpower, plus this easy-to-follow boot camp regimen, and you're on your way . . .") to everyday conversation; I swear I once overheard a tiny pregnant woman saying, "I'm trying to gain zero pounds, but I have no willpower." It had apparently not occurred to her that a weightless fetus would be unlikely to thrive, or that a gestating body asks for more nourishment because it *requires* more.

But here's the thing about willpower and the fat lady: If we accept as definition "the strength of will to carry out one's decisions, wishes, or plans" (*American Heritage Dictionary*), then the average Round Ruby has willpower in spades. Simply to go forth in the world is, for us, an act of supreme courage, a tamping down of panic, a setting aside of the knowledge that we will be stared at and remarked upon and scorned. When the office workers go to lunch, we walk alongside them, pretending our 200 excess pounds weigh no more than a hiker's day pack. We enter cafés and restaurants hoping for sizable seating, and if it doesn't exist, we cope with the spectacle of wedging ourselves, publicly, into booths. We order the salad, refuse the cheesecake, smile and nod as the others discuss—sometimes pointedly—their diets and exercise regimens and "disgusting, repulsive cellulite" (an actual quote from memory).

And we have, as does anyone else, lives punctuated by crisis and tragedy—which, as does anyone else, we surmount in whatever ways we can. In my case, I was attacked by sled dogs (I was raised in Alaska) at age seven, lost an eye and cheekbone, and spent many years having surgery—much of it complicated and bleak. I was an unwed mother at sixteen, lost my own mom at nineteen, took in my terminally ill father at twenty-nine, and survived his death at thirty-two. I have endured house fires and floods and the suicide attempts of loved ones, have carried my child to emergency rooms, have survived cancer and job loss and depression. These are not all, I acknowledge, uncommon events, but they were hard, and to manage them took—need I say it?—willpower times ten.

So inner strength, per se, is not a key deficiency in this—nor necessarily in any—fat lady's makeup. Some will say that the real question is about choice—at what we choose to direct our willpower—and this makes some sense. If (a) I do have willpower and (b) I am fat, then (c) I must have aimed the laser beam of my will at something other than my own adipose tissue. Consider this logically, however: Given the excruciating circumstances I have already mentioned—achy joints, dearth of wardrobe choices, and public mockery—what fat person in her right mind would *not* decide to be smaller? Then consider your own observations: Have you once met a fat person who has never dieted, never resolved firmly to conquer the behemoth that is her body? In my experience (and I have known hundreds of sizable folk), the larger the person, the more individual weight-reduction schemes she has followed—the low-fat plan, the low-carb, the all-lettuce, the grapefruit, the cider vinegar, the amphetamine, the liquid protein, the vitamin "milk shake," the exercise-till-you-drop, and so on. It is not, then, that we are fat because we've never intended otherwise; we've intended otherwise *over and over again,* and have grown, over time, ever larger. The reasons for our perpetual *avoirdupois* vary from genetics to discouragement to socioeconomics—but I acknowledge outright that in the end, for some of us, it is a matter of altered choices, a dawning conviction that enough, as they say, is enough.

In my case, this conviction came during graduate school, when I was fulfilling coursework, teaching as many classes as some full professors, writing a thesis, and abusing the goodwill of my dear siblings, who stepped in constantly to look after my young daughter. As I recall it now, I rarely slept, rarely ate a full meal, and was ill a good deal of the time with recurring ear infections, colds, flu, and the general malaise that accompanies exhaustion. Expressing parental guilt one day to a friend, I said, "I see my little girl only thirty minutes a day." The friend said, "That's more quality time than a lot of kids get," and I responded, "I'm not talking quality time. I literally see her thirty minutes a day, driving to and from day care." Meanwhile, I was working out with Jane Fonda, skipping breakfast and sometimes dinner, and once in an eon (on payday) splurging on an egg salad sandwich in the student union. I weighed 250 pounds.

I had been put on my first diet at nine years old, after I'd spent two consecutive six-week periods in a hospital bed—confined there while some grafts healed—and expanded (not surprising, given my Slavic ancestry) from an undernourished thinness into a moderate plumpness. My younger sister had been chubby since birth, so both of us were fed an egg at breakfast, bread and bologna at lunch, and something minuscule at dinner. During frequent hospital stays, my days were enlivened mostly by visits from the meal cart, and now the at-home periods took a similar turn. At play, at rest, in church, hunger was a scratchy, raw sensation, obscuring most other perceptions. I recall my mother saying that if I could stick to a reducing plan for three months—such an eternity, I thought!—I would have lost "all my weight" and be back to normal. I also recall that I lost almost nothing, and eventually our money ran out anyway and we were all back to bulk-purchased noodles and wild mushrooms from the woods.

Between then and adulthood I pursued dozens of diets, both informally and under medical supervision. I even, at one point, joined one of those pyramid schemes—"Your friends are your built-in customers!"—so I could buy my milk shake diet drinks for 60 percent less than retail. Regardless of the regimen, though, the pattern and results were the same: A brief, sudden weight drop (10 gratifying pounds in 2 days, mostly water) followed by an inching down of the scale indicator, followed by what is called a plateau—a period, often months long, when no matter how much less you consume, your weight stays steady and unyielding. Food is constantly on any dieter's mind, but in plateau times it becomes an obsession—not only its ingestion, but also its avoidance. A cousin of mine, who'd dieted down to 102 pounds and wanted to be an even 100, literally leapt backward one day at the sight of a carrot. Waving it off with her hands, she said, "I can't eat *anything*. Yesterday I had just one glass of orange juice, and today I'm one hundred and three."

One hundred pounds is far below what many people strive for (frankly, I'd be happy at *two hundred*), but the mechanics of the game are similar at any weight. At some point—sometimes an early point—in the weight loss process, the body simply stops shedding pounds, regardless of daily exercise, and the most reliable way to pass the "plateau" is to eat less, literally, than is required to sustain life. Don't get me wrong: This method does work. The problem is that once you're on a starvation diet, you must remain on it indefinitely, perhaps for the rest of your life. The task of maintaining a diminished body requires constant vigilance, and such vigilance is exhausting, overwhelming, and, to my mind, unrewarding. For the very wealthy, some relief is available—cooks can be hired, and personal trainers; nannies can distract the kids while Mommy works out; personal secretaries can run errands, housekeepers maintain the home, laundry services wash, dry, and fold. A friend once called to read me an article revealing the daily fitness routine of a crash-dieting TV star—*x* number of sit-ups followed by *y* number of leg lifts, then *z* minutes on the stair climber, *q* miles of jogging, and so on. For enlightenment's sake, we decided to estimate the time involved in such a regimen, assigning one second to each sit-up or leg lift, eight minutes to each jogged mile, and so on. By our calculations, the television star spent *seven hours daily* simply exercising, which inspired my friend to remark, "I'd go that route, too, if I had a staff running the rest of life."

But, in fact, most of us have many fewer time-saving buffers, and poor people none at all. For me, during school, my family took on much of my parental and homemaking burden, providing precious "extra" minutes in the day for studies and odd jobs and Jane Fonda. About that time, it occurred to me that I was succeeding in the world with only part of my brain engaged. While a tenth of it was devoted to school, a tenth devoted to my daughter, and perhaps another tenth devoted to family crises and illnesses, the other 70 percent of my mind was constantly focused on food—the calorie count of a grape, the filling bulk of popcorn, the clever use of water as a placebo. *How much farther,* I thought, *can I go in the world if I use that 70 percent more wisely?*

And so I began it. Henceforth, I declared (privately, so as not to invite disgrace), I would banish all concerns regarding pounds or inches, all self-urgings (don't eat that, don't eat that) that I deemed wasteful, unproductive, or thankless. Like a debtor devising a budget, I found myself sorting, evaluating, checking off—only the currency at hand was not dollars but units of thought. Whereas formerly I'd responded to hunger pangs by (a) fantasizing about food, (b) struggling not to fantasize about food, or (c) glancing wildly around for an inspiring thin woman, now I would simply locate some palatable food, purchase or prepare it, then chew, swallow, and pursue in full consciousness some unrelated project that would make me proud tomorrow. The diet production was over, the fat lady had sung, this operagoer was moving up the aisle, headed for the bright and substantial real world.

At first, my only confidante was the friend who, years later, would read me the celebrity fitness article, and she made a pronouncement now that became my motto: They don't put your weight on your tombstone. (Well, my own family might, as a joke, but still.) When they're summing up your life, she said, they tell what you've achieved, not that you've stayed the same weight since infancy. It was worth remembering, I thought, and I called it to mind many times over the next years as I passed through tragedies large and small, as I summoned the courage to focus on them—and as my body did, in fact, expand.

I would like to say that after abandoning the weight loss life, I became, ironically, more fit than ever; but such is not the case. Liberated abruptly from famine, every one of my cells said, "Party!" and stocked up against the day when I might again cut off supplies. A petite woman with whom I stayed for a week marveled, "You eat no more than I do," and she was right, but this body was making up for lost calories; gradually the pounds added up, the hefty dimensions increased, and I became a cautionary tale for young hedonists.

But I experienced much joy. This body was now a temple, not an icon; the housing, not the jewel. The circumstances of my life had not changed: I was still poor, still weary, still the oldest of four motherless siblings, still struggling to raise a child. But when my father, 100 miles away, became ill or broke a leg, I had a full mind to devote to retrieving him; when my daughter was afraid, I was fully present to hear her; when a school project approached, my whole brain set itself to the task. I felt smarter, more competent, less a failure, for I was succeeding at big things rather than failing, day by day, at a small one.

Few people approve of my choice, this decision to suspend body-related thought. Some of them call insults from cars, some decry loudly to children ("Yes, you'll get fat if you eat too much"), some send me clippings about stomach stapling. Doctors admonish me at every visit, until I mention the fat ladies I know who, afraid of being shamed, never brave a medical office until they are too sick to be helped much at all. Grudgingly, then, my physicians withdraw their assault, sometimes all at once, and sometimes with a last token lecture about health risks. The ones who don't withdraw, I never see again, taking my surly self off to better climes.

It's not that the naysayers don't have a point. I will die young. I will, perhaps, suffer diseases like diabetes, arteriosclerosis, and joint deterioration. But I will have written books. I will have parented well. I will have taken care of an ailing father and survived his death, as well as the death—young, herself—of my mother. My headstone will not read "She never let herself go," but neither will it say "She was as big as a barge." It will, I hope, say something like "She knew Truth and Substance and abided in them." It's the best I can ask, anyway, because I'll not again—understand this—do otherwise.

The Middle Way

Learning to Balance Family and Work

Ellen Gilchrist

AYBE YOU HAVE to wait for happiness. Maybe the rest is only words.

. . .

When I was a child I had a book about a small boy in Scotland whose father was a Highlander and whose mother was a Lowlander. All his life they argued in his presence about whether he was a Lowlander or a Highlander and each tried to persuade him of their case.

In the winters they lived with his mother's people and farmed and cared for domestic animals. In the summers they stayed in the Highlands with his father's people and he hunted the high hills with his father and his uncles. He was a strong boy and the altitude caused him to grow powerful lungs. When he called the goats and cattle on his mother's farm, his voice rose above the rest. In the hills he sometimes stood and called out across great distances to the other hunters. So he grew until he was almost as tall as a man.

The year he was sixteen, as they were making their way from the Highlands to the Lowlands, they came upon a man sitting on a rock playing bagpipes. The boy had never heard such heavenly music. He begged his parents to let him stay and learn to play bagpipes. Finally, when the man agreed to teach him, his parents left him there. And there he stayed the rest of his life, halfway between the Lowlands and the Highlands, playing beautiful music and looking up and down at the worlds he had left behind. Because his lungs were strong from working on the farm and climbing in the hills, he was able to make music so fine it could be heard from miles away.

I loved that story the most of anything I had ever read. I can still see each page of the book in my mind's eye, and I think I have finally found a place between the worlds where I can live in peace and do what I was meant to do. The middle way, the Zen masters call it. Ever since I first heard of that I have known that is what I was seeking.

Family and work. Family and work. I can let them be at war, with guilt as their nuclear weapon and mutually assured destruction as their aim, or I can let them nourish each other. In my life, as I have finally arranged it, the loneliness of being a writer and living alone in the Ozark Mountains is balanced against the worry and control issues of being a mother and a grandmother. I move back and forth between these two worlds. Somewhere in the middle I play my bagpipes and am at peace.

Of course, it wasn't always this easy. I have written two books of poetry and eighteen books of fiction about the struggle to free myself from my family and my conditioning so I could write and/or live as an artist with a mind that was free to roam, discriminate, and choose. I will leave the details of that struggle, which included four marriages, three cesarean sections, an abortion, twenty-four years of psychotherapy, and lots of lovely men, to your imaginations and go on with the story of where I landed, on this holy middle ground that I don't feel the need to fortify or protect, only to be grateful for having, as long as my destiny allows. I tell myself I am satisfied to be here now, but, of course, I would fight to keep my life if I had to, with sharp number two lead pencils and legal pads, my weapons of choice for all battles.

Still, I don't remember the events of my life as a struggle. I think of myself as a thinking, planning, terribly energetic competitor in games I believed I could win. It's all perception. If I cried I thought of the tears as some sort of mistake. Later, I knew that tears are unexpressed rage. But my father was a professional baseball player until I was born. At our house we had no respect for crybabies. We believed in Channel swimmers and home run kings and people who learned to walk after they had polio. My daddy set the bar high. He taught me it didn't matter if you won or lost, it was how you played the game.

. . .

Practically speaking, I have worked it out this way. Part of the time I live on the Gulf Coast near my family and participate in their lives as hard as I can. I don't change my personality to do that. I am a bossy, highly opinionated person and I say what I think. On the other hand, I love them deeply and help them in every way I can. They don't have to ask for help. I see what is needed and I act.

Then, when I have had enough of trying to control the lives of people just as willful and opinionated as I am, I drive back up to the Ozark Mountains and write books and run around with writers, artists, photographers, fitness experts, professors, and politicians. Sometimes I stay away from the coast for months and don't even think about my family unless they call me. If they need me I am here.

Because I don't like to fly on airplanes or stay in hotels, I have to make the life I live in Arkansas as rich as I can figure out how to make it. If I have a good life here I can leave my children alone to live their lives without interference. I want to help them but I don't want to need them.

Two years ago I decided I was getting stagnant, so I asked the university here to give me a job teaching writing. I had never taught but I thought I would be good at it. I wanted to be with younger people who were not related to me. Also, it was the year my oldest grandson went to college, a rite of passage for both of us. I think subconsciously I wanted to be with other young people who were experiencing what he was. I have always participated very deeply in his life. Perhaps teaching at a university was one more way of staying near him. So, now, to add to my happiness, I am teaching. What I do aside from that is get up at dawn every day and run or walk or work out at the health club. I love endorphins and I love to write and I love to read. I read and read and read. I live like a nun. I eat only fresh vegetables and high-protein foods. I drink only water and coffee. On Sunday afternoons I have a group of friends who come over and read the plays of William Shakespeare out loud. We've been doing that for fifteen years. Talk about bagpipes, this is the World Series of intellectual endorphins.

. . .

I think I am happy because I have quit trying to find happiness through other people. No one else can give you happiness after you become an adult. Happiness is self-derived and self-created. I derive happiness from the fact that my children and grandchildren are alive and breathing and that I am here to watch their lives unfold. Aside from that it's up to me. "To be alive becomes the fundamental luck each ordinary, compromising day manages to bury," it says on a piece of paper I have tacked up in the room where my children stay when they come to visit. I have internalized that knowledge. I want them to begin to learn it, too.

What else? I have learned to wait. I no longer have to *always* be the one who makes things happen. Sometimes I write every day for months on end. Sometimes I immerse myself in teaching. Sometimes I go to the coast and try to control my progeny's lives. Sometimes I don't do a thing but watch tennis on television and exercise obsessively and read books and go shopping at the mall. I have written and published twenty-two books. I have been the best mother I knew how to be and a better grandmother. In the light of that I refuse to feel guilty about a thing, past, present, or forevermore.

Who knows how long my happiness will last? It won't last forever. That's for sure, but I have a plan for when it ends. When I can no longer call the shots about my life or if I become ill with a disease that would make me an invalid, I will, I hope, cheerfully kill myself. I will find a fast, chemical way to do it and go somewhere where I won't leave a mess and get it over with. Whatever I was will rejoin the dazzling, star-filled carbon mass from which it came. I'll leave my DNA in three sons and twelve grandchildren and that's enough for me. I have told my family for twenty years that is how I intend to die and they all know it's true. No one will be surprised and the ones who loved me will know better than to be sad.

I believe with all my heart and soul that happiness begins with great good health and is nurtured in solitude. Perhaps the reason so many young mothers are stressed and unhappy is that they never get to be alone long enough to calm down and play the bagpipes. When I am taking care of small children I can't find time *to take a bath*.

Also, women in my generation had children when they were very young. A nineteen- or twenty-year-old girl is a much different mother than a highly educated, thirty-year-old woman who has had a responsible job or a career and interrupts it to have children. I was a child myself when I had my first two children and I played with them as if I were a child. I'm still pretty childish, which is why small children like to be with me. I lapse back into a childhood state quite easily, as I have a wonderful, inventive mother who taught me to believe that fairies played at night in my sandpile and left footprints on my castles. She would go out after I was asleep and walk around the castles with her fingers. Also, she told me that beautiful fairies hid behind the leaves of trees to watch over me. She is ninety-three and still a lovely, ethereal creature.

It may be easier to be a mother when you have never had any real achievements until you produce a baby. Here it is, the reason for existence, and you created it! I think older women probably make better mothers in many ways. But young women are more selfish and you have to be selfish to demand time for yourself when you have children. Young women are closer to the time when they were manipulative and childish and they don't let their babies manipulate them as much as older mothers do. These are only my conclusions from watching children in grocery stores. I love to watch them work on their mothers to get what they want, and because I am always a child, I'm pulling for them to get the candy and get it NOW. The other day I watched a little blond beauty pull her mother's face to her and lay her hands on her mother's cheeks and kiss her nose. Needless to say, they opened the bag of cookies then and there.

One of the reasons I am happy now is that I did the work I had always dreamed of doing. But I didn't start doing it seriously and professionally until I was forty years old. I have always loved books and always thought of myself as a writer but didn't have an overwhelming desire to write and publish things until my children were almost grown. I had published things off and on during my life and I enjoyed the process but I had no sustained desire to be a writer. It was just something I knew I could do if I wanted to. I was busy falling in love and getting married to three different men (I married the father of my children twice), and having babies and buying clothes and getting my hair fixed and running in the park and playing tennis. During those years my desire for literature was satisfied by reading. If there was something that needed writing, like the minutes for a PTA meeting or a play for my husband's law firm's dinner party, I wrote it and everyone liked it but I didn't want to keep on writing. To tell the truth, I was forty years old before I had enough experience to be a writer. I barely knew what I thought, much less what anything meant.

. . .

I wouldn't be happy now if I had no progeny. The reason I don't fear death is that every chromosome of me is already in younger people, spread around in all my lovely grandchildren. Some of them have my red hair. Others have my temperament. A few have my verbal skills. One has my cynicism. Several have my vanity and pride.

The years I spent raising my sons are as important to my happiness as the books I have written. If some of that time was frustrating, if occasionally I wondered if I was wasting my talents, then that was the price I had to pay for being happy now. There are always dues to pay.

. . .

The month my first book of fiction was published was also the month my first grandchild was born. "I don't know which thing makes me happier," I told Eudora Welty in July of that year, just weeks before the two events occurred.

"They aren't in competition, Ellen," she answered.

When I think of that conversation I remember running into her once on the Millsaps College campus, years before, when she was my teacher there. I had my three little redheaded boys with me. They were four and five and two, gorgeous, funny little creatures, fat and powerful, with beautiful faces. I had never mentioned to Eudora that I had children. I suppose it took her by surprise to see me coming down the path with my sons. I think they were wearing white summer outfits. When they were young I loved to dress them in white sailor suits or buttoned-up shirts with ruffles down the front.

"Oh, my," Eudora said. "Are they yours? Do they belong to you?"

"They're mine," I answered. "Aren't they funny?"

"Why would you need anything else?" she said. "Why would you need to be a writer?"

I did not understand what she was saying to me but I do now. Eudora had no children of her own and that year she had lost her father and her brother. Her mother was in a nursing home. Think how my riches must have looked to her.

In the end happiness is always a balance. I hope the young women of our fortunate world find ways to balance their young lives. I hope they learn to rejoice and wait.

What Independence Has Come to Mean to Me

THE PAIN OF SOLITUDE.
THE PLEASURE OF SELF-KNOWLEDGE.

Vivian Gornick

I STAND DRINKING coffee at the window of my apartment in downtown New York, looking out onto a street I have been looking at for twenty-five years, thinking about how it looked to me when I first moved in, and how it looks to me now; or rather how *I* looked to me then, and how I look to me now. This year I turned sixty-five, the year that society decides you're ready to be put out to pasture. For me, the year has been one of reckoning: an assessment of the past undertaken for the sake of getting on with the future. Behind such an act always lies the unspoken question: Who am I, and how did I get here?

I take another sip of the cooling coffee, stare at the street, and, inevitably, begin to brood on what now looks to me like a lifelong struggle to become a human being: an independent human being. Looking back on this struggle, I see that this question of "becoming" is a preoccupation of mine that has found its way repeatedly into my work. Much of what I have written over the past twenty years is riddled through with it. For instance, consider the following:

> It's Sunday morning, and I'm walking up Columbus Avenue. Couples are coming at me on all sides. They fill the street from building line to pavement edge. Some are clasped together looking

raptly into each other's faces; some are holding hands, their eyes restless, window-shopping; some walk side by side, stony faced, carefully not touching. I have the sudden conviction that half these people will, in a few months, be walking with someone else now walking on the avenue as one half of another couple. Eventually that arrangement will terminate as well, and each man and each woman will once again be staring out the window of a room empty of companionship. This is a population in a permanent state of intermittent attachment. Inevitably, the silent apartment lies in wait.

Who could ever have dreamed there would be so many of us floating around, those of us between thirty-five and fifty-five who live alone. Thirty years of politics in the street opened a door that became a floodgate, and we have poured through in our monumental numbers, in possession of the most educated discontent in history. Yet, we seem puzzled, most of us, about how we got here, confused and wanting relief from the condition. We roam the crowded streets, in naked expectation of the last-minute reprieve.

I wrote these paragraphs eight or nine years ago. They were the beginning of an essay called "On Living Alone." In a certain sense, I'd come to realize, I'd written often about living alone because I couldn't figure out why I *was* living alone. Now, in this essay, I rehearsed as honestly as I could the history of my own solitary condition. I spoke of how I had married young, felt subsumed in marriage, and taken flight; discovered first the pleasures of solitude and the promise of revolutionary feminism; and then the loneliness that came with what I took to be independence. I also wrote of the romance I had made out of that loneliness—turning it quickly into a political position ("this is what we must endure to become ourselves")—as well as the wisdom I acquired (slowly and unwillingly) when I faced up not to the lie but to the half-truth at the heart of that romance.

Inclined by nature toward polemics, and now on the barricades for radical feminism, it had been easy for me to make a simple article of faith out of living alone. But the reality turned out to be less than simple. The reality was that I was alone not because of my politics but because I did not know how to live in a decent way with another human being. In the name of equality I tormented every man who'd ever loved me until he left me: I called them on everything, never let anything go, held them up to accountability in ways that wearied us both. There was, of course, more than a grain of truth in everything I said, but those grains, no matter how numerous, need not have become the sandpile that crushed the life out of love. Suppressing the contradictions of what I was *actually* experiencing—that much of my loneliness was self-inflicted, having more to do with my angry, self-divided personality than with sexism—began to feel bad. The worse I felt, the more polemical I became. I found myself trapped inside my own rhetoric, imprisoned by a flash of insight that had congealed into dogma.

Some years later I wrote another piece in which I spoke even more openly about the divided feeling behind my "position" sentences. Work, I had once written, had come to seem everything, the element of life I had determined to no longer live without. Loving a man, I had decided, would never again be uppermost in my concerns. Now, in this piece—titled "What Feminism Means to Me"—I examined the matter once more, and this time looked a bit more clearly at the consequence of what I so easily claimed could be dispensed with—love, that is:

> Perhaps, in fact, the two [work and love] were incompatible. Love-as-I-had-always-known-it was something I might now have to do without. I approached this thought blithely, as though it would be the easiest thing in the world to accommodate. After all, I'd always been an uneasy belligerent, one of those women forever complaining that men were afraid of "women like me." I was no good at flirting; it was a relief to be done with it. All around me relationships were falling apart because one or both partners were suddenly conscious of deep inequities in their shared situation, and the enraged helplessness such consciousness had brought to the surface. If love between equals was impossible—and it looked as

though it probably was—who needed it? I pressed myself against my newly hardened heart. . . . The only important thing, I told myself [again], was work. I must teach myself to work. If I worked, I'd have what I needed. I'd be a person in the world. What would it matter then that I was giving up "love"?

As it turned out, it mattered. More than I had ever dreamed it would. Yes, I could no longer live with men on the old terms. Yes, I could settle for nothing less than grown-up affection. Yes, if that meant doing without I was prepared to do without. But the idea of love, if not the reality, was impossible to give up. As the years went on, I saw that romantic love was injected like dye into the nervous system of my emotions, laced through the entire fabric of longing, fantasy, and sentiment. It haunted the psyche, was an ache in the bones; so deeply embedded in the make-up of the spirit it hurt the eyes to look directly into its influence. It would be a cause of pain and conflict for the rest of my life. I love my hardened heart—I have loved it all these years—but the loss of romantic love can still tear at it.

This piece had grown out of years of struggling to look ever more closely at the truth of some of my actual experience. As, for instance, the following:

- I was in love with "the feminist community"—or so I claimed—yet I found myself bored and irritated by the conversation of more than half my "sisters."
- I claimed work was everything—yet was unable to cure myself of a crippling self-doubt that, year after year, allowed me to remain largely unproductive.
- I had, in the midst of feminism's long struggle for legal abortion, had an abortion myself, and had been startled to feel myself gripped by a primitive sense of dread at what I was doing—as though I was committing a sin and retribution would be mine.

- Known as a liberated woman, I had affairs with men who shared my politics, yet in love it was I who remained fantasy-ridden—needy, passive, belligerent, and distinctly self-involved.

In short, I came, over the years, to see that no matter what my choice—what*ever* I said yes or no to—the decision was complicated not only by the externals of my situation, but by inner divisions of my own that repeatedly took me by surprise. No choice was ever without serious contradiction or regret on my part. Not because I was a consciously dishonest or falsely motivated person, but because I did not know myself well enough to understand the depth of my own anxiety—I seemed unable to both work and love at the same time, it was always one or the other—to see that what I was calling my "choices" weren't really choices at all, they were simply the impulses of a conflicted being: one of them had to be acted upon. And thus, more often than not, after I had "chosen" I'd end up feeling stranded; confused and disappointed; surprised it was all turning out this way; and as shut up inside myself as before—neither free nor independent. Ah, there was the rub. Not independent.

Consciously, I was undivided in my desire for autonomy. Independence, I thought, was what I valued above all else. But it was turning out that I had not understood the meaning of the word at all. For years I had mistaken rebelliousness for independence. I thought that every time I treated the man in my life badly because "work comes first" I was asserting my independence. I thought dressing like a depressed slob meant defying the social code. I thought reciting the history of women's oppression ad nauseam explained all the writing I wasn't doing.

What I didn't understand was that the kind of independence I am talking about is not a thing one demands or pleads for but a thing one earns; not a gift granted but a condition pulled out of one's own reluctant self; not a passive but an active state of being. As Chekhov said, "Others made me a slave, but I must squeeze the slave out of myself, drop by drop." Which I interpret to mean, You work hard to acquire self-knowledge so that you may look directly at the cards that life has dealt you, and learn to play them rather than regret them, thereby giving yourself the greatest single strength a human being can possess: knowing what you can live with and what you can't live with—and why. That, I came to realize, is independence.

It's the true subject of *Walden*. Thoreau went to the forest to ask himself, What exactly is it I need, and what am I willing to pay to get it? The question was being asked by a man who wanted to put himself to the test: to know himself so that he might live in a state of inner independence *with* people, not without people. That, he thought, required as stripped-down an atmosphere as he could devise, so that he could sort out real needs from the ones rooted in fantasy. The reward would be encountering the world as it is, in the person that he knew himself to be.

. . .

So where does this leave me at sixty-five? And where, for that matter, does it leave the rest of us would-be independents? Living in a just and benevolent world where all wounds and deprivations stem only from our own neurotic and childish selves? Hardly. The dissatisfactions of women as women are very real. Our unhappiness at having been born into the "wrong" sex has risen to crisis levels every fifty years for the past two hundred—since Mary Wollstonecraft laid it out in 1792 in *A Vindication of the Rights of Woman*—and rightly so. Each time it does, yet another wave of Women's Liberation washes over us, so astonishingly vigorous in its initial force that it's hard to believe it will recede again. It does, of course, recede, but it leaves in its wake thousands of lives forever changed for the better.

I count myself lucky to have come into my maturity during a time when the second wave of American feminism was rising steadily. Because it deepened my understanding of myself as a person born into the wrong sex, feminism clarified immensely the lifelong task of sorting out What is me? What is the world? What is being done to me? What am I doing to myself? Though feminism hasn't, alas, solved my contradictions—the need for companionship in conflict with the need to begin and end with myself—it has allowed me to spend my life exploring them, analyzing them, making ever better sense of them.

So, putting down my coffee cup at the window of the apartment that's mine and mine alone, I come to my conclusion, or at least one of them: I am, simply, a person living a life partly that I chose and partly that chose me, a life that, though filled with friends and family and colleagues, is primarily one of solitude, one lived autonomously. And though this is far from ideal at all times—and though some days loneliness plagues me—for the most part, this is a life, *my* life, that I have come to embrace and appreciate. For how impossible it would have been to live it only fifty years ago! And what a privilege it has been to live it now. To be alive in times that make room for me and my kind: women living out the conflicts rather than the fantasies. Times that allow us to struggle actively with ourselves in order that we may *become* ourselves. Times that I and my generation of feminists helped create. (And that's where the romance of work, of polemics, *does* pay off; I can look back and feel fulfilled and filled by it now.) Mine is a life that embodies an extraordinary education; the one that comes with living out the discrepancy between the cocky, hard-edged declarations made from the barricades and the shocking reality of doing daily battle with one's own self-ignorance. This is the true exhilaration of revolutionary rage: the one that leads to *real* independence.

The Perfect Equality of Our Separate Chosen Paths

Becoming a Mother. Or Not.

Pam Houston

TWO WEEKS AGO I celebrated my thirty-ninth birthday. My graduate students decorated my office with balloons and streamers. They sang to me and brought me a cake from Baskin-Robbins.

"Is it your first thirty-ninth birthday?" several of my colleagues asked.

I realized that I hadn't yet reached the age where I'd been tempted to lie about it, but perhaps it was fast approaching.

My students asked me if there was anything I would try to accomplish in this last year before my status officially changed to over-the-hill.

I took stock of my life's résumé. Three books published, fifty countries visited, a tenure-track teaching job in northern California, a ranch in the Colorado mountains at 9,000 feet. Friends and dogs and horses I adored, respect of my peers, a growing inclination toward consciousness and generosity.

There were also a couple of glaring omissions, and I summed them up by singing the words of Shawn Colvin:

> I gave nobody life,
> I am nobody's wife
> And I seem to be nobody's daughter

Some of my colleagues smiled in recognition.

I have spent the last five years waiting to see in my own eyes the same panic I see in the eyes of nearly all my childless friends, to quake with the desire to breast-feed, to be willing to endure everything from painfully long needles to painfully dull men to satisfy this one desire, this one need that completely consumes them.

Until very recently, it has not been there at all, and even now, the version I have of it seems speculative and equivocal compared to the passionate single-mindedness I have seen among my friends.

"Didn't Shawn Colvin eventually have a baby?" somebody said.

I am keeping a careful eye on myself, since it is my own reserve I trust least of anything.

"Yeah," somebody else said, "I'm pretty sure she finally did."

. . .

I did three things immediately when I came home from the post office and found the note from Randy, my fiancé, that said he had left me. That said, Don't try to contact me ever again. That said, I really did love you, Randy.

I made an appointment with my therapist, I wrote to the Chinese embassy to ask for a visa that would allow me to go to Tibet, and I went to my favorite bookstore to purchase a book on international adoption. They were the first three things I could think of, things that I had expressly not been doing because I feared Randy would find them threatening, and I was trying, stupidly, in those days, above all else, not to threaten Randy.

The shelves in the bookstore were teeming with adoption assistance. Staring out at me in bold black and yellow was the title *Adoption for Dummies.*

"What can they be thinking?" I said to the salesclerk.

"You don't understand," she said. "It's part of a series."

But I did understand. "Computers, maybe," I said, "wine making, feng shui," I said, "but not this."

When she was gone I hid the "dummies" book behind the others, weighed a book in my hand on international adoption, took it to the counter, and purchased it without once cracking open the cover.

. . .

In 1992, just before my first book came out, I found out I was pregnant for the first time. The father was a good man, and though I didn't know him very well when I found out I was pregnant, I ended up marrying him, and staying married to him for a few good years.

I kept the news of the pregnancy to myself for a few days, and then I told him, and then my editor and then my mom. The father said, "I think it's a miracle, but I just never know when I'm going to be moving on down the road."

I ended up having an abortion, at the advice of my editor and my mother, who shared a rare opinion—though only my mother was brave enough to say it out loud. She said, "You have a very special talent, a very special gift, and a lot of people have invested in that gift and expect you to deliver. As soon as you have that baby you become ordinary, exactly the same as everybody else."

. . .

For the better part of my life I would have made a pretty poor mother. I was as afraid to be dependent as I was to have dependents. I couldn't remember nine-tenths of my own brutal childhood. I couldn't tell the difference between what felt good and what felt bad.

Then I found the world's greatest therapist, who taught me how to face my fears and my losses, who taught me that I was an adult capable of making my life into anything I wanted, who taught me the thrill of being present and fully conscious in the rich and fluid center of my life.

Now both he and my dearest friends say I would make a sensational mother, but the weight of history presses still. I know now, beyond certainty, that I won't repeat the crimes of the past, but does the past somehow have a life of its own, some regenerating principle like the starfish that grows another arm, huge and unstoppable no matter what we human beings do?

. . .

I just happened to be in Vail on the day Kate gave birth to Truman. Normally Kate and I live six hours of Colorado mountain driving apart, but I was in Vail skiing with friends and she needed to deliver in a hospital of some size. It was her second baby. A vaginal birth after cesarean, and they were afraid to touch her in her little town.

She knew of Randy's departure the week before, but we hadn't really talked about it. I walked into the room three hours and twenty minutes after Truman's birth. I brought with me a gift bag in which I had put goat cheese, a stuffed animal, three or four very sweet minneola tangerines and, because they've always suggested womanhood to me, a perfectly formed butternut squash. Kate took one look at me and burst into tears. Her husband, John—one of the good ones—gave me a huge happy hug.

"For a while the pain was so unbearable I started to hallucinate about farmers in a field."

John looked at me and shrugged. "Crazy," he said. "You want to hold Truman?"

His fingers were way out of proportion, long for the rest of him, and every now and then he opened his eyes. It was hard to believe in the existence of a being that tiny. I felt like I could have sat in that rocker with him until the end of time.

"I'm going to go to your wedding," I told him, "and I'm going to be the old woman with the long gray braid who's crying like crazy, and you're going to say, 'Hey, Mom, who is that maniac over there making such a fool of herself?' And your mother will say, 'You remember Pam, she held you for a whole hour when you were just three hours old,' and you'll roll your eyes and kiss your bride and look over at me pityingly."

When Kate stood up to change her gown, the blood poured out of her as if from a pitcher.

"Is that what's supposed to happen?" I asked.

Kate waved a hand in the air. "You think that was bad, you should have been here a couple hours ago."

. . .

I have never been with a man I trusted enough to trust with the care of my children. I suspect, as my therapist would say, that this is just a symptom of the problem, rather than the problem itself.

. . .

My mother was obsessed with weight and physical appearance. Not just hers or even mine (though that's clearly where she lay her focus) but really everyone's, in my life, in her life, even on TV. In her mind there was no amount of intelligence, wit, charm, or goodness that could overcome five or ten extra pounds of body weight.

"If they look at you and see a fat girl," she was famous for saying, "then a fat girl is all you will forever be."

Her daily challenge for us both each day was to "see if we could make it all the way to dinner without eating anything," and then to "stop eating the second our stomachs ceased to growl."

It's completely astonishing to me that she allowed herself to gain the weight that her pregnancy with me must have required. It is my fervent hope that I have not avoided having children all these years because I'm afraid of what my mother would say (from the grave) when I reached my ninth-month weight.

. . .

My friend Sarah and I sat in a Thai restaurant last weekend, with her seven-month-old baby, Collier, between us. When she had her first son, Ben, Sarah endured hours of back labor and then months of severe postpartum depression. When Collier was born, he couldn't breathe at Colorado's high altitude, so the family was forced to move to the coast.

Ben, now an adorable five-year-old, was off watching motocross with his dad. Collier was breathing the California air with ease, and Sarah, across the table, looked as happy as I had ever seen her.

We were expending a fair amount of energy keeping Collier entertained and therefore quiet, so we wouldn't become a bother to the other diners.

He tried to pull my thumb and forefinger apart for a while. Then he enjoyed making marks with his one tooth on the tips of each of my fingers. Then he sucked on my silver bracelets one at a time. Then he ate a lot of mashed banana and something out of an organic baby food jar that was an alarming color of green.

He'd hardly uttered a sound, hardly let a scrap of food fall to the floor, and still the women around us were eyeing our table with the strictest disapproval. Sarah just kept smiling at them and at Collier while I made up stories about their pathetic lives.

This one had fertility treatments for eight years and never maintained a pregnancy. That one lost her only child in a terrible custody battle with her spouse. Sarah said they just feared the untimely end of their peaceful dinners, but I said what looked like so much disdain on their faces surely must have been hunger, very thinly disguised.

I put my hand on Collier's head protectively. It was not lost on me for a moment that I had appeared, and could again appear, to be one of them.

. . .

I am a person who has suffered a lot of physical pain in her life: more than ten broken bones, including a radius, an ulna, a tibia, a fibula, and a femur. The broken bones occurred either during my violent childhood or in my willful and stubborn adult recreation of those years.

I have to admit that I have been hesitant about knowingly signing up for the pain of childbirth. I suspect that this is just a symptom of the problem, rather than the problem itself.

. . .

It was our third day in Laos's northernmost region, and about the thirtieth village in which we stopped. The woven huts sat quiet, bleaching in the sun. Pigs rooted around in the bushes. A couple of turkeys pecked in the dirt. In the late-morning air there hung the scent of wood smoke, and just under that the sweeter, thinner smell of burning opium.

There are sixty-eight different minority groups in Laos, and our guide, Xai, was bent on Randy and me meeting at least one person from each group. We stood around in the dirt yard waiting for something to happen. An old woman, her teeth stained with betel nut, came to her door and peered out at us. Then three little boys exploded out the door around her, tumbling out into the courtyard more like puppies than kids.

There was one in particular. He wore a red shirt embroidered with Buddhism's eight auspicious signs, and a gray-striped cloth tied around his waist like a sarong. He had a round face and huge dimples, a broad nose and deep intelligent eyes, short black hair and straw sandals. He stopped dead in his tracks when he saw me, struck a pose, and flashed me a smile like he was Miss America and I was Bert Parks. He was no more than four years old.

I offered a greeting in what I hoped was the correct one of the sixty-eight languages, and he offered it back, perhaps imitating my accent just a bit. His smile broadened further. He pointed to my camera and I raised it and shot. The other kids tried to get his attention, but his gaze never left my face.

Already Xai was herding us back toward our van.

I have read plenty of accounts of childnapping. Of barren women so overcome by desire at the sight of a child that they snatch the baby and go hurtling off down the shopping aisle, through the airport terminal, along the flower-lined streets of Disneyland. Until that moment I had always thought those women were of some species so apart from me and my experience that they may as well have been the stuff of fairy tales.

More and more children poured out into the yard. At least four or five for every hut, I found myself thinking. The smiling boy still contemplated me as I walked backward toward the road. And then the unconscionable thoughts began: Would his absence lighten the burden of poverty? Is he destined, like so many villagers, for a future laced with opium? Is he destined to have a future at all?

I sat heavily in the backseat of the car and rolled down the window. Still he watched me.

I tried to guess how many of the children were his brothers and sisters. It wouldn't matter if there were a hundred, I knew. That little boy would surely be missed.

I waved to him and he waved back. Both Xai and Randy were completely oblivious to how my life had just changed.

I would not grab the boy and run down the dirt road with him. I would not presume to believe that I could make a better life for him than he was having in Laos's Golden Triangle.

But if his mother had been watching through the window. If she had looked in my eyes and seen what was true. If she had come out of the house and asked me how much I would pay, or if she had come out of the house and put his hand in mine and said, "He go to America and grow big and strong," or if the old woman in the doorway had said, "Such a pity, both parents dead, and not enough food to feed all of them," there wouldn't have been the slightest hesitation from me.

The van started and we rumbled away from the village. I keep that photo in my wallet like a prayer.

. . .

And then there are the days when I simply love my life: my dogs, my friends, my freedom. I love being able to get on an airplane with a name printed on the nose in some language I can't begin to decipher, and know that when the plane touches down again I'm going to be in a world different from any I have ever seen before—Bolivia, Tibet, Antarctica, or Bhutan. I love not caring what food I eat or how sick I get or whether or not the whole country goes on strike and I have no idea when I'll ever get home.

I love staying up all night to write if the spirit moves me.

I love playing the role of good parent with my students, of believing in their abilities completely, of helping them to believe they can be anything they want.

I love sitting around the table with writers and poets when the room smells like Scotch and cigarettes and the conversation moves farther and farther away from anything anybody would want their children to hear.

I ran into Katy, an old college friend, at the Peet's Coffee and Tea near my house. We were English majors at Denison University together, had almost the same birthday; we both went west to find ourselves after school.

She was there with her youngest son, his brother off in first grade, and as I flew in the door between a morning of writing and an afternoon of teaching, she sat in the sun helping her son feed muffin crumbs to the birds with a look on her face and a posture in her body that said, I might just sit here all afternoon.

I took the time to sit with them for a minute. She bemoaned the fact that she was almost forty and felt she should have done more with her life. I said I often wondered if I should have done less.

When we parted I wrote her number on the back of a Parisian optician's card I had in my wallet. She wrote my number on the back of a yearlong membership to the local petting zoo.

I said, "Well, that just about sums it up, doesn't it?"

And later I worried that it might have sounded snotty, when what I was really feeling was the perfect equality of our separate chosen paths. We both envied the other's life, both felt we had missed out somehow, and yet neither of us could or would think of trading.

On the way home it occurred to me that nothing on earth was stopping either of us from venturing down the path not taken. I eyed the international adoption book on the shelf when I got home.

. . .

"Everything was perfect with your father and me until you were born," my mother used to say, almost daily. And then she would pour herself another glass of vodka and turn on *What's My Line* on TV. I suspect that this was just a symptom of the problem, though we may be getting closer to the problem itself.

When I was barely in my twenties, I had a friend, I'll call her Anna, who lost a baby to sudden infant death syndrome. I didn't know her very long, in the grand scheme of a life. We became friends during her pregnancy, the baby lived some part of a year, and she and her husband moved away not too long after the baby died. That baby's was the first funeral I ever attended.

I remember a conversation we had a few months after the death. Anna's marriage was in trouble, and they were hoping the move would help put the past away.

"I can't even imagine," I said, "what kinds of things you've been feeling."

"No," she said, "you can't." Young as I was then, Anna was younger still, but she looked out at me from dark eyes that looked as though they no longer had a soul in them.

"I'm not even twenty years old," she said, "and as much as I want it not to be, I know my life is over."

I remembered all her doubts about the pregnancy. About the marriage. About tying herself to a baby before she had made a success of her own life. All of that vanished with the birth of the baby, and all that was left in its place now was grief.

I lost touch with Anna long ago, but I think of her often. When my mother died in 1992, when my best girlfriend died in 1993, and just last year, when a man I had loved more truly than any other died of cancer before I even knew he was sick.

What I have had, instead of children, are dogs—Irish wolfhounds—and I have made them my children in all the predictable ways that women do. When my Dante, the most magnificent and dearest dog I have ever known, was diagnosed with osteosarcoma at the age of four last year, I saw how I had been protecting myself from all the other losses. How I had walled myself off from the deaths of my parents and friends, how I feared Anna's words in my own mouth so much that I kept a part of me back in the face of their illnesses—not desertion so much as withholding—and in that withholding I let them down, and also myself.

I vowed not to do that with Dante. I vowed not to do it ever again. I broke through the wall that fear of loss had made inside me, and that breaking felt physical. I vowed to love Dante every day until he died, completely and consciously.

Against all medical odds he's still alive, and I understand that every day with him is another gift, and I haven't yet broken my promise. I also understand that even more than the fear of losing my autonomy, even more than the fear of seeing my mother's rage reborn in me, in fact even more than any other I can come up with, the real reason I haven't had children is that I have not been able to contemplate the thought of losing something I would love so completely.

I knew if I kept writing long enough I would come upon something that was not a symptom, but the heart of the problem itself.

It was quiet in the house last night when I took down the book on adoption. The wolfhounds were sleeping soundly and the nighthawks were calling from the field across the street. I peeled back the cover and sank into the couch with Dante.

"Congratulations," it said. "You've just taken the very first step."

Afterword

SINCE THE HARDCOVER publication of *The Bitch in the House,* with full credit to the twenty-six contributors whose words fill its pages, I can happily claim that the book has struck a deep and vibrating chord among women in this country and abroad. Within weeks it became a surprise national bestseller, widely reviewed and discussed; long after publication, this discussion is still going strong. The book became, in short, exactly what I'd hoped for but had barely allowed myself to imagine: a spark for fiery dialogue on the issues it presents—an ongoing conversation about the conflicts of women today—that is provocative, important, and wise.

In my view, two things in particular ignited this spark: the raw nerves the book exposes with its honest and passionate revelations, and the validation it fosters through shared experience. Days after publication, the *New York Observer*, known for its snide, smart exposés, ran a lengthy cover article about *Bitch* entitled "Mommy Maddest," which, underneath an illustration of a professional woman bawling at her desk, gleefully proclaimed that contemporary women "got what they asked for. And it's hell." *New York* magazine followed with a cover story about the friction, if not downright animosity, between the city's working and stay-at-home mothers. *Glamour* magazine received piles of letters when it excerpted Kristin van Ogtrop's essay about the stresses and struggles of an ambitious working mother who cherishes the calm and her power at the office compared to the chaos of home, both from readers who fully identified with her dilemma and readers condemning her for the choices she'd made. Hannah Pine's piece, about her open marriage, elicited a similar flood of mail at *Elle*, as did others excerpted in magazines.

Ultraconservatives tongue-lashed the book's contributors for daring to have jobs outside the home, while ultraliberals chastised the same women for having the gall to discuss their "problems" when so many in the world have it so much worse. Writing in *The Atlantic Monthly*, Caitlin Flanagan presented *The Bitch in the House* as evidence that part of why today's marriages include less sex than old-fashioned, traditional marriages is because contemporary women are too "liberated," adding that "the rare woman—the good wife, and the happy one—is the woman who maintains her husband's sexual interest and who returns it in full measure," in part by "adopting a good attitude." (Yikes!) Writing in the *Pittsburgh Post-Gazette*, Judy Wertheimer announced that she'd stock a "saferoom" —a place her family could survive for three days in the event of a terrorist attack—with "a corkscrew and a good cabernet, hermetically sealed cookies from Prantl's bakery, and a copy of *The Bitch in the House*, a collection of essays in large part about how women screw up their lives when they get married and have kids." (She goes on to add that she's "joking, of course" about the screw-up-their-lives part.) And so on. The book has been heralded and dissected, pummelled and lauded and expanded upon.

Something's up here, is it not? It turns out that contemporary women lucky enough to have choices (and it goes without saying, in these times of world upheaval and spreading poverty in our own nation, that anyone with choices, not to mention a roof over her head and three meals a day, is, truly, lucky) are hungry for meaningful material to help them figure out their messy and complex lives—lives complicated in ways largely unknown to past generations of women. Strong, ambitious, highly competent women—the very ones for whom the Feminist Movement opened the doors to power and success—find themselves at a difficult crossroads today, a time when one major need, desire, biological urge (to love, to nurture, to have children, to be the good mothers our own mothers were, or weren't) is in direct conflict with another: that of not only contributing a necessary share of the family income, but of fulfilling the intellectual and professional ambitions for which we've been groomed and primed, often for our entire young lives. And one path to consolation, if not a step toward solution, is to talk about it. We women need to share our lives and dilemmas and frustrations, to tell the truth whenever and wherever we can—even if it means contradicting each other, even if it means being called difficult or demanding or *bitchy*. As the Chinese fortune I have taped in my workspace reminds me, "Discontent is the first step in the progress of a man or a nation."

In this spirit, I'd like to close this edition of *Bitch* by offering a letter from a woman blissfully unafraid either to share her life or to contradict—in this case, her own daughter, who happens to be one of the book's contributors. I should say first that one of the many things that surprised me in compiling *The Bitch in the House* was how many of the writers, myself included, talked about our mothers. We women are, I realized—for better or worse—profoundly affected by the women who raised us, whether we love or despise them, whether they were there every hour of our childhoods or rarely around, whether they're someone we want to emulate or hope never to become. And sometimes perhaps we project things on our mothers that simply aren't there—because they grew up in a different generation with different expectations and conflicts, or simply because they're different people than we are. (As Kristin van Ogtrop points out in her essay, some of us turn into not our mothers but our fathers with ovaries.)

The letter is to E. S. Maduro, the first and youngest contributor to this book, from her mother, a fifty-five-year-old special education teacher who married at age twenty-one (to a man she met and started dating at age thirteen) and raised two children before she went back to work. E. S. herself is now a twenty-six-year-old graduate student attending, on scholarship, one of the finest Ph.D. programs in the country. She's also a woman torn with ambivalence about her current relationship—with a man she likes, and maybe loves, who has said he wants to marry her—because she wants to be free right now to focus on her work; a woman who wants, deeply, both to have a partner and children someday, and to make a difference in the world. And if her past career success is any indication, she surely will. In the first essay in this book, E. S. talks about growing up with a stay-at-home mother. Here is what her mother has to say in response:

Dear E:

I read your essay for *The Bitch in the House* with much interest. As always, you are perceptive and thoughtful about all the issues of your life. However, I find myself wanting to respond to some of what you said about mine. This note is not written in anger, nor is it motivated by hurt feelings; but it is written with the conviction that there is a misperception on your part about my feelings about my role as wife and mother. Perhaps it is hard for you and your peers to understand my perspective—because of differences in age, experience, situation. So I have decided to try to explain some of my experience and thoughts in this letter, in hopes of broadening your understanding of my take on issues that appear to be vitally important to you.

First, we are indeed of different generations. I grew up in a household with a mother who never worked outside the house but who also, once there was enough money, didn't clean, do much cooking, or spend a lot of time with her kids doing activities that were of interest to them. Not unlike some other women of her day (post-Depression era) and station (wife of a successful professional), she played (golf, bowling, cards), socialized, and shopped. I came home for lunch in elementary school to a housekeeper and made my own meal while I watched soap operas. Most days, my mother walked into the house at 5:00 or so with just enough time to supervise the finishing of a dinner made by the housekeeper so that dinner would be on the table at 5:30, my father's requested time to eat. She was in bed watching television by 7 P.M., and pretty much unavailable to me emotionally or physically. In the summer, I was shipped off to camp.

By the time I was 20 or 21, several of my close friends were already married. In my circles, the woman who went to graduate school or work was the exception rather than the rule. Your father and I wanted to live together, and the only way was to get married, so we did. Since he was going to graduate school, with plans of becoming a professor, it was up to me to go to work. I did this gladly, thinking it a great thing, not just in and of itself (I would be a teacher, something I thought noble and exciting), but as a way to demonstrate that I was not going to be like *my* mother and spend my time frivolously.

Almost from the start, I liked my work very much. The fact that I did all the shopping and cooking and cleaning at home was just part of the territory; all the women I knew did this, and I never thought to question or resent it. (In fact, only looking back on it from the perspective of today does it occur to me that it might have been different.) I was living a life very different from my mother's, and to me, it was infinitely superior, as I was engaged with my surroundings.

I had always wanted children, and after several years, I got pregnant and cut back to part-time work throughout the pregnancy. When I was close to having the baby, I quit; I had always planned to be home with my children once I had them, and by then, your father had finished school and could comfortably support us.

When you and your sister were growing up, I was what your generation calls a "stay-at-home mom." As you point out in your essay, I did all the shopping, cooking, cleaning, and much of the activity required for raising two children. I can say now that those were some of the happiest years of my life. I was enchanted by my daughters, and watching them grow from little helpless blobs into wonderful people was the most rewarding experience I have ever had. I didn't then and still do not consider it a job. It was joy. Of course, there were times when it was trying, sad, or frustrating, but overall, it was wonderful. I wanted to be enmeshed in every aspect of running a household. Need it be said? Unlike my mother.

During this time, along with learning a lot about how children develop—which is vitally important to the work I do now—I also learned to cook (something I still love) and to appreciate and fix up old houses (which, as you know, is now a passion for me). I also developed friendships with many women who, like me, were home raising children. I don't remember any of us feeling conflicted about what we were doing. For the most part, we were happy and productive and we enjoyed ourselves.

Eventually, as you and your sister got older, I decided to go back to school to become professionally qualified to do the activity that I loved—teaching children. I added taking classes to my daily roster of activities, and though I was very busy those years, and sometimes bone-tired, I was not angry or resentful. I had chosen this life. And now, more than a decade later, I still love my work, and I think I am good at it. I also know that all the courses in the world could not have prepared me better for the work I do now—for having empathy with young children—than my years of being a mother. The fact that I did not start this career until I was 45 doesn't bother me at all, nor do I remember pining for it before it came. I have had sixteen years and expect a few more, and that's plenty for me.

You seem to feel in your essay that I have some anger about all I did, particularly the domestic roles that fell to me. But I do not now, and don't believe I ever did, feel angry about these roles and tasks. Yes, there are dissatisfactions in my life—as there are in most if not all people's lives—but they have little to do with my role as a wife and mother. I never felt I was thwarted from doing what was important to me, and in fact, the two things I cared most about—having my own children and working to help other ones—have both been mine. I feel grateful and lucky for this.

I hope this letter has helped you understand more about me, and perhaps some other women of my generation, who may strike you as unfulfilled and silently angry. Perhaps if my mother were alive today, she would write me a similar letter and tell me the glories of running a household by proxy, and how very important that was for someone who came of age in the Depression, where her mother had no money to do it that way. Perhaps we're all a little too quick to judge our mothers. It'll be interesting to see what your own daughter, if you have one—and I hope you do—will write in 25 years. Perhaps part of our role as daughters is to try to do it a little bit differently. And perhaps, as you grow, you'll develop your own style, be comfortable with it, and won't end up being "the bitch in the house."

I love you.

Mom

I love this letter, and it's exactly the sort of response, and subsequent dialogue, that I hope this book will continue to foster. It is worth noting that the years this writer credits as some of her happiest occurred more than two decades ago. I wonder if, twenty years from now, some of the contributors in this book—myself included—will likewise look back on these tumultuous times as the best years of our lives. Certainly that doesn't seem out of the question. The stress, exhaustion, and seeming incompatibility of exploiting all the many choices before us—or of choosing from among them—doesn't necessarily preclude happiness; and there is no denying the ecstasy of falling in young love, of discovering your passion in work, of marrying your lover, birthing a baby, observing your toddler take his first steps—even if you're on deadline and the phone is ringing and the sink full of dishes while you do it. Perhaps we'll even wonder, through the haze of nostalgia, what we ever had to be dissatisfied about, when our lives were so full and vital and healthy. Or perhaps by then we'll have entered another phase of life with its own set of conflicts and liberties, and we'll be on to figuring out that one.

Here's to having time and space to find out. And here's to keeping the dialogue open.

—CH, February 2003

Contributors

LAURIE ABRAHAM, editor at large for *Elle* magazine, is the author of *Mama Might Be Better Off Dead: The Failure of Health Care in Urban America* (University of Chicago Press). Until May 2000, she was the features editor at *Mirabella* magazine. She has written for *The New York Times Magazine, The New Republic, Health,* and the *Village Voice,* among other publications. A piece she wrote for *Mirabella,* "Landscape of Desire," was selected as a notable essay of 1999 by *Best American Essays* (Houghton Mifflin).

NATALIE ANGIER, a Pulitzer Prize–winning science reporter and writer for the *New York Times,* is the author of *Woman: An Intimate Geography,* which was a finalist for the National Book Award, as well as *The Beauty of the Beastly* and *Natural Obsessions*. She has worked as a writer and/or editor for *Time, Discover, The Atlantic Monthly, Parade, Natural History, Ms.,* and many other print and online magazines. She lives in Takoma Park, Maryland, with her husband, Rick Weiss, and their daughter, Katherine.

JILL BIALOSKY is the author of two books of poetry, *The End of Desire* and *Subterranean* (Alfred A. Knopf), and most recently a novel, *House Under Snow* (Harcourt). She lives in New York City with her husband and son.

VERONICA CHAMBERS is the author of the memoir *Mama's Girl* and several books for children. Her articles appear regularly in *O* magazine, the *New York Times,* and many other publications. The 2001–2002 Hodder Fellow at Princeton University, she lives in Princeton with her fiancé, Jason Clampet, and is working on a novel.

KATE CHRISTENSEN is the author of three novels, including the forthcoming *The Epicure's Lament* (Doubleday, Spring 2004). She has published essays and articles in various publications, including *Salon, Elle, Mademoiselle,* and the *Hartford Courant.* She lives in Brooklyn with her husband.

CHITRA DIVAKARUNI is the author of *The Mistress of Spices* and *Arranged Marriage,* for which she won an American Book Award. Her latest novel is titled *The Vine of Desire.* Her work has appeared in *The Best American Short Stories, Atlantic Monthly,* the *New Yorker, Ms., Zoetrope, O* magazine, and others. She divides her time between northern California and Houston, where she teaches creative writing at the University of Houston.

HOPE EDELMAN is the author of three nonfiction books, including the bestseller *Motherless Daughters,* which was a *New York Times* Notable Book of the Year. She is the recipient of a Pushcart Prize for creative nonfiction. Her essays have appeared in numerous publications, including the *New York Times,* the *Dallas Morning News, Self, Parenting, Real Simple, The Iowa Review,* the *Crab Orchard Review,* and the forthcoming anthology *Toddler*. She lives with her husband and two daughters in Los Angeles, where she is working on her next book, *Motherless Mothers*.

ELLEN GILCHRIST has published nineteen books of fiction, two books of poetry, and a book of essays, and is the recipient of the National Book Award for Fiction. She lives in Fayetteville, Arkansas, and Ocean Springs, Mississippi, and teaches creative writing at the University of Arkansas.

VIVIAN GORNICK is the author of eight books, including the memoir *Fierce Attachments* and the essay collections *Approaching Eye Level* and *The End of the Novel of Love.* Her newest book, which grew out of fifteen years of teaching nonfiction writing, is *The Situation and the Story: The Art of Personal Narrative.* She lives in New York City.

KERRY HERLIHY, who teaches ninth-grade English, has contributed essays to anthologies including *Motherland: Writings by Irish American Women About Mothers and Daughters.* She lives with her daughter outside of Boston.

PAM HOUSTON is the author of two collections of short stories, *Cowboys Are My Weakness* and *Waltzing the Cat,* and a collection of essays, *A Little More About Me*. Her work has appeared in many magazines and anthologies, most recently *O* magazine, and most notably *The O Henry Prize Stories* and *Best American Short Stories of the Century*. She recently finished her first stage play, *Tracking the Pleiades,* and her novel, *Sighthound,* will be published by W. W. Norton in 2004. She lives in the mountains of southwestern Colorado and teaches in the masters program at the University of California, Davis.

KAREN KARBO's three novels, including *Motherhood Made a Man Out of Me,* have all been named *New York Times* Notable Books of the Year. She is the recipient of an NEA Grant and a past winner of a General Electric Younger Writer Award. Her most recent work is a memoir, *The Stuff of Life,* about her relationship with her father. Her nonfiction, essays, and reviews have appeared in *Vogue, Elle, Esquire, Entertainment Weekly, The New Republic,* and *Sports Illustrated for Women*. She lives in Portland, Oregon.

CYNTHIA KLING is a gardener, writer, and editor who lives in upstate New York with her husband, the writer Philip Weiss, and her dogs, Franklin and Mercer.

NATALIE KUSZ is the former director of Harvard University's creative writing program, and now teaches in the MFA program at Eastern Washington University. Her work, including the 1990 memoir *Road Song,* has been published in four countries and has earned a Whiting Writers' Award, an NEA fellowship, a Pushcart Prize, and other honors.

E. S. MADURO is the pseudonym for a writer and youth counselor who divides her time between New England and Central America.

JEN MARSHALL is publicist at large for Vintage Books and Anchor Books. She lives in Williamsburg, Massachusetts.

HAZEL McCLAY is the pseudonym for a writer of fiction and nonfiction born and raised in the Midwest.

DAPHNE MERKIN is the author of the novel *Enchantment,* which won the Edward Lewis Wallant Award, and of the critically acclaimed essay collection *Dreaming of Hitler.* She writes regularly for the *New Yorker,* the *New York Times Magazine,* and other publications.

SARAH MILLER has written for various publications, including *Details, Glamour, Cosmopolitan, TV Guide,* and the *New York Press,* and has contributed to the radio program *This American Life.* She lives in Los Angeles.

CATHERINE NEWMAN writes and edits in western Massachusetts, where she lives with her family. She is a contributing editor at *FamilyFun* magazine and the author of *Bringing Up Ben,* a weekly journal on parentcenter.com.

HANNAH PINE is the pseudonym of a novelist living and working in the United States.

ELISSA SCHAPPELL is the author of the novel *Use Me,* which was a *New York Times* Notable Book, a *Los Angeles Times* Best Book of the Year, and a finalist for the PEN/Hemingway Award. She is editor at large of *Tin House* magazine, which she cofounded with her husband, Rob Spillman, and is a contributing editor at *Vanity Fair,* where she writes the "Hot Type" column. She is also coeditor of the forthcoming anthology *The Friend Who Got Away*. She teaches in the low-residency MFA program at Queens College in North Carolina, and lives in Brooklyn with her husband and children.

HELEN SCHULMAN writes novels, stories, and screenplays. Her last book, *P.S.,* is soon to be a major motion picture. She is teaching in the MFA program at the New School.

SUSAN SQUIRE is the author of *For Better, for Worse,* a nonfiction narrative about the impact of parenthood on five contemporary marriages. She is at work on her next book, *A Brief History of Marriage,* to be published by Bloomsbury USA.

KRISTIN VAN OGTROP is the managing editor of *Real Simple* magazine. She has also worked at *Glamour, Vogue, Premiere,* and *Travel & Leisure*. Her writing has appeared in *Seventeen, Vogue, Outside, Equity,* and the anthology *Child of Mine*. She lives in the New York suburbs with her husband and two children.

NANCY WARTIK has contributed features, reviews, and other stories to a wide range of publications, including the *New York Times,* the *Los Angeles Times, Harper's Bazaar, Glamour,* and *Self*. She is a former staffer at *Ms.* magazine and is an adjunct instructor in the film and media department at Hunter College. She lives in New York City with her husband, Dennis Overbye, and their recently adopted daughter, Mira Kamille Overbye.

Acknowledgments

So many people helped me with this book, I could fill every page thanking them all. Instead, I'll narrow it down to a few, and hope the others forgive me. I am grateful to every one.

This book would not have come about without four amazing women. The first—reader, soul mate, muse, and dear friend—is Kate Christensen, with whom the idea for the project was born during one of our many passionate discussions at my kitchen table, and whose encouragement and wisdom propelled me every step of the way. My agent, Elizabeth Kaplan, responded with her trademark speed and finesse. Marjorie Braman, tirelessly attentive editor, provided the perfect combination of freedom, hand-holding, enthusiasm, and expertise. And Rory Evans—writer, thinker, friend—appeared just when I was about to give up to buoy me with her rational counsel and then connect me to some of the book's most exciting contributors.

Many other women—and a few good men—also helped along the way, some of them contributors to this book, others not, though for me they are here in spirit. Robbie Myers, voice of reason and restraint, lent an ear many times and supplied her usual acumen and impeccable judgment. Katha Pollitt shared thoughts that both aided with the book and taught me some valuable life lessons. David Handelman and Daphne Merkin gave insightful eleventh-hour feedback. Susan Squire, Cynthia Kling, Hope Edelman, Deb Addis, Joan Berzoff, Alison Brower, Liz Egan, Jeanie Pyun, Kristin van Ogtrop, Margot Guralnick, Chris Russell, Gina Russell, Ted Conover, Lisa DeLisle, Holly Welker, Karen Mockler,

Veronica Chambers, Lois Feldman, Vera Jones, and—especially—Amy Hanauer and Elizabeth Feldman, as well as Bette, Judy, and Lonnie Hanauer, generously proferred time, suggestions, and conversation. Kate Bernheimer and Helen Schulman offered early advice. Lorraine Yasinski listened and said all the right things.

Among the book publicists who assisted me in working with authors: Nicholas Latimer, Sally Marvin, Kimberly Burns, Suzanne Williams, Jen Marshall, Katherine Beitner, Sarita Varma, Sandee Yuen, Irene Reichbach, Jane Beirn, Sharyn Rosenblum, Paul Slovak, Theresa Zoro, Alison Rich, Brant Janeway. (The others are in my mind, if not on this page.) Literary agent Susan Ramer also was particularly helpful.

The stellar Donna Cavanagh furnished endless hours of loving child care for my son, Nathaniel, while I worked on this book, and both Nathaniel and his sister, Phoebe, endured me saying, more times than I'd want to tally, "Not now, I'm working!" Dan Jones—where to start?—gave more than any husband should have to throughout this project. Night after night, he agreed to let me read him one more essay by a woman who's pissed off, responding with encouragement, humor, crucial feedback, and creative help. It came to a head the night he said, with a smile, "I can't believe I'm married to the bitch in the house." True, alas, and all I have to say about it is, Lucky me.

Last but not least, I thank the contributors to this collection: for their talent, their patience, their honesty, and their bold and beautiful words. The credit for this book goes to them, of course, and I offer it fully, humbly, and with eternal thanks.

Copyright Notices